T0305418

The Gold Standard
at the Turn of the Twentieth Century

Columbia Studies in International and Global History

Columbia Studies in International and Global History

The idea of "globalization" has become a commonplace, but we lack good histories that can explain the transnational and global processes that have shaped the contemporary world. Columbia Studies in International and Global History will encourage serious scholarship on international and global history with an eye to explaining the origins of the contemporary era. Grounded in empirical research, the titles in the series will also transcend the usual area boundaries and will address questions of how history can help us understand contemporary problems, including poverty, inequality, power, political violence, and accountability beyond the nation state.

CEMIL AYDIN
*The Politics of Anti-Westernism in Asia:
Visions of World Order in Pan-Islamic and Pan-Asian Thought*

ADAM M. McKEOWN
Melancholy Order: Asian Migration and the Globalization of Borders

PATRICK MANNING
The African Diaspora: A History Through Culture

JAMES RODGER FLEMING
Fixing the Sky: The Checkered History of Weather and Climate Control

Steven Bryan

The Gold Standard at the Turn of the Twentieth Century

*Rising Powers, Global Money,
and the Age of Empire*

Columbia University Press   New York

Columbia University Press
Publishers Since 1893
New York   Chichester, West Sussex
Copyright © 2010 Columbia University Press

Library of Congress Cataloging-in-Publication Data
Bryan, Steven.
The Gold Standard at the turn of the twentieth century : rising powers,
global money, and the age of Empire / Steven Bryan.
p.   cm. — (Columbia studies in international and global history)
Includes bibliographical references and index.
ISBN 978-0-231-15252-5 (cloth : alk. paper) — ISBN 978-0-231-52633-3 (electronic)
1. Gold standard—Japan—History. 2. Gold standard—Argentina—History.
I. Title. II. Series.

HG1272.B79   2010

332.4′2220952—dc22

2009046546

⊗

Columbia University Press books are printed on permanent and durable acid-free paper.
This book was printed on paper with recycled content.
Printed in the United States of America

c 10 9 8 7 6 5 4 3 2

References to Internet Web sites (URLs) were accurate at the time of writing.
Neither the author nor Columbia University Press is responsible for URLs
that may have expired or changed since the manuscript was prepared.

For John and Sarah Bryan

Contents

Tables

Acknowledgments

I gratefully acknowledge the assistance and support of the many people and institutions who have allowed me to write this book. First and foremost, thanks go to my professors and advisers at Columbia University. Above all, to Carol Gluck, who provided guidance and support from beginning to end. To Hugh Patrick and David Weiman, who graciously supported my interest in economic history and assisted in countless ways over the years. To John Coatsworth, who kindly agreed to help on short notice and provided invaluable advice about how to frame the material for a wider audience. To Adam McKeown, who read multiple drafts and always managed to cut to the essence of the argument. To Itō Masanao and the faculty and staff of the Graduate School of Economics at the University of Tokyo, who provided a research home in Japan. To the staff of the Biblioteca Nacional and Archivo General de la Nación in Buenos Aires, who provided kind assistance on my maiden voyage to Argentina. To the faculty and staff of the Economic History Department at the London School of Economics, who provided the starting point. Finally, this book would not have been possible without the financial assistance of Columbia University, the Weatherhead Foundation, the Economic History Association, and the Japan Foundation. I thank them all.

Introduction

Pasts Imperfect

The financial panic of 2008 marked at least a temporary interruption in the market fundamentalism that emerged out of the 1970s in Anglo-American society. But this idealized view of markets and classic English economics was, and remains, immensely influential. Its influence has been particularly strong as applied to ideas of globalization and global economic history.

In the years after the fall of the Berlin Wall it became common in Anglo-American society to look toward the turn of the twentieth century as a globalized mirror of the present. This mirror image served not only as historical déjà vu but also as validation of the market-dominated turn of the twenty-first century. In both periods, goods and capital flowed around the world, businesses boomed, and prosperity reigned for most. For globalization enthusiasts looking back at the 1890s, it was almost as if their world had once before existed—before two world wars, fascism, communism, the Great Depression, and a century's worth of history had so rudely interrupted. Looked at in this mirror, the twentieth-century world economy seemed at its close to have come full circle.[1]

At times there were also popular images about a brave new world of unprecedented change.[2] But both images addressed matters from a similar starting point using similar tools. Being presented as largely an economic story, the globalization tale leaned toward being one of guidance for present-day public policy focused on the concerns, methods, and viewpoints of current day Anglo-American society. Elements of the late nineteenth-century world economy that pointed away from those of the late twentieth century slid to the background. The Depression and post–World War II years became detours and digressions. The experiences of other countries were ignored or framed in terms of the degree they had or had not adopted ostensibly universal, Anglo-American norms.

Primarily, it became a story framed in terms of modern Anglo-American social science: neoliberalism and neoclassical economics, and their ancestor nineteenth-century English liberalism.

In this way the late twentieth-century globalization tale as popularly referenced by Britons and Americans merged with an older story among English speakers of British triumphalism and Pax Britannica.[3] This produced a tendency in society at large not only to frame the years before World War I in terms of modern social science but also to present a world economically dominated by English ideas and institutions even where it was not. In large part this was the understandable tendency of people to place themselves at the center of the world and the center of history. It is why children around the globe grow up with maps placing their country at the center of the world even when this means slicing other countries and continents in two.

For native English speakers coming out of the 1980s, 1990s, and 2000s, this meant an image of English liberalism and American neoliberalism hovering over popular ideas of globalization and implied a history largely written in the British image. In short, this particular neoliberal variant on the Anglo-American view of the world has presented a turn-of-the-century belle époque of sorts, not only of globalization and liberal economics but also of nineteenth-century English and twentieth-century American dominance in both ideas and institutions.

This was not, however, how people outside Anglo-America necessarily viewed their world in the late nineteenth century. Nor did it necessarily determine how they shaped their world.

Although cognizant of both the theory and the practice of British ideas and institutions, individuals in countries that sought political and eco-

nomic power at the turn of the twentieth century reacted far more pragmatically to British ideas and institutions than Pax Britannica implies.
Even when adopting the forms of British institutions, they did so from a
different mindset than that assumed by English liberalism and neoclassical
economics. In short, they made British institutions their own—adapting
and modifying them for their own purposes, developed in light of their
own view of how the world worked.

The history of the modern world economy has also been a history of
shifting powers. Rising economic powers have traditionally favored more
activist state roles in their national economies and international economic relations than established powers.[4] They have also generally sought to
change or adapt existing rules of international economic conduct to their
own purposes. Nor historically has it been rare to see countries pursue activist state policies when their economies and industries were developing,
only to discover the logic of markets in later eras. The English and American ideological shifts from protectionism to free trade in the mid-nineteenth century and after World War II are only the most notable examples
of this tendency.

English liberalism certainly existed in the late nineteenth century and
was certainly influential—most notably, and most unremarkably, among
Englishmen, the majority of whom could imagine little but English ideas.
But it was only one model, and far from the dominant one by century's
end. Early moral philosophers such as Adam Smith and David Hume developed English economic liberalism from English experience and modeled it on English needs. These ideas reached their practical peak with
the height of British manufacturing in the 1850s and 1860s. By 1890 the
model, for all intents and purposes, ruled only in Britain, and even there
it faced mounting opposition as economic conditions, social change, and
the balance of international power pointed in a different direction.

The nineteenth century's second applied model came from those such
as the German Friedrich List and the American Alexander Hamilton who
sought to use industrial protection and nationalist ideas and institutions
as a means to challenge British economic and political power.[5] This model dominated even at midcentury in those countries such as the United
States and Prussia that sought to duplicate, and even surpass, the English
Industrial Revolution of the late eighteenth and early nineteenth century.
By the end of the nineteenth century the ranks of those countries seeking
to follow the United States and Germany, rather than Britain, included

most independent countries worldwide with pretensions to industrial or military power.

In short, the global economy before World War I combined laissez-faire, cosmopolitan liberal ideas with statist, nationalist ideas. Mass capital and immigration flows—while they lasted—fit perfectly into liberal ideas of borderless movements of people, goods, and money.[6] Coexisting with these liberal trends were liberalism's opposites of trade protectionism, infant-industry promotion, and a large state presence in the form of empire building and military spending—with ideas and a nationalist point of view far different from cosmopolitan liberal thought to back them up. This was acknowledged as a commonplace in the years before World War I. It was not, however, so often acknowledged in the interwar years or in popular images of globalization dominant in the English-speaking world in the 1990s and 2000s.[7]

This popular tendency to frame world history in terms of liberal ideas and institutions was hardly limited to the neoliberal heights of the 1990s and early 2000s. In the 1920s policymakers and the most serious of serious opinion latched onto the idea that the secret of worldwide prosperity prior to 1914 had been the dominance of English ideas and institutions. In particular, they became convinced that the secret of worldwide prosperity before the war had been a presumed adherence to laissez-faire capitalism expressed through an international financial system constructed on the adoption worldwide of the British gold standard.

As the economist and economic historian Joseph Schumpeter wrote in the 1950s, the gold standard came to be viewed (as Schumpeter himself viewed it) as "a perfectly 'free' or 'automatic'" standard that was "part and parcel of a laissez-faire and free-trade economy" and "extremely sensitive to government expenditure . . . foreign policy . . . and, in general, to precisely all those policies that violate the principles of liberalism."[8]

This, indeed, was the belief of most policymakers and popular opinion in the 1920s. But it was a belief that ran head on into reality, as countries sought to reinstate a gold standard that had been ripped from its historic context, and deflated their economies in order to match presumed rules of conduct prescribed by English theory. Their attempts to recapture a lost age of laissez-faire economic glory helped lead to a global downturn and, then, the Great Depression.[9]

A large amount of material on the gold standard in Europe and the United States has shown these policy decisions to be a primary factor, if not the primary factor, in bringing about the Great Depression. Work by scholars such as Barry Eichengreen, Peter Temin, Harold James, Christina Romer, and Ben Bernanke has been particularly noteworthy in this regard.

This book adds to this insight about the 1920s by showing that the gold standard as established worldwide in the 1890s was different from the rigid, deflationary gold standard that policymakers in the 1920s believed they were emulating. In short, they sought to reinstate a gold standard that looked more like the standard of mid-nineteenth-century laissez-faire, liberal English theory than it did the flexible, devalued, and antideflationary standard that governments adopted in the 1890s.

To date, studies that have linked the return to the gold standard in the 1920s to the onset of the Great Depression have not looked to see if the gold standard that policymakers sought to reinstate in the 1920s was fundamentally the same as the gold standard of the 1890s. They have looked at particular technical details. But they have not looked at the underlying reasons and purposes for adopting the gold standard in the 1890s nor examined how countries adapted the gold standard to suit those purposes.

Nor have global accounts of the late nineteenth-century world economy and the gold standard generally included contemporary, non–English language sources. In giving priority to the beliefs of late nineteenth-century Englishmen, such accounts have inevitably placed Britain at the center of the late nineteenth-century world, even as rising powers such as the United States and Germany gained equivalent or greater economic and political power. Nor have they generally looked out from Europe and North America to the rest of this globalizing world and addressed that world on its own terms, rather than as a travelogue of views from Europe.

This book is about the gold standard and how it came to be adopted worldwide at the turn of the twentieth century in ways and for reasons that had less to do with fealty to English power or English theory than with realpolitik concerns of national power, prestige, and anti-English competition. It was a use of the gold standard distinct from neoclassical ideas, English influence, and late twentieth and early-twenty-first-century ideas of market economics.

This book seeks to complicate and nuance a more geographically limited, British Empire account that centers discussions of the gold standard principally within the British Empire and views countries outside of Europe primarily in terms of how technical, day-to-day changes in the

London financial markets and Bank of England interest rates affected gold inflows or outflows in those countries.

In this, the book draws on, and seeks to add to, the work of numerous historians and economists. In particular, Arthur Bloomfield's classic work in the 1950s and 1960s showed how the nineteenth-century gold standard in practice differed from the laissez-faire ideas of the most influential scholars, policymakers, and commentators of the 1920s. Bloomfield was most influential in first suggesting that the nineteenth-century gold standard as viewed from the 1920s was not the same as the nineteenth-century gold standard viewed from the nineteenth century.

Barry Eichengreen and Marc Flandreau have presented fuller historical pictures of the gold standard. Eichengreen, in particular, has provided valuable insights about the interwar period and the relation of the gold standard to the coming of the Great Depression. Marc Flandreau has brought power politics into the equation showing, most notably, how in nineteenth-century Germany and France the gold standard emerged less from economic rationality and a belief in laissez-faire economic ideas than from domestic interests and international political and military rivalry.

For reasons of language or geographic preference the emphasis in English has been first on Europe and second, the United States. Scholars such as A. G. Ford, Jorge Braga de Macedo, Jaime Reis, Alan Taylor, and Gerardo della Paolera have provided valuable insights about the gold standard in what has been known as the periphery—that is, areas, such as Argentina, seen as peripheral to a British-centered world. Other scholars working in Spanish, such as Ezequiel Gallo, and Japanese, such as Nakamura Takafusa, Chō Yukio, Hugh Patrick, Kojima Hitoshi, Itō Masanao, and Mark Metzler, have provided notable accounts of the gold standard treating countries outside of Europe in their own right, not simply as peripheral appendages to a British-centered world. Metzler, in particular, has been at the forefront of introducing Japanese economic history into world history.

Historians such as Roberto Cortés Conde, Fernando Rocchi, Timothy Duncan, Paula Alonso, Natalio Botana, Roy Hora, Pablo Gerchunoff, and Lucas Llach have redefined the political and economic history of Argentina at the turn of the twentieth century by focusing on Argentine political and economic institutions as they developed internally rather than as a simple function of commerce with Britain. I hope the current book adds at least a bit to their insights and shows that Argentina was not alone in the world in its turn-of-the-century concerns. I will consider the book at least a partial success if readers can see events and ideas in Argentina and Japan as part of a larger, late nineteenth-century world, rather than as segregated national histories irrelevant to the wider world and students of that world.

I owe a debt to all these authors and to others. The book could not exist in its current form without the benefit of their work.

I believe the time has come for a new look at the gold standard as a global system, not from the perspective of a British center, but with what has been more commonly called the periphery occupying center stage. The point is not to see these countries as exceptions to a British system, or adopting a yes-no attitude of either accepting or rejecting British institutions and ideas. Rather, it is to ask what ideas were at play and what were the characteristics and purposes of the institutions adopted in these countries. The book also seeks to show how the particular ideas and institutions these countries adopted—and the interests competing over these ideas and institutions—helped shaped the late nineteenth-century world.

The gold standard in practice meant that countries fixed the value of their currencies to gold. By state fiat one yen equaled X ounces of gold, one dollar equaled Y ounces of gold, and so on. Since Britain had been the first country to fix the value of its currency to gold in the nineteenth century—and was by the mid-nineteenth century the world's primary financial and trade power—setting a fixed value of one's currency to gold meant, in practice, fixing the value of one's currency to the British pound sterling. It was, in short, similar to countries in the 1990s, such as Argentina and Thailand, that fixed the value of their currencies to the U.S. dollar.

By adopting the gold standard, countries enacted something vaguely resembling a single world currency and thereby limited control over their own money. A country gained gold either by selling more goods to the rest of the world than it bought, or otherwise borrowing or attracting foreign capital. According to a piece of English theory first developed in the eighteenth century by David Hume, a country importing more goods than it exported would suffer a net outflow of gold that would lead to declines in the money supply, consumption, and prices. As prices deflated, a country would be able to sell its goods more cheaply abroad leading to an expansion of exports and an increase in gold inflows.

In theory, this self-regulating process would yield a balance of currency and goods at a perfectly equilibrated, and perfectly efficient, price. Practice was something quite different, however, as states sterilized gold flows, intervened in currency markets, and sought to accumulate specie irrespective of their trade balances.[10] The gold standard in its pre–World War I incarnation was a system pragmatically, even cynically, applied by many states in a way sharply divergent from the image of the cosmopolitan, liberal system presented in English theory. Quite simply, state leaders were more interested in promoting their own view of national interests than the tenets of a century-old theory.

Individuals and groups outside of government also competed, attempting to shape government actions to advance their own private interests as well as their particular perceptions of the national interest. Not surprisingly, their perceptions of national interests often, but not always, reflected their private interests.

But the ultimate adopters of the gold standard were governments. These governments were not completely free of the pressures of parliaments and outside interests. But they were able to manipulate the process, and benefit from divided opponents, in such a way that their final monetary choices reflected their ideas of the national interest.

The chapters that follow show how the gold standard emerged outside of Europe in the late nineteenth century as a tool of nationalists and protectionists intent on fostering domestic industry and imperial expansion. In so doing, the book shifts the center of gravity for the gold standard from a cosmopolitan world of free markets, economic liberalism, and laissez-faire to one in which nationalist concerns with infant-industry protection and military power dominated. Where this contradicts the way English-language readers in recent years have come to think about the global economy at the turn of the twentieth century, it is because English-language sources and interpretations have been predominantly concerned with the gold standard, and indeed the entire turn-of-the-century global economy, as a British-based system infused with British ideas, British interests, and British institutions.

The book draws a distinction between the mid-nineteenth-century height of European free trade and laissez-faire ideology and a late nineteenth-century backlash to the mixed results of those policies.[11] Just as the twentieth century went through periods in which greater or lesser degrees of internationalism or nationalism, free trade or protectionism, and state intervention or laissez-faire predominated, so too did the nineteenth century. Nor should this be particularly surprising given the continual historic waxing and waning of periods of greater or lesser nationalism or internationalism, and greater or lesser roles for the state in economic activity and society in general.

In looking at the years before World War I, what is so striking is not how the global economy at the turn of the twentieth century lacks growth, trade, internationalism or, indeed, globalization, which it does not, but the fact that these global activities and institutions coexisted with, and in many ways were founded on, the antithesis of late twentieth-century globalization in terms of ideology and institutions.[12]

Whereas free trade, deregulation, and a supposedly vanishing state constituted the cornerstones of late twentieth-century globalization, global economic activity in the years before World War I was most remarkable for combining expanding trade, growth, and industrialization with a range of statist economic institutions, restrictions on trade, and nationalist ideology united in pursuit of the dominant goals of the age: industry and empire.

This book is divided into three sections and an epilogue, which together make the argument that the dominant ideas and institutions of the world economy at the turn of the twentieth century were unique to that era and not merely a reflection of the ideas and institutions of the present day. I argue, historically, that the world economy has come in various forms, been underpinned by a range of ideas and institutions, and been influenced by a variety of political and economic interests. Finally, I argue that as much as those raised in an English-language tradition may naturally view the world from an English perspective, this does not necessarily mean that the rest of the world has followed suit.

The book is meant for scholars in various fields and for general readers. The individual parts of this story should be familiar to specialists. It is, however, not uncommon for American, Asian, and European specialists, historians, economists, and political scientists to talk less across academic fields than within them so that what is familiar to one set of readers may be unfamiliar to another. I aim to build on the insights of existing scholarship in history, economics, and political science by shifting the focus to the less-often-considered powers of Asia and Latin America: Japan and Argentina.

Why specifically Japan and Argentina? Quite simply because Japan and Argentina were the most important independent countries politically and economically in Asia and Latin America at the turn of the twentieth century. India was part of the British Empire; China never adopted the gold standard; and Russia's status as a non-European country is arguable. Both

Japan and Argentina were comparatively well off, economically and politically ambitious, and obsessed with national advancement—obtaining civilization and progress as those terms were defined at the turn of the twentieth century.

Other countries are addressed briefly in chapter 3 to place the Japanese and Argentine experience in context and to show that they represented common trends of their age rather than being exceptions. Presenting more than two examples in detail would have required a far longer book than the current one.

In this book I look at the views of society at large, rather than presenting a survey of scholarly interpretations dominant now or in the past. Above all, my purpose is to look at the turn-of-the-century global economy and its central institution, the gold standard, through the eyes of the late nineteenth century, not those of the pre- or postcrisis twenty-first.

I also look at the ideas, institutions, and interests dominant in late nineteenth-century Argentina and Japan through Argentine and Japanese eyes, not as those elements were viewed from Britain, the United States, or any other country. For the purposes of the book, the views of late nineteenth-century Britons and Americans are less important than the views of their Argentine and Japanese contemporaries.

For those seeking a discussion of the current state of scholarly debate, the footnotes provide a review of scholarly literature and notable references on specific points. Full publication information can be found in the References.

Part I (chapters 1, 2 and 3) sets out the international context of industrial development, protectionism, and imperialism from when the gold standard became a European system in the 1870s with its de facto or de jure adoption in Germany, France, and other continental countries, and then in the 1890s when it became a global system with its adoption by Russia, Argentina, Japan, and other countries removed from the center of Europe. Chapter 1 outlines the major elements of the late nineteenth century that shaped the world currency system—trade and protectionism, empire, warfare, finance, and foreign borrowing—and then looks at how the trio of industrial development, empire, and warfare were linked to turn-of-the-century prosperity.

Chapter 1 also introduces a chronological and ideological distinction between two nineteenth centuries: one of English dominance at midcentury supported by cosmopolitan ideas of English liberalism; the other, dominant in the years before World War I, based on nationalist ideas of empire and Listian developmentalism.

Chapter 2 turns to the gold standard itself, looking at it as a national institution, and sets out the issues of foreign borrowing and currency depreciation versus appreciation that affected currency decisions in the late nineteenth century. Chapter 3 looks at the different countries that adopted the gold standard, and draws a distinction between those countries with purely economic ambitions and those with political ones as well

Parts II and III take a closer look at two specific countries, Argentina and Japan—the former belonging to the ranks of countries primarily interested in economic and industrial progress, the latter from the ranks of countries with not only industrial ambitions but also political, imperial, and military ones.[13]

I focus in particular on the interplay of ideas and interests that shaped each country's monetary choices. In this way, this book is a story of the interaction of institutions, ideas, and interests. Above all, I focus on how and why these countries came to adopt the currency systems they did: Why leaders in each country made the choices they did; which interest groups and segments of society influenced these choices; what contemporary Argentines and Japanese believed they were doing; and how they interpreted the systems they were enacting.

I pay particular attention to the thinking of the primary architects of the respective Argentine and Japanese currency systems, Carlos Pellegrini and Matsukata Masayoshi, in parts II and III. I do so not only because these men were responsible for designing their country's currency system—and forcing through their adoption in the face of lukewarm to openly hostile domestic opinion—but also because their ideas about currency, and the role of the state, reflected views typical of a certain type of activist bureaucrat-politician prevalent in economically and politically ambitious states at the turn of the twentieth century.

Like Bismarck in Germany and Sergei Witte in Russia, these individuals viewed national progress in the form of industrial strength or imperial expansion. The same can be said of the United States, where the mercantilist tradition of Alexander Hamilton merged with the imperial preferences of William McKinley and Teddy Roosevelt in the 1890s to create an American governing majority founded on industry and empire.

In Pellegrini's case, the primary goal was industrial development. For Matsukata, the goal was great power imperialism. Both Argentina and

Japan were very much of their time in being self-consciously new nations in the late nineteenth-century hierarchy. With Argentina coming into political existence in the mid-nineteenth century and Japan becoming a modern centralized state after the Meiji Restoration in 1868, each country soon went about acquiring the accoutrements of nineteenth-century nationhood: public schools, railroads, constitutions, national myths, and, eventually, the gold standard. Each country addressed the expansion of the gold standard worldwide in the 1890s in terms of the same technical issues that countries such as China regularly face today: whether to have a fixed-rate currency system, what rate to set, and whether to link that rate to silver, gold, or something else. As with currency decisions today, the institutional choices rested on a mixture of the prevailing economic and political ideas and the interests of the age.

Part II (chapters 4–6) examines the adoption of the gold standard in Argentina in 1899 and argues that it was a system rooted in the second nineteenth-century model of Listian development and, more specifically, in the desire to devalue the peso and protect domestic industry. Chapter 4 lays out the dominant industrial development model of infant-industry protection and currency devaluation, particularly as advocated by Carlos Pellegrini, and contrasts it with its opponents—the supporters of free trade and appreciated, metallic currency. Chapter 5 discusses the odd alliances of parliamentary supporters and opponents of the Argentine gold standard and how this was rooted in the use of a means borrowed from the first, liberal English model of economic development (metallic currency) to accomplish the ends of the second, Listian model (currency devaluation and industrial promotion). Chapter 6 addresses the question of whether the Argentine currency system can even legitimately be considered an example of the gold standard as that system came to be interpreted by contemporary Englishmen and in the rearview mirror of the 1920s and the turn of the twenty-first century.

Part III (chapters 7–9) looks at adoption of the gold standard in Japan in 1897 and the parallel tracks of economic and political factors leading to its adoption. Unlike Argentina's desire for industrial protection, which drove adoption of the gold standard, the Japanese government was primarily motivated by a desire to attract foreign capital to finance projected great power wars. Chapter 7 sets up the basic economic and political arguments for a gold standard in Japan and examines the particular issues of trade and stability. Chapter 8 looks at the interests of exporters and merchants who shared the Argentine enthusiasm for depreciating currency and whose potential opposition to the gold standard was undercut by uncertainty about world events. Chapter 9 shifts the focus to the state and argues that rather than seeking primarily to promote industry and commerce, as was the case in Argentina, Japanese leaders concentrated on political and national security concerns: great power priorities and issues of imperial management.

The epilogue looks at how the loose money, protectionist, and intensely political and militaristic currency systems of the 1890s came to be lumped in the 1920s into a sanitized vision of the late nineteenth-century world. This vision—cut off from prewar history—saw a gold standard rooted in liberal English political economy and World War I as a deus ex machina interrupting a turn-of-the-century world of peace, prosperity, and liberal economics. In so doing, governments turned what thirty years earlier had been an expansionary monetary order into a contractionary one, and with it set the stage for the Great Depression of the 1930s and the collapse of the interwar world that followed.

PART ONE

Gold and the
Late Nineteenth-Century World

1

The Late Nineteenth-Century World

In the early nineteenth century Britain emerged as the predominant political and economic actor of its age. The Industrial Revolution of the late eighteenth and early nineteenth century, the end of Napoleon's military dominance on the European continent in the 1810s, and Britain's use of military and economic means to cobble together trade and colonial centers all contributed to Britain's global power and influence. This influence peaked during the 1850s and 1860s, giving way to a relative decline vis-à-vis other countries in the last quarter of the nineteenth century.[1]

The economic side of this so-called Pax Britannica of relative English dominance was not limited to Britain's industrial and manufacturing strength; it also included London's role as the world's financial center. Although by the 1890s Britain had lost its manufacturing superiority to Germany and the United States as textiles gave way to chemicals and heavy industry, Britain retained its financial power. If anything, London's financial role was, in absolute terms, more notable immediately before World War I than in the 1870s, when English manufacturing strength first began to wane. British funds flowing overseas totaled 17% of total British wealth in

1870, in 1913 they reached 33%. Britons held 370 million pounds in foreign assets in 1860; by 1913 they held 3.9 billion pounds.[2]

The rise of English industrial and financial power brought varied responses from the rest of the world: challenging it, allying with it, or seeking protection from it. Other countries did not necessarily seek to mimic late nineteenth-century English ideas and institutions, even in cases when they might appear to have adopted the forms of those institutions. In most cases, the point was not to imitate English institutions for the sake of imitation, but rather to accrue political or economic power and then use that power for national purposes. Most often, countries looking to Britain in the late nineteenth century viewed British ideas and institutions as suitable only to the particular interests of mature powers such as Britain, not to countries such as themselves seeking to develop their own political and economic power.

British ideas and institutions were most influential from the 1850s to the early 1870s, which coincided with the height of European free trade and a midcentury boom in trade, prices, and income. Free trade treaties were the norm, with the Anglo-French treaty of 1860 quickly followed by similar treaties among Britain, France, Prussia, Belgium, the Netherlands, and the Piedmont (Italy).[3] Although military force was used to promote European commercial interests in Asia, Latin America, the Middle East, and Northern Africa, the hyper phase of nineteenth-century imperialism kicked in only at the end of the century.

The world from the 1870s through the early 1890s was one of declining prices, economic unease, protectionism, and increased military expenditures linked to a revived enthusiasm for empire and military expansion as values unto themselves. It was also a time when rising powers were rapidly industrializing. In the late nineteenth century, industrialization first became a worldwide phenomenon. It brought a reordering not only of economic and political power and interests but also of prevailing ideas and institutions.

In 1870 Britain, Belgium, and France produced almost half of the world's industrial output.[4] By 1913 these countries produced barely one-fifth. In 1870 Britain produced 32% of the world's industrial output, the United States 23%, and Germany 13%. By 1913 Britain produced 14%, Germany 16%, and the United States 36%.[5] In 1870 British iron and steel production was greater than the combined production of the United States and Germany. By 1913 the combined production of the United States and

Germany was six times that of Britain.[6] In 1880 Britain consumed 47% of the world's raw cotton; by 1913 it consumed only 18%.[7]

In the years before World War I, more cosmopolitan and less nationalistic workers parties came to favor international socialism or, as in Argentina, became ardent supporters of classic English political economy and free trade. The more nationalistic and militaristic parties and governments of the right leaned toward the state-centered policies of the U.S. treasury secretary Alexander Hamilton and the German nationalist Friedrich List, himself heavily influenced by Hamilton, in a preference for industrial promotion and trade protectionism.[8] The McKinley-era U.S. Republican Party, the protectionist Partido Autonomista Nacional in Argentina, and the Meiji oligarchs in Japan all followed this route.

After World War II the political left was most often associated with protectionism and industrial promotion—in the image of Soviet communism, import substitution in Latin America and India, and labor unionism in the United States and Europe. But this was not the case in the late nineteenth century when protectionism and industrial promotion formed, along with imperial expansion, the basic economic and foreign policy creed of the political right.

The changed economic environment of the late nineteenth century appeared most notably in a wave of declining prices that led contemporary observers to call the twenty years from the early 1870s to the 1890s "the Great Depression." The uneven pace and distribution of these declines favored certain interests and industries and harmed others. This led to increasing economic and social discontent, with wealth shifting from debtors to creditors, and increased global trade meaning boom times for some individuals and industries and disaster for others.

The cause of the price declines remained unclear for years. Even when a set of explanations emerged, the wildly different interests helped or harmed by declining prices led to wildly different judgments regarding those explanations. The most common explanation linked the price declines to a lack of money. More specifically, it linked the declines to a lack of gold for those countries basing their currencies on gold. Gold production started to decline in the 1870s from peak levels reached in the 1850s and 1860s just as the number of countries using gold currency was increasing. As the supply of gold slowed and demand for it increased, the value of gold rose and prices declined. Although there had been a 60% increase in gold currency from 1850 to 1866 as newly discovered Australian and

California gold flooded the market, from 1867–80 the amount of gold currency increased by only 31%.[9] Gold production declined steadily between 1871 and 1880, just as Germany and other countries in continental Europe were shifting from silver currency to gold, and then dropped substantially from 1881 to 1883.[10]

Product prices for these periods showed a 50% increase for 1850–66 followed by a 30% decline for 1867–80. From 1880 to 1896 a 30% increase in the amount of gold currency worldwide was accompanied by a 27% decline in prices.[11] From 1865 onward business profits shrank, new businesses and industries grew more slowly, and interest earned on capital declined.[12] British prices increased by 51% between 1849 and 1873, decreased 45% between 1873 and 1896, and increased by 39% between 1896 and 1913.[13] The pattern was similar in the United States, where prices declined an average of 1.7% per year between 1875 and 1896.[14]

This price deflation caused recessions in the 1870s and 1880s in Europe and, to a lesser extent, in the United States. In the United States criticism erupted about an American "Crime of '73," a reference to Congress prohibiting the free minting of silver, which opponents believed had brought about the price declines by restricting the supply of money to gold and, in turn, causing the value of the dollar to appreciate. Since the dollar was then worth more, prices fell to compensate. As the supply of gold failed to keep pace with demand, the value of gold appreciated and prices fell.

As with most economic change, in the long run, and in theory, all these changes in supply, demand, and prices would be expected to work themselves out as individuals adjusted their activities and purchases. In the real world these changes took time and happened at different speeds, causing hardships and disruptions to some groups and individuals and providing windfalls to others. It was one thing to say that declining agriculture prices meant that a certain numbers of farmers should stop farming in order to cause farm prices to rebound. It was quite another to put this into practice. Changing one's life is considerably easier in theory than in practice.

How much of the price declines were actually caused by the appreciation of gold was, and still is, disputed.[15] The contemporary concern with the appreciation of gold, however, was real and led to government silver purchases in the United States and a series of monetary conferences in the 1880s aimed at promoting silver and potentially moving to a global bimetallic system that would use both silver and gold to make up for the limited gold supplies.[16] This interest in bimetallism only died out after a new flood of gold discoveries appeared in the mid-1890s, rendering concerns about limited gold supplies moot. Before that could happen, however, declining prices and appreciating gold brought about a fundamental reordering of the late nineteenth-century world economy in another way: a revival of protectionism.

Trade and Protectionism

Protectionism was the dominant form of state economic policy in the seventeenth and eighteenth centuries. It meant favoring exports over imports, and domestic producers over foreign, by tacking on various surcharges or taxes—that is, tariffs—to the prices of imported goods. In this way, domestic products became less expensive than imported ones, meaning that consumers bought more domestic goods than foreign, and domestic producers were freed from worrying about competition from foreign producers. This, of course, also meant that consumers paid more than they would have had they been able to purchase foreign goods without the tariffs.

The dominance of protectionism began to fade in the late eighteenth century when English theorists such as Adam Smith and David Hume shifted the focus of economics away from the state and onto individual producers and consumers.[17] The shift to free trade and liberal economics gained impetus in Britain as industrialization made tariff-free trade of benefit to English manufacturers whose products easily dominated, in price and quality, those of other less industrialized countries. This process culminated in 1846 when Parliament repealed the last of Britain's protective tariffs, sacrificing British agriculture to the interests of manufacturing.

After the flurry of European free trade treaties in the 1860s proved of little benefit to most countries, and the late nineteenth-century price declines made matters worse, the tide turned back to protectionism. The new protectionism came repackaged in the form of the Americans Alexander Hamilton and Henry Carey, the German Friedrich List, and a post–French Revolution emphasis on nationalism.[18] The most immediate result of late nineteenth-century deflation was thus the reemergence of protectionism in Europe, a strengthening of protectionism in those countries such as the United States where free trade had never taken hold, and an eventual shift to protectionism even in countries such as Argentina that had close ties to Europe and depended on European capital and trade.

Except for Britain, the Netherlands, and Belgium there was virtually no independent country in the late nineteenth century that was not protectionist, often virulently so. This was readily acknowledged and widely supported.[19] The story was different for countries that were either formal colonies or, subject to semicolonial treaties (e.g., China and Japan) that removed their freedom to set tariff rates. This enforced adoption of free trade was fiercely opposed by the majority of those countries subjected to colonial or semicolonial status.[20] It was also a practice that was centered, as in Europe, in the mid-nineteenth century. The Asian tendency toward lower tariff rates changed from the late 1880s as Japan and other Asian countries regained tariff autonomy.[21]

As one English observer wrote in 1896, "It is a common-place of economic history that during the last thirty years a wave of protectionism has spread over Europe and America. It has been due partly to wars, partly to agricultural depression, partly to the great fall of prices in gold-using countries, partly to the growth of an economic theory which prefers national to cosmopolitan considerations, and to which the writings of Frederick List and [Henry] Carey have given a wide popularity and influence."[22]

Germany shifted to export promotion in the mid-1870s and from 1879 moved sharply from free trade leanings to a policy of protective tariffs.[23] Agricultural tariffs expanded rapidly not only in Germany but also throughout Europe from the 1870s with Austria-Hungary, France, Germany, and Italy having tariffs of roughly 40% on wheat in the years before World War I.[24]

More important for adherents of Listian developmentalism were tariffs on manufactured goods. In developing countries such as the United States, Argentina, Brazil, Mexico, and Russia these averaged two, three, or more times those in Europe.[25] Nor did tariffs decline in the years before World War I. In France, where protection became synonymous with that "apostle of protectionism" Jules Méline and the Méline Tariff of 1892, tariff rates did not reach their peak until 1910.[26] In most countries they increased until the war. As of 1913 average tariffs on manufactured goods were 13% in Germany, 18% in Austria-Hungary, 18% in Italy, 20% in France, 26% in Canada, 28% in Argentina, 30% in Japan, 41% in Spain, 44% in the United States, 40%–50% in Mexico, 40%–60% in Colombia, 50%–70% in Brazil, and 84% in Russia.[27]

Even the degree to which Britain actually practiced free trade has been questioned, with some observers arguing that Britain used excise taxes on luxury goods to obtain the same trade benefits that other countries sought through protective tariffs.[28] But given the prevalence of free trade rhetoric in Britain, the absence of protective tariffs, and the commitment of the Liberal Party of William Gladstone and David Lloyd George to free trade doctrines, the dominance of late nineteenth-century protectionism is not immediately apparent if one looks solely at Britain and the British Liberal Party.

But in Britain another current in society and politics by the turn of the century more accurately reflected developments in the rest of the world. Increasing competition from American and German manufacturers produced a shift in British opinion in the 1890s, with newspapers, magazines, and popular books such as Ernest Williams' *Made in Germany* (1896) and Frederick McKenzie's *American Invaders* (1902) trumpeting the menace of foreign manufacturing and imports.[29] In response, protectionist ideas and policies experienced an upsurge in Britain, championed by such figures as Lord Salisbury and Joseph Chamberlain.

This turn-of-the-century revival of British protectionism only increased the certainty of those countries that looked to Britain and saw not the triumph of free trade as either idea or institution, but rather a self-interested application of fungible means to the ends of national economic and political power. When mercantilism served British purposes, Britain was mercantilist. When free trade served British purposes, Britain was free trade. And when free trade no longer provided benefits, it could be jettisoned as well.

Rather than seeing a triumph of scientific truth, these countries saw a Britain that had abolished its protective tariffs and adopted free trade in 1846 "due to the superiority of its manufacturing industry over those of other nations, which made competition virtually impossible."[30] In response, proponents of industrial promotion in virtually every country that sought to develop industry in the late nineteenth century viewed their adoption of protective tariffs and industrial promotion as indistinguishable from British adherence to free trade. Both were the pragmatic application of the means best suited at the moment to secure national economic power.

Although Germany and the United States were the most successful in their challenge to British industrial and political power, they were not alone. From the 1870s increasing economic and political nationalism abandoned the cosmopolitanism of English liberalism for doctrines better suited to promoting national power. In this way, developmental protectionism became accepted state policy in countries seeking internal renewal, such as

France and Russia, and in self-consciously new or radically reformed nations like Germany, Japan, Italy, the United States, and Argentina.

In these countries Listian ideas flourished and industrial promotion most often meant protection of infant-industries.[31] The governments of Otto von Bismarck in Germany, Joseph Méline in France, Francesco Crispi in Italy, Eduard Taafe in Austria-Hungary, and Sergei Witte in Russia all based their economic systems on promoting and protecting industry. American protectionists—from Alexander Hamilton to Henry Clay and his "American system," from Abraham Lincoln to the turn-of-the-century Republican Party embodied by William McKinley—did so as well.[32]

Like other nineteenth-century promoters of nationalism and industrialization, List accepted free trade for a country like Britain that had already developed industry. He did not, however, accept it for other countries. List and the majority of late nineteenth-century protectionists saw infant-industry protection as an intermediate step on the way to British-style free trade. As List put it, "In order to allow freedom of trade to operate naturally, the less advanced nations must first be raised by artificial means to that stage of cultivation to which the English nation has been artificially elevated" by its own past mercantilist policies.[33]

English trade theorists did not necessarily challenge the infant-industry argument despite the dominance of free trade doctrine in universities in Britain and, to a lesser extent, the United States. In the United States the academic tilt toward free trade coexisted with advocates of a protectionist "American system" of Listian policies such as Matthew Carey (1760–1839) and his son Henry (1793–1879), considered at the time as the most noted American economist. Henry Carey, not surprisingly given his proindustry and nationalist views, gained popularity and influence among politicians and industrialists—including Abraham Lincoln and most of the East Coast manufacturing establishment.[34]

John Stuart Mill, the midcentury paragon of English liberalism, accepted the need for protective tariffs to aid infant-industry while urging that they be discarded as quickly as possible.[35] Similarly, Mill's late nineteenth-century replacement as Britain's most noted economist, Alfred Marshall, also accepted List's arguments for infant-industry protection in developing countries. So, too, did Marshall's successor as most eminent establishment economist of his generation A. C. Pigou. As Pigou put it in 1906, "Of the formal validity of List's [infant-industry] argument there is no longer any dispute among economists."[36]

In France, a sizable liberal school remained since its midcentury zenith with the theoretically liberal Paul Leroy-Beaulieu succeeding to the chair of liberals J. B. Say and Michel Chevalier at the Collège de France. But by the 1890s, in France as well, liberal theory was being challenged. Not only Listian economic nationalism but also the empiricism of the French historical school and arguments of racial and political imperialism that Leroy-Beaulieu himself would come to favor in the face of German protectionism came to challenge the liberal dominance.[37]

Leroy-Beaulieu remained staunchly free trade even as he embraced imperialist ideas politically. But other predominantly liberal economists such as Charles Gide (1883) and Léon Poinsard (1893) adopted protectionist ideas. Gide and Poinsard argued that while free trade might be better in theory, the circumstances of the late nineteenth-century world required France to adopt limited infant-industry protection. More markedly protectionist was Paul Cauwes' *Cours d'économie politique* (1878) that, with its defense of Listian developmentalism, drew from the views of both List and Cauwes' contemporary Augustin Cournot and attracted considerable support among politicians and businessmen even as it ran up against the dominance of liberalism within French academia.

In Germany, Gustav von Schmoller and the inductive, nationalist, and protectionist historical school dominated and owed a clear, and openly acknowledged, debt to List.[38] In Japan the ranks of free traders and protectionists—or, in Japanese usage, advocates of "free trade" and "protected trade"—split according to whether the university in question was public or private.[39] The two private universities—Fukuzawa Yukichi's Keio University and Ōkuma Shigenobu's Waseda University—overwhelmingly housed free traders. At imperial universities, such as the University of Tokyo, protectionists predominated. In contrast to English theory, however, which remained overwhelmingly deductive, free trade supporters in Japan argued, like Listians, inductively from practice, contemporary examples, and historical analogy.

For advocates of free trade at the turn of the century, such as the Harvard economist Frank W. Taussig, the best that could be said was that "the doctrine of free trade, however widely rejected in the world of politics, holds its own in the sphere of the intellect."[40] But Taussig, like his English counterpart Alfred Marshall, accepted infant-industry protection as an exception, in theory as well as in practice, to free trade even while advocating free trade on both theoretical and practical grounds. In arguing for the

benefits of free trade, Taussig in 1905 summed up turn-of-the-century ambivalence about free trade: "So far as the doctrine of free trade is concerned,
enthusiasm has been supplanted by cautious weighing or open doubt. Free
trade would seem to be the waning doctrine . . . [and] has no more sanctity
or authority than any other part of the obsolete system of natural liberty,
and the advantages or disadvantages of tariff restrictions are to be coolly
weighed for each country itself, in the light of specific experience."[41]

As was the case with their Anglo-American forefathers, the historical fact
of turn-of-the-century protectionism has attracted the attention of present-
day economic historians.[42] Approaching the matter most often through the
lens of neoclassical theory, many have been puzzled by the presence of protective tariffs during a period of high growth. They have also been puzzled
by why countries would enact protective tariffs when present-day studies
tell us that high tariffs decreased growth rather than increased it.

To understand why individuals in the late nineteenth century acted the
way they did, it is important to understand not only whether their calculations were correct or not in light of present-day theory and calculations but
also how they themselves approached the issue. Rational or not according
to neoclassical theory, the dominant way for late nineteenth-century governments to see the world was through the lens of Listian development,
nationalism, and great power politics, not the cosmopolitan rationalism of
midcentury English liberalism.

If industrial protection in the late nineteenth century was accepted in
theory, it was positively embraced in practice. But rather than an all or
nothing case where one either practiced protectionism or not, there were
degrees of support for particular national industries at the expense of foreign competitors. If the dominant form of protectionism was tariffs, it was
possible to aid industry in other ways. And countries were creative enough
with their institutions to do precisely that. And that is, indeed, what many
of them did when they sought to adopt the gold standard in order to devalue their currencies and thereby promote exports, block imports, and
protect their developing industries.

Turn-of-the-Century Prosperity

The relative and much remarked upon prosperity of the decade and a half
before World War I had its roots in increased gold production, declin-

ing interest rates, and rising prices after the deflation of the previous decades.[43] Notably, this array of forces produced the seeming paradox of a globalization not only coexisting with protectionism, but one in which increased trade accompanied increased protectionism. After the tight money world of the 1870s, '80s, and early '90s, the combination of gold discoveries, declining interest rates, and expanding money supplies marked a fundamental change in the world economy.[44] From 1896 to 1913 world trade increased from less than US$8 billion to more than US$18 billion.[45] Increased prices provided a stimulus to economies such as Japan's and Argentina's that relied primarily on exports. Increases in Japanese silk exports closely tracked increased inflation and overseas demand.[46]

The increase in gold production was not the only cause of the worldwide boom. Part of the monetary expansion was due to increased use of substitutes for metal even in countries with metallic currency standards.[47] Between 1885 and 1913 global gold reserves increased three and a half times while demand deposits increased fivefold.[48] By the early 1900s grain production had increased as production expanded from the United States and Canada to Southeast Asia and Australia, which exported their excess harvests to England and continental Europe.

The economic development of Argentina and other states in South America that formed after the collapse of the Spanish and Portuguese empires in the early nineteenth century, and the expansion of European imperialism into Africa with its demand for military and civilian provisions also contributed to the worldwide boom. Although the world economy was dominated by Britain, Germany, France, and increasingly the United States, countries such as Australia, Argentina, and Japan were central motors in this newly increased worldwide economic activity.

Military expenditures also contributed to worldwide inflation. Although food products showed relatively small price increases, copper, iron, and other products with industrial and military uses showed comparatively large price increases.[49] Imperial warfare itself helped propel economic activity, with demand from the Russo-Japanese War causing an uptick in the U.S. and European economies in 1904 and 1905.Even in Japan, where the Russo-Japanese War was far from the unalloyed economic success that the decade-earlier Sino-Japanese War had been, the conflict spurred economic activity and produced increases in commercial shipping and port construction.

It is impossible to discuss the global boom from the late 1890s to the outbreak of World War I without taking into consideration the central role that warfare played not only in establishing the gold standard but also in world trade and industrialization. Indeed, despite the efforts of industrial developmentalists in Argentina to promote domestic industry on the back of protective tariffs, Argentina's agricultural export model came to be solidified under increased demand from Britain for wool, beef, and wheat during the Boer War of 1899–1902.[50]

Military power was regarded as a sign of civilization in tandem with industrial technology. Countries such as mid-nineteenth-century Japan, which were "ignorant of all the methods of production as of modern wars," were regarded as feudal, backward, and outside the global flow of progress and civilization.[51] Only with the acquisition of military power could these countries be considered fully civilized. But military endeavors cost money. So, too, did the hypothetical wars around which the turn-of-the-century "armed peace" among the great powers revolved. Thus the worldwide expansion of the gold standard in the 1890s and the increased gold production beginning in that decade were accompanied by increased hording of gold by European governments and central banks in the form of war treasuries to finance anticipated wars.

As the economist and champion of French imperialism Paul Leroy-Beaulieu put it in 1899, "The real cause why there is not an excess of gold is the new policy of the large national banks that insist on indefinitely increasing their reserves beyond what could be necessary for economic needs, and this policy of the great banks has had as its cause the exaggerated armaments system and the maintaining or rather the augmentation of genuine war treasuries." Whereas previously, central bank coverage ratios—the amount of gold and silver held to redeem convertible paper—had ranged from 40% to 59% of the amount of paper in circulation, with roughly half of that in silver, by the 1890s the average gold reserve ratio alone had moved to the 60%–70% range. As Leroy-Beaulieu put it, "Gold is not in reality deposited in the banks; it is a prisoner: once it has entered, it is no longer able to leave."[52]

Between 1880 and 1914, total military expenditures for Germany, Austria-Hungary, Britain, Russia, Italy, and France rose from 132 million pounds sterling in 1880 to 158 million in 1890, 205 million in 1900, 288 million in 1910, and 397 million in 1914.[53] Between 1880 and 1914, warship tonnage increased from 367,000 to 532,000 in Britain, 426,000 to 891,000 in Germany, 543,000 to 910,000 in France, 246,000 to 444,000 in Austria-Hungary, and 791,000 to 1.352 million in Russia.[54] Nor were

Table 1.1
Annual Gold Production, Worldwide

Year(s)	Francs (in millions)
1851–55 (annual median)	686.7
1856–60 (annual median)	694.9
1861–65 (annual median)	637.4
1866–70 (annual median)	671.7
1871–75 (annual median)	599.0
1876–80 (annual median)	572.0
1881	533.9
1882	528.6
1883	494.4
1884	527.2
1885	562.0
1886	550.2
1887	548.1
1888	571.1
1889	640.0
1890	615.6
1891	677.1
1892	760.0
1893	816.2
1894	939.0
1895	1,032.9
1896	1,051.0
1897	1,211.7

Source: Paul Leroy-Beaulieu, "De la producción y el empleo del oro en el mundo," *El Economista Argentino*, June 3, 1899, 7.

these trends limited to Europe. In the United States, warship tonnage increased from 34,000 in 1880 to 164,000 in 1914. In Japan, warship tonnage increased from 15,000 in 1880 to 41,000 in 1890, 187,000 in 1900, 496,000 in 1910, and 700,000 in 1914.

But the price increases on which that prosperity rested brought their own adjustments and, eventually, interest rate increases that began to slow economic activity. By 1912 the increase in gold production, which had seemed so inconceivable in the 1880s, and so durable in the early 1900s, had largely run its course. Prior to the enormous expansion of gold production in the 1890s annual gold production had never exceeded 800 million francs even in the 1850s at the time of the Australian and California gold discoveries.[55] Production had declined to the 500 million franc level by 1882, where it remained throughout the 1880s. It was only thereafter that the true explosion of gold production began. Annual production figures passed 1 billion in 1895, 2 billion in 1906, and by 1908 had reached 2.3

billion. But production in 1909 increased by barely 70 million francs. By 1920 annual production fell by 4 million francs. And with this decline in production, the original motor of the turn-of-the-century boom passed.

The Two Nineteenth Centuries

One might say that there were two nineteenth centuries, each with its particular ideological influences and practical characteristics. The first began in roughly 1846 when Britain abolished the Corn Laws, gave up protectionism, and became the global exemplar of free trade. The second began in 1871, with the conclusion of the Franco-Prussian War, or possibly in 1873, with adoption of the gold standard by a newly united Germany. In this second nineteenth century the movement toward free trade that dominated at midcentury was replaced by a renewed protectionist tilt as well as a political shift internationally from an emphasis on English liberalism and legal rights and process to one based more squarely on state promotion of industry and empire.[56]

This distinction between these two nineteenth centuries marks the gold standard. During the first nineteenth century, the gold standard was limited to Britain and founded upon principles of eighteenth-century English political economy. During the second nineteenth century, the gold standard expanded to a continental Europe preoccupied with industrial promotion, protectionism, empire, and a social Darwinist sense of nationalism. From the 1890s these second nineteenth-century trends coalesced into a turn-of-the-century burst of nationalism, protectionism, and empire. Expansion of the gold standard worldwide in the 1890s reflected these second nineteenth-century trends. Just as the first nineteenth century of free trade and expanding English liberalism was qualitatively different from the second nineteenth century of protectionism and empire, so too was the gold standard of the first nineteenth century qualitatively different from the gold standard of the second nineteenth century.

In short, if the twenty years from the 1850s to the 1870s were a nineteenth century based at least roughly on the tenets of classic English political economy, the second forty years of the long nineteenth century from the 1870s to World War I followed another model: that of gold and iron. It was this model that shaped state currency choices as much as it did decisions to pursue armaments, colonies, and protective tariffs. Or as one late

Meiji advocate of the gold standard put it in describing the development of "national civilization" (*kokka no bunmei*):

> Bismarck said that there are only two things: iron and blood. I, on the other hand, believe that there are only iron and gold. Now, nations compete for monetary advantage: they pursue commercial relations in pursuit of gold, they develop industry to acquire gold, they pursue railroads and shipping to acquire gold, they expand to markets around the world in pursuit of gold. However, the propulsive power in acquiring this gold is iron. Textile machines, ships, railroads—every kind of industrial equipment is made of iron. Even the military is based on iron from which all the new weapons are made. Iron and gold are both the means and the ends.[57]

2

National and International Money

The gold standard as it developed worldwide at the turn of the twentieth century was not the first use of international money. For centuries, trade and the precious metals to pay for it had passed through various lands as a matter of course. With the establishment of European trade and colonies in the Americas in the 1500s, silver from Latin American mines joined silver from Asia as the de facto currency of international commerce. It remained so through the early nineteenth century.[1]

But the changed ideological and institutional context of the late nineteenth century made the expansion of the gold standard different from the earlier dominance of silver. The emergence in the nineteenth century of nation-states along ostensibly ethnic lines meant the replacement of the multilingual and multiethnic empires, city-states, and kingdoms that had dominated prior to that time. In their place, there arose centralized, national political units resting on an array of nationalist institutions and ideas.

Thus the key to understanding the gold standard in the years before World War I is not its international character, but its national one. As much as the gold standard was an international monetary institution establishing a common global reference for international trade and finance, it was also an explicitly national institution. It flowed out of efforts in the nineteenth century to create strictly national currencies. Under centralized government control, these currencies replaced the more flexible and borderless currencies of the pre-nineteenth-century world.[2]

Under the gold standard the values of individual national currencies were fixed relative to each other. In this way, the gold standard promoted international trade and finance by removing the uncertainty of exchange rate fluctuations. But this advantage lay not with gold per se but with the fact that the exchange rates were fixed. In this, the gold standard was little different from the post–World War II Bretton Woods system, Argentina's currency board of the 1990s, the European Monetary System of the 1980s, or China's current exchange rate regime of fixing the value of the yuan to other currencies. Dramatically different is the current system of floating exchange rates between the dollar, yen, euro, and most other major currencies.

The gold standard was a national system in embodying the culmination of the nineteenth-century process of establishing national currencies: centralized, national government control over money. Currencies had traditionally been legal tender regardless of geographic boundaries, with their value coming from their intrinsic metallic worth. But during the nineteenth century, national currency consolidation accompanied national political consolidation. It was as central to the assertion of central government control, and national identity, as the establishment of other national institutions and ideas such as national armies, schools, and histories.[3]

Most notably, governments established central banks simultaneously with the expansion of the gold standard.[4] They used these banks to control financial flows, which under English liberal theory were supposed to occur automatically and be free from state control. The State Bank of Russia (1860), the German Reichsbank (1876), the Austro-Hungarian Bank (1877), the Bank of Japan (1882), and the Bank of Italy (1893) were all part of the process of monetary consolidation and control that continued with adoption of the gold standard. Even Austria-Hungary and Italy, which did not officially go onto the gold standard, used their central banks to stabilize their exchange rates and intervene in currency markets when gold flows appeared to threaten monetary stability or the preferred exchange rate. In essence, they acted like central banks do today when they buy or sell their own or foreign currency in order to influence exchange rate markets.

Silver and Gold

The currency of worldwide use prior to the nineteenth century was silver not gold. But silver was a global currency in ways that the gold standard of the late nineteenth and early twentieth century was not. Whereas the gold standard served as a means to link national currencies that could only be used as legal tender within national geographic boundaries, silver currency flowed freely without regard to national distinctions. It was the metal itself that mattered, not the government that turned it into coins. Thus from the 1500s silver from Peru, Chile, or China was as accepted in Asia and Europe as it was in South America with no need to exchange into any other currency. From the early nineteenth century the most common currency used for trade in East Asia was not Chinese money but the Mexican silver peso.

Not until the second quarter of the nineteenth century did gold currency replace silver and principles of national power and control come to determine the nature of local and global money. This was after the French Revolution had established the idea of nations, national identity, and citizenship to replace belief in the divine right of monarchs; after the disintegration of the pre-nineteenth-century Spanish, British, and French empires in North and South America and their replacement with national boundaries where none had existed; and after the reintegration of remnants of the old Roman and Holy Roman empires into the new nations of Germany and Italy

The gold standard evolved historically through three phases during the nineteenth century, distinct geographically, politically, and economically.[5] When gold standard enthusiasts in the 1920s thought they were replicating the global gold standard as it had come into existence in the 1890s, they were actually evoking the first phase of the gold standard—and in the most extreme cases the eighteenth-century English theory on which it was inconsistently based.

In the first phase, from the 1820s through the 1860s, gold was confined to Britain, Australia, Portugal, Brazil, and Turkey; silver was used in the German states, Austria, Holland, Scandinavia, Mexico, and Asia; and bimetallic systems, incorporating both silver and gold, were used in the United States, France, Switzerland, Italy, and Belgium.[6] This phase coincided with the first period of nineteenth-century economic growth commencing in the 1820s with the end of the Napoleonic wars and continuing through the 1850s and the height of British manufacturing predominance. Helping fuel this period of economic prosperity were the almost simultaneous gold discoveries in California and Australia in the late 1840s and early 1850s, which produced a massive increase in worldwide gold production in the 1850s and 1860s.

The second phase began in 1873 when a newly unified Germany adopted the gold standard. Fresh from defeating Napoleon III's armies in the Franco-Prussian War, Bismarck's government used its war indemnity from France to abandon its French-associated silver standard. In the process it sold thirty-two hundred tons of silver and flooded world markets.[7] This mass of silver, as well as the continued French-German animosity that had propelled Bismarck's abandonment of silver in the first place, prompted the Bank of France in its "Crime of '73" to refuse purchases of German

Table 2.1

Price of Silver in London and Silver to Gold Exchange Rate, 1870–95

Year	Average Price of Silver in London (pence per ounce)	Market Ratio (silver:gold)
1870	60 (9/16)	15.57:1
1871	60 (1/2)	15.57:1
1872	60 (5/16)	15.65:1
1873	59 (1/4)	15.92:1
1874	58 (5/16)	16.17:1
1875	56 (7/8)	16.62:1
1876	52 (3/4)	17.77:1
1877	54 (13/16)	17.22:1
1878	52 (9/16)	17.92:1
1879	51 (1/4)	18.39:1
1880	52 (1/4)	18.06:1
1881	51 (11/16)	18.24:1
1882	51 (5/8)	18.27:1
1883	50 (9/16)	18.64:1
1884	50 (5/8)	18.58:1
1885	48 (9/16)	19.39:1
1886	45 (3/8)	20.78:1
1887	44 (11/16)	21.11:1
1888	42 (7/8)	21.99:1
1889	42 (11/16)	22.10:1
1890	47 (3/4)	19.77:1
1891	45 (1/16)	20.92:1
1892	39 (3/4)	23.68:1
1893	35 (9/16)	26.70:1
1894	28 (15/16)	32.57:1
1895	29 (13/16)	31.57:1

Source: Laughlin 1886: 223–24; U.S. House of Representatives 1903: 512; Laughlin 1931, 1:514; Gallarotti 1995: 166.

silver. This pushed bimetallic France onto a de facto gold standard. In the process it destroyed Europe's silver-based, multinational currency system, the Latin Monetary Union.[8] With Germany and France effectively now on the gold standard, the rest of continental Europe hastened to adopt gold as well: Scandinavia in 1873, the Netherlands in 1875, Belgium and Switzerland in 1878. This German-led abandonment of silver in favor of gold led to plummeting demand for silver and substantially increased demand for gold.[9]

Finally, the 1890s saw the gold standard's third, and first genuinely global, phase. As vast new gold discoveries and declining interest rates fueled a reverse of twenty years of price declines, countries around the world began to adopt one form or another of currencies convertible into gold: India in notably awkward stages throughout the 1890s, Japan and Russia in 1897, Argentina in 1899, Austria-Hungary in 1902, Mexico in 1905, Brazil in 1906, and Thailand in 1908. These countries were not committed to English-style political economy nor did they adopt their gold standards in furtherance of those principles. Rather, they pursued gold currency within the context of a new age defined by protectionism, industrial promotion, and colonial expansion, as well as lingering concerns from the 1870s and 1880s over the deflationary effects of appreciating currency.

For colonies like India, the choice was largely dictated from abroad, with less concern for domestic benefits than the greater good of the empire. For relatively independent nations such as Japan and Argentina the situation was different. For these countries, the economic goal was not to deflate prices or preserve existing exchange rates but to preserve the industrial benefits of depreciation that they had previously enjoyed due to the declining value of silver. Politically, the goal was to acquire the accoutrements of a great power and the access to the foreign loans, and war treasuries, it was believed a gold standard would provide.

Finance and Foreign Borrowing

One of the most popular late twentieth-century theories for explaining why countries adopted the gold standard has focused on the presumed benefits of a gold standard in enabling borrowing from English financial markets.[10] And, indeed, capital markets are the rare aspect of the late nineteenth-century world economy that do, more or less, match up with the English ideal of free markets, free-flowing goods, and borderless cosmopolitanism and the 1990s move to dismantle Depression-era regulatory controls.

Although tariff restrictions on trade were at least as high at the turn of the century as they were in the interwar years and in developing countries through the 1970s, controls on capital were distinctly different. Controls on foreign capital, popular in the years after World War II, played virtually no role in the late nineteenth century. This resulted in the world's major financial markets having a cosmopolitan character absent in the nationalistic world of trade. It also left them easier to spin out of control in crisis.

Finance and capital flows were not, however, devoid of national significance. Global finance was central to late nineteenth-century industrial and military development, imperial expansion, and imperial management. Not only did the Franco-Prussian War of 1870–71 start the shift of the world's major currencies from silver to gold, it also marked the emergence of Britain as the world's dominant financier. Between 1861 and 1872, the value of government loans floated in London and Paris was roughly equal. Only after France's defeat in the Franco-Prussian War did London begin its fifty-year reign as the center of international finance.[11]

Although London in the 1890s was indisputably the world's largest financial center, its interest rates were consistently higher than those in France, Belgium, and the Netherlands. It had also been losing relative ground as a financial center since the immediate post-Franco-Prussian War peak. But where Britain's relative decline in manufacturing was in respect to the United States and Germany, its relative decline in finance was primarily with Paris and Frankfurt and not yet with the New York markets, which became a strong international competitor only at the start of the twentieth century.[12] Rather than self-funding through New York, the United States was still dependent on huge inflows of borrowed capital, mostly from London, to finance industrial and railway expansion after the Civil War.

Rather than remaining constant, British capital exports fluctuated, depending on factors at home and abroad.[13] Between 1861 and 1872 net British foreign investment rose from 1.4% of GNP to 7.7%, then fell back to 0.8% in 1877. Net investment climbed to 7.3% in 1890 before dipping below 1% in 1901. In the years immediately prior to World War I, investment increased once again, reaching a peak of 9.1% in 1913.[14]

Foreign capital financed much of the infrastructure and military expenditures of the age's developing countries, and this, in turn, has led to a tendency for economic studies to look at bond rates in London for clues as to why countries adopted the gold standard at the end of the nineteenth century. Although there is no consensus regarding whether adoption of the gold standard did, in fact, lower interest rates, governments considered it might in adopting the gold standard.[15] Still, foreign borrowing concerns were not equally important for all countries, nor were they necessarily the determining factor in decisions to adopt the gold standard.

In two of the more notable cases—Japan and Argentina—foreign borrowing played very different roles. In Japan's case, military funding was, key to the decision to adopt a gold standard. Meiji leaders spoke openly of foreign borrowing as a factor in their decision. In Argentina, however, the assumption turns out to be false. Although Argentine governments borrowed enormous sums in London, foreign borrowing played virtually no role in the decision to adopt the gold standard.[16]

Very simply, Argentina was a favored venue for English investment regardless of the currency used and this was a state of affairs readily acknowledged within Argentina. Few countries attracted more ridicule in the Argentine press than Chile, which was derided for its disastrous attempts to adopt a gold standard out of exactly such foreign borrowing concerns. Far from seeing the gold standard as a route toward obtaining funds in London, Argentines were vocally proud of the fact that they could obtain ample funding in London regardless of their currency system.[17]

Depreciation and Appreciation

There is no great mystery to the appeal of depreciating currencies for countries relying on exports and intent on developing industry. Overlooked, however, has been the role that a desire for depreciated currency played in economic decision-making in the late nineteenth century and in the adoption and functioning of the gold standard in the years before World War I.

In broad strokes, depreciating currency aids exporters, and industries that rely on exports, by decreasing prices of exported goods in foreign currency. Depreciation also makes goods imported from foreign countries more expensive in local currency. This is as true today as it was in the 1890s, and it is why sudden, relative currency appreciation in major exporting countries so often leads to financial and broader economic crises, particularly when tied to borrowing in foreign currency.

Appreciating currency relative to their trading competitors helped spark the economic crises in Thailand in the late 1990s and Argentina in the early 2000s. Various studies have found that currency appreciation played a role in Japan's "lost decade" of the 1990s either by itself or by prompting attempts to combat appreciation that led to Japan's asset bubble of the late 1980s and subsequent bust.[18] Rapid appreciation of the yen relative to the dollar since late 2008 has helped pushed Japan's economy into crisis, with record declines in exports and for companies and industries relying on exports.[19]

The export advantage of depreciating currency is also why countries have used, and continue to use, currency depreciation explicitly to promote exports. Argentine economic policy since the depths of the economic crisis in 2002 has been based on a conscious policy of depreciated currency to promote exports combined with domestic subsidies on food and energy to promote consumption.[20] The Chinese yuan has similarly been viewed as being consciously undervalued for purposes of promoting exports.

Even countries not particularly dependent on exports, and far from the infant-industry stage, such as the United States, have continued on and off to rely on currency depreciation in hopes of promoting exports and blocking imports. The U.S. departure from the Bretton Woods system in the early 1970s, the Plaza and Louvre agreements in the mid-1980s, and periodic calls for Japanese and, more recently, Chinese currency appreciation have all been attempts to gain for the dollar the advantages of a depreciating currency.[21]

Given the worldwide concern beginning in the mid-1870s that the gold standard and the demonetization of silver had led to deflation and economic stagnation, it was not surprising that the dominant currency concern in the early 1890s was currency appreciation—or "the money question," "currency question," or "currency problem," as it was referred to in numerous countries.[22] Most often this was a concern about gold appreciating and was tied to calls for bimetallism, free coinage of silver, and various international conferences meant to deal with a perceived shortage of gold and its effects on the world economy.[23]

It was commonplace in the last quarter of the nineteenth century to find claims from American and European economists that currency appreciation was "one of the worst evils that can threaten humanity" and that it meant "ruin for the industrialist, misery for the worker, discontent and universal suffering."[24]

British finance ministers, future prime ministers, and other Victorian notables joined in the calls for giving "to Queen Silver her conjugal relations. . . without dethroning King Gold."[25] For these eminent Victorian critics of gold appreciation, that appreciation had converted English currency "into an immensely deceitful standard .. . [that] worsens the situation of the debtor and gives creditors an illegitimate benefit," "weighs over men and those who have a spirit of enterprise, who try to develop the agriculture and industry of the country, [and] increases the burden that weighs on the country's industry," and, if left unchecked, would "cause a crisis more disastrous than all those that the commercial world can recall."[26] Alfred Marshall, the dominant English economist of his generation—who, along with his contemporary F. Y. Edgeworth urged Britain's Gold and Silver Commission in 1886 to adopt bimetallism—worried in 1898 that "the precious metals cannot afford a good standard of value."[27]

This concern was particularly acute in those countries already on the gold standard, which faced increasing foreign competition. French textile manufacturers and silk producers sought protection from lower-priced Japanese thread. In the United States in the late 1880s and early 1890s, farmers and miners found themselves at a price disadvantage against the weaker currencies of non–gold standard primary products producers such as Argentina, India, Brazil, China, and Russia. Mixed in were also racial fears—particularly of the presumed danger of Asian immigration, the "yellow peril," and the threat this was seen to pose to the Anglo-Saxon way of life. As Winston Churchill's uncle put it, "The yellow man using the white metal holds at his mercy the white man using the yellow metal."[28]

Concern with deflation and its economic and social effects helped fuel the rise of the Populist Party in the United States and the takeover of the then probanker, pro–hard money, and pro-gold standard Democratic Party by William Jennings Bryan and his silverite supporters. The silver movement dominated American politics in the mid-1890s, with Bryan declaring that mankind would not be "crucified on a cross of gold." It also made its presence felt in children's literature when the Kansas Populist L. Frank Baum wrote his book *The Wonderful Wizard of Oz* as an allegory of silver politics. The yellow brick road symbolized the gold standard; Dorothy's silver (not ruby, as in the movie version) slippers represented the silver standard; and the Wizard was meant to be William Jennings Bryan.[29]

Support for silver and depreciating currency was strongest in the United States not only because of the interests of silver miners but also because of the decline in values, the disruption of prices, and the increase of debts and taxes that resulted from currency appreciation and the "inferiority" these imparted "in the competition with other nations."[30] Depreciation also played a substantial role in Argentine monetary policy in the late nineteenth and early twentieth century, as well as in Brazil and Chile.[31] Governments in the last quarter of the nineteenth century thus made it a priority "to avoid [having] their money [appreciate] and [to] limit the international superiority that is provided to other nations by a relatively cheap and expansive currency."[32]

It was this perceived national competitive disadvantage from appreciated currency that led Nelson Aldrich, the dominant financial figure in the U.S. Senate—protectionist, architect of the Federal Reserve System, and father-in-law of John D. Rockefeller—to push repeatedly for international monetary conferences into the late 1890s. Aldrich argued that "the decline in the price of silver has as an effect to provide to silver countries . . . the means to sell their products at a premium, with great prejudice for American producers."[33]

Although advocates of bimetallism remained vocal into the 1890s, they were running up against more than currency preferences and new gold discoveries. To make bimetallism work there needed to be the sort of international agreement that would establish the Bretton Woods system at the end of World War II. This, however, was unlikely in the context of the nationalistic basis of much of the late nineteenth-century world. Bimetallism rested, as did the Latin Monetary Union of the mid-nineteenth century, on a supranational mindset and set of institutions. This was much as envisioned in classic English political economy. But this was not the general mindset of the 1890s and early twentieth century. Rather than focusing on international institutions, states at the turn of the century dedicated themselves to the national interest and worked to protect and expand national power in all its forms.

In the 1890s it was, above all, nationalism that drove currency choices.[34] In this environment, the new nations of North and South America, as well as Japan, were seen as being in a Darwinian struggle to equal, or surpass, the levels of civilization achieved by the handful of imperial powers in Europe.[35] In late nineteenth-century parlance, this meant military, industrial, and financial power.

3

Nations and Gold

New nations came to adopt the gold standard in the late nineteenth century for similar reasons, drawing from a common pool of economic, political, and cultural ideas and interests. Above all, the ideas of the age were nationalistic. But the particular weight of these elements varied from country to country. Their influence on adoption of the gold standard varied as well.

This did not mean that all policymakers necessarily saw their national interests in the same way. Different policymakers had different ideas of what the national interest meant to their country. Nor did they necessarily use the same tools to advance those interests. Most often nineteenth-century state leaders saw their national interests linked to industrial development, military power, or both. The two often went hand in hand, but not always. Nor did the nationalistic goals of policymakers lessen the private interests of different segments of society or their subjective visions of the national interest.

In all countries there existed a variety of public and private currencies, with significant amounts held in paper unbacked by any metal. In Latin America the move toward centralized, national currencies was as strong as it was in nations such as Germany, Italy, the United States, Russia, and Japan. But a lack of gold and silver reserves made reliance on paper money inevitable.

The gold standard was part of industrial promotion (Argentina), industrial and military promotion (Germany, Russia, and Japan), great power political maneuvering (Germany, France), or a question of colonial management imposed from abroad (India). It was also a matter of the relative political power of specific economic interest groups seeking policies serving what they saw as their own interests. And in countries such as Japan, Argentina, and Russia there was a tendency to find, as was the case earlier in Germany, one or two central bureaucratic figures who believed adopting the gold standard was paramount for national advancement and proceeded to do so even when opposed by major segments of society.

For these new nineteenth-century nations, the differences in their currency choices rested ultimately on the relative mix of economic and political ambitions—offensive or defensive, national or international, economic or political. Their different choices also rested on their relative power and whether they viewed the gold standard primarily as a signifier of civilizational, national, and racial worth or as a practical means to concrete ends.

Finally, there were the odder cases of Britain and the United States. For Britain, gold currency emerged as a matter of happenstance and then piggybacked on the rise of British economic and political power. In the United States relative physical isolation and a large internal market meant currency was more of an independent choice. But this did not mean that the United States was exempt from the dominant ideas and institutional choices of the age. It, too, shaped its economic institutions around ideas of industrial protection and military expansion, as well as the various private interests that made up late nineteenth-century American society.

The Powers That Would Be

In financial, as well as industrial and military, matters the defining late nineteenth-century distinction was between those countries that aimed to be great powers and those that did not. The former category included the United States and the major countries of northern Europe.

BRITAIN

Until the early nineteenth century Britain did not restrict its currency to gold; it used silver as well.[1] Despite the centrality of the gold standard to late nineteenth-century British finance, Britain was officially on a bimetallic standard until 1821. As a practical matter, silver disappeared from circulation in the early eighteenth century after Isaac Newton, then master of the mint, established official exchange rates for silver and gold that undervalued silver in relation to market rates, thus leaving only gold in circulation.

The gold standard thus came de facto into effect in Britain by accident rather than by any conscious political or economic decision. David Hume's "specie flow" theory of the late eighteenth century was used in the nineteenth and twentieth centuries to explain the presumed scientific workings of the gold standard. But the specie flow theory did not limit itself to gold. It attempted to describe any monetary system using precious metals, be they silver, gold, or any other. Not until 1821 did Britain make its de facto gold standard de jure and officially become the world's most prominent gold standard country.

It was virtually the only one. Prior to 1873 the only countries using gold currency—or backing their paper currency with gold—other than Britain and Australia were Portugal (which traded heavily with Britain and adopted gold in 1854), Portugal's effective colony Brazil, and Turkey. The rest used either silver or were bimetallic, using a combination of gold and silver. It was only as British political and economic power expanded in the nineteenth century that the gold standard did as well.

The Franco-Prussian War and politics in France and Germany played a decisive role in the expansion of the gold standard after 1870. But the development of British trade and finance made gold attractive for those who sought to purchase British goods, sell goods in Britain, or borrow British funds. With gold they were spared worrying about variations in exchange rates between silver and gold changing the amount of money they actually spent or received.

London's financial market sat at the center of the gold standard partly because the nineteenth-century gold standard as an institution began in Britain and because the ideology of the gold standard rested on English political economy for support. In addition the world's gold market was centered in London. Where the tenets of English political economy and the practical working needs of the London financial markets conflicted, the practical considerations took precedence.

English theory imagined a world in which central banks and state treasuries sat idly by and watched gold flow freely in and out of the country—inflating or deflating prices, filling central bank vaults, or being pulled out in financial panics. But this was theory, not reality. In practice, Britain, like all other states, sterilized gold flows, intervened in currency markets, and sought to accumulate specie irrespective of its trade balances. Britain's management of the gold standard was as focused on national political and economic self-interest as any other country's.

The primary difference was that the world's financial and commodities markets were centered in London. Britain thus had more influence over the worldwide operation of the gold standard than did any other country. When gold outflows during the worldwide financial crisis of 1873 threatened Bank of England reserves, the bank pushed interest rates up to historic highs rather than allow gold to flow overseas. Because of the size and influence of London's financial markets, the Bank of England could get away with such drastic moves whereas smaller countries had less freedom to manage their currencies on a day-to-day basis.[2]

GERMANY AND FRANCE

The clearest links between gold and nationalism appeared in Germany and France where the gold standard emerged as a direct consequence of the Franco-Prussian War.[3]

Prior to 1873 France was at the center of the European bimetallic system, using both gold and silver. In 1865 France, Belgium, Italy, and Switzerland formed what came to be called the Latin Monetary Union and agreed to set their currencies at a standard ratio of 15.5 grams of silver to 1 gram of gold and freely exchange their currencies. They were later joined by Spain, Greece, Romania, Austria-Hungary, Bulgaria, Venezuela, Serbia, Montenegro, San Marino, and the Papal States/Vatican. Although the union officially lasted until the 1920s, in practice it shifted along with the rest of Europe from a bimetallic system to a de facto gold standard during the 1870s.

As the largest country, with the dominant central bank and most active financial markets, France stood at the center of the union and the operation of gold and silver exchanges. Effectively, the Bank of France acted as the ultimate intermediary between gold and silver countries, buying and selling silver and gold in order to keep the exchange rate steady. This could only continue, however, for as long as the Bank of France was willing to freely exchange gold and silver at the set 15.5:1 ratio—which it was until Germany abandoned silver for gold in 1873.

French and Prussian rivalry had been ongoing in various degrees since the end of the Napoleonic wars and grew over the course of the nineteenth century as Prussia's political and military strength increased. This rivalry climaxed with Prussia's victory in the Franco-Prussian War of 1870–71 and the unification through that war of the various German principalities into a single nation-state. With the Treaty of Frankfurt in May 1871, a newly united Germany under the control of Prussia gained territory and 5 billion francs as a war indemnity. Germany ultimately used this indemnity to establish a gold conversion fund to convert its silver currency system to gold.

There was no particularly compelling economic reason for Germany to switch from silver to gold. The breakdown of countries having silver, gold, or bimetallic systems had remained basically unchanged since earlier in the century. Continental Europe was still silver or bimetallic and Britain remained the sole major gold standard country. Nor was Bismarck particularly interested in abandoning silver for gold. Popular pressure moved the country away from reliance on France and all French-influenced institutions. This included the use of silver currency, which placed Germany on a similar standard to bimetallic France. Adopting a British-centered gold standard would free Germany from the possibility of French financial pressure and Bismarck was forced to use the war indemnity to establish a gold conversion fund and begin to sell off Germany's extensive silver reserves.

Germany's abandonment of silver in 1873 started the process of rapid silver depreciation and gold appreciation that characterized the deflationary years of the 1870s and 1880s. These German silver sales caused a massive increase in the amount of silver being brought to the Bank of France for exchange into gold. In all of 1871 and 1872 the French mint had received 5 million francs of silver for conversion to coin, whereas in 1873 alone 154 million francs were received. Due to political animosity toward Germany stemming from France's defeat and concern over the massive increase in silver inflows, the Bank of France stopped exchanging silver for gold. This pushed France onto a de facto gold standard. The other Latin

Monetary Union countries agreed in 1874 to limit the free conversion of silver on a temporary basis. By 1878, with no recovery in the silver price in sight, Latin Monetary Union members stopped minting silver entirely and effectively went onto de facto gold standards.

RUSSIA

With the German silver sales in the 1870s, and French refusal to accept them, the European continent became almost entirely a gold standard region. The one exception was Russia, which by the late 1890s remained the only major European power on a silver standard.[4] When Russia finally adopted the gold standard in 1897, the decision rested not on English liberalism but on a combination of Listian developmentalism, authoritarian political power, and great power ambitions.

Although acknowledged as a political and military power in the other major capitals of Europe, Russia at the turn of the century straddled an uncomfortable divide between European great power, unstable empire, and late developer. A desire for rapid economic development coupled with Russia's enormous military, authoritarian tradition, and great power maneuvering produced a monetary system rooted squarely in both the industrial and imperial prongs of late nineteenth-century currency choices.

As in Argentina and Japan, adoption of the gold standard in Russia was, institutionally, a top-down phenomenon driven by a bureaucrat-politician convinced of the nation's needs, versed in the latest theories of scientific truth from Europe, and skilled in political maneuvering in a country in which mass political participation was limited to nonexistent. In all three countries a primary advocate and a small number of associated finance ministry officials effectively designed the currency system. They then pushed it into effect, despite considerable opposition, with rubber-stamp legislative majorities and by skirting administrative and legislative requirements. If administrative rules were bent or finessed in Argentina and Japan, advocates of the gold standard in Russia took advantage of the authoritarian government to bypass nominally required lower councils and go directly to the tsar to have the gold standard enacted by unilateral, imperial proclamation.

In turn-of-the-century Russia, Sergei Witte occupied this central bureaucratic role, as Carlos Pellegrini did in Argentina and Matsukata Masayoshi did in Japan. Director of railway affairs within the Finance Ministry from

1889 to 1891, transportation minister in 1892, and then finance minister from 1892 to 1903, Witte, like many of his contemporaries, was a follower of Friedrich List's ideas of national economics, state-sponsored industrial development, and protective tariffs.

Like Bismarck in Germany, segments of the Partido Autonomista Nacional in Argentina, and William McKinley and the Republican Party in the United States, Witte accepted industrial and military power as the measure of national success and sought to develop industry rapidly behind a wall of protective tariffs. Like the others, Witte borrowed British forms but emphasized their practical, realpolitik application rather than the theoretical niceties of academic discourse.

Witte resembled other late nineteenth-century leaders in his preference for Listian developmentalism. But his explicit reliance on List was particularly notable in that, shortly after entering the Finance Ministry in 1889, he published a book describing List's thought and introducing List's *National System of Political Economy* to Russian readers.[5] Witte, like List, acknowledged the side effects of high tariffs in terms of increased consumer prices, retaliation from other countries, and the tendency for industries to rely too heavily on tariffs. He also believed, like List, that these disadvantages were outweighed by the inability of infant industry to develop in the face of foreign competition. In particular, Germany had been exporting large amounts of industrial products duty free to Russia, which Witte attempted to counter by imposing protective tariffs on iron, steel, and manufactured goods. After an extended tariff war with Germany, the two countries eventually set minimum and maximum tariff scales for their respective products.

As in other late nineteenth-century industrializing countries, Witte placed particular emphasis on heavy industry and industrial infrastructure: steel and railroads. Prior to becoming finance minister, Witte oversaw construction of the Trans-Siberian Railway, which linked Moscow and western Russia with Vladivostok and Asia and was critical for Russian industrial and military planning. Witte argued that a gold standard would allow Russia to obtain foreign funding more readily for its military and industrial endeavors.

Like Matsukata in Japan, Witte sought foreign borrowing not only for industrial development but also to pay for military expenses needed for imperial expansion and foreign wars. That both Russia and Japan had colonial designs on Korea and Manchuria, and that each one regarded the other's military as the prime threat to those imperial ambitions, made their shared concern with military funding easily understandable. This shared belief that the gold standard would ease foreign funding of those ambitions was further reinforced as they moved forward simultaneously toward adopting a gold standard, with each being fully aware of the other's moves.

In Russia there was a third reason for adopting the gold standard: the gold standard served as the final step in withdrawing excess paper currency from circulation and consolidating the central government's control of money. As in other nineteenth-century countries, warfare resulted in a substantial increase in the amount of paper money in circulation. As the Union government did during the U.S. Civil War, as Meiji Japan did during its wars of national consolidation in the 1870s, and Argentina during the Paraguayan War (1864–70) and its own wars of national consolidation, the Russian government resorted to the issue of massive amounts of paper currency to pay for its expenses in the Crimean War of 1853–56. Unable to borrow in the main European financial markets of its adversaries, London and Paris, and lacking sufficient tax revenues, the Russian government resorted to printing paper money to pay its debts.

Russia established a silver system in 1860, but paper remained the primary form of currency in daily use. From 1892, when Witte became finance minister, the government attempted to acquire sufficient gold reserves to establish a gold standard. Russia lacked, however, the one-off war indemnities that Germany acquired after the Franco-Prussian War and Japan after the Sino-Japanese War in 1895. Nor had Russia succeeded in acquiring sufficient gold reserves by the time the gold standard was officially proclaimed in effect by the tsar in 1897. Although the system was nominally gold, in reality it remained a system of paper currency representing silver rubles and convertible into silver. As was the case in Argentina, the label "gold standard" was applied, but without sufficient gold reserves to actually establish a fully working gold currency system.

Witte devalued the ruble in going onto the gold standard both to aid industry and to avoid disrupting the economy. In devaluing the ruble, Witte belonged with figures such as Matsukata, who sought defensively to avoid deflation while enacting a gold standard primarily for other reasons—specifically, to acquire foreign loans. They did not in general use it offensively as a tool meant to expand exports and inhibit imports as did Argentina.

Regardless of whether these states were focused primarily on promoting exports and blocking imports, as was Argentina, or on military development and industrial-use industry, as were Russia and Japan, the focus of all three rested squarely on their positions within a broader world context.

THE UNITED STATES

Although the United States was distant from the European balance-of-power concerns that drove adoption of the gold standard in France, Germany, and Russia, nationalist economics played a role in the United States as well.[6] As in Japan, government support for the gold standard rested in part on a belief that adopting the gold standard would ease borrowing in London and thus speed American industrialization.[7] As in Argentina, support for the gold standard in Congress was closely linked with support for protective tariffs.[8] And, as in both countries, and elsewhere, private interests argued for the monetary policy that best served their own interests: primary products versus manufactures, debtors versus creditors, imports versus exports.

The United States went de facto onto the gold standard in 1873 when the federal government stopped minting silver coins. Because of the ensuing deflation and harm to debtors, farmers, and western mining interests, the government's move became known as the "Crime of '73." It began thirty years of ongoing battles between creditors, bankers, and other hard-money advocates of gold and deflation, on the one hand, and debtors, farmers, western miners, and other advocates of inflation, silver, and bimetallism, on the other. Although government silver purchase acts passed Congress in 1878 and 1890, they only allowed the federal government to purchase set amounts of silver in order to prop up silver's price and keep gold from further appreciating. They did nothing to allow the free minting of silver, which became the leading demand of silver partisans.

As in Russia, at one level the gold standard was the most recent stage of late nineteenth-century attempts to consolidate national currencies and deal with massive amounts of paper money issued to pay for wars. In the United States, the Union government's issuance of unbacked paper currency, "greenbacks," to pay its Civil War expenses led to currency depreciation and rapid price inflation that aided debtors and those, such as farmers, who borrowed early in the year, when prices were lower and the real value of their debts after inflation were higher, and then sold at the end of the year, when prices were higher and the real value of their debts lower. Bringing inflation and currency depreciation under control meant, by definition, mass withdrawals of currency from circulation, deflation, and monetary appreciation.

Just as inflation and depreciated currency aided debtors, appreciation and deflation aided banks and other creditors. In the postbellum United States, the debtor-creditor divide tracked geographic and industrial divisions that, to some degree, were variations on the prewar economic divides between an agricultural South and an industrial North that had helped bring about the Civil War. These divisions also reflected changing demographics as U.S. national boundaries pushed to the West.

The two defining economic issues of the 1890s in the United States were currency and tariffs: gold versus silver and, if not free trade versus protectionism given the dominance of protectionist ideas and the Civil War defeat of the traditional Southern bastion of free trade, than at least differences in the degree of protectionism advocated. Just as the idea of cutting taxes lodged itself at the core of Republican Party economics in the late twentieth century, in the late nineteenth century the idea of raising tariffs played a similar role in the McKinley-era Republican Party.

Rather than challenge the dominance of protectionism, the Democratic Party occupied itself with the currency question. The Democrats were pro-gold in the 1880s and early 1890s under the control of the Grover Cleveland wing of the party, which had its base in New York financial circles. From the mid-1890s the party turned pro-silver with the selection of William Jennings Bryan as its presidential nominee in 1896 and the absorption of Populist support into the Democratic Party.[9] Bryan's last-minute selection as the presidential nominee after a speech proclaiming that mankind would not be "crucified on a cross of gold" marked the centrality of the silverite cause to the 1896 Democratic campaign.

For the Republicans, currency allegiances were more fluid and subject to shifting coalitions and political horse trading, unlike protective tariffs that functioned as the economic raison d'être of the late nineteenth-century Republican Party.[10] It was tariff policy that sat at the center of late nineteenth-century Republican Party economic policy, not the gold standard. McKinley had a history of supporting bimetallism and during the 1896 campaign repeatedly called for an international conference to remonetize silver.[11]

The Populist and silverite call for increased coinage of silver was only one part of a set of ideas that would be mainstreamed into American life over the coming decades: a progressive income tax, eight-hour workday, direct election of senators, and curbs on lending practices and interest rates. In fact, the call for silver currency and the denunciation of the gold standard was one of the few planks from the 1896 Democratic Party platform that almost immediately lost relevance, so much so that when Bryan ran again as the Democratic nominee for president in 1900, silver was nowhere to be found.[12]

This latter twist resulted from increased gold production in the Transvaal and other regions that did away with fears of deflation after the turn of the century. But in 1896 the cross of gold imagery summed up a wider set of complaints and a deeper sense of economic grievance that had spawned, first, the Populist movement and then the effective takeover of the Democratic Party by Populist supporters. Although it acquired urban supporters as well, Populism was primarily a movement of farmers. Prices for agricultural products were low; rents farmers paid were rising; transportation, credit, and product monopolies ran small producers out of business and increased the prices farmers, and all consumers, had to pay for their supplies.

Into this critique came silver. For the Populists, the demonetization of silver was the logical outcome of policies meant to benefit creditors and the wealthy at the expense of debtors, industrial workers, and farmers. In this view, silver had been demonetized intentionally to cause appreciation and fatten usurers, bankrupt enterprise, and enslave industry.

In short, the Populists, the silverites, and the Bryan campaign formed in their image wished to increase the money supply sufficiently to reverse deflation and ease the burdens of debtors. In this, they failed. But the increased gold production of the 1890s would make the issue moot almost as soon as it hit its peak in 1896. Thereafter, under a Republican governing majority, the gold standard worked together with protective tariffs to promote both industrialization and a Republican political majority.

The Others

At the end of the nineteenth century Britain, France, Germany, Russia, and the United States were all, in one way or another, leading imperial and economic powers. The situation was very different for other countries. Industrially, countries such as China, India, and Japan lacked control over their own tariffs due to formal or informal colonial ties with the great powers. Some, such as India, also lacked control over their own currencies. Other countries did have control over their currencies and either continued without substantial change, as in China; mimicked foreign institutions for the sake of mimicry, as in Chile; or, for the most ambitious like Argentina and Japan, used currency as a tool to aim at great power status themselves.

Even when not reflecting formal colonial status, many of these countries' tariff regimes represented the darker side of the era of European free trade treaties in the 1850s and 1860s. Starting with Britain's Opium War against China in the 1840s, the major European powers and the United States established various commercial treaties through military force or military threats. These "unequal treaties"—imposed first in China and then in other countries—removed from local governments the power to set tariff rates. Instead, they set notably low rates that opened these markets to foreign products and removed the option of infant-industry protection. Along with the principles of most favored nation (MFN), which extended favors extracted by one treaty power to all the others, and extraterritoriality, which exempted foreign nationals from local laws and jurisdiction, the lack of tariff autonomy defined the colonial or semicolonial relationships constructed in the mid-nineteenth century to foster European and North American trade and industry.

But formal colonial or treaty restrictions were not the only limits imposed on colonies, semicolonies, and those countries uncomfortably close to falling into those categories. For countries, such as India, on silver standards, fluctuating exchange rates between silver and gold could mean sudden windfalls to exports and debt repayment, but it could also mean sudden losses. So too, the fact that depreciating silver made exports cheaper but debt repayments more expensive, and appreciating silver made debt less expensive but exports more so, created a constant conflict between the interests of exporters and manufacturers on the one hand and importers and creditors on the other.

In the case of India these were domestic Indian problems as well as problems of British imperial management.[13] India was on a bimetallic standard from 1836 to 1852; a silver standard from 1853 to 1893; an ill-defined, transitional phase meant to lead from silver to gold from 1893 to 1897; and then a pound sterling standard from 1898 under which British gold coins were made legal tender in India in order to match

Indian currency fully with that of the British metropole. Although India stopped coining silver in 1893, silver continued to circulate throughout the 1890s as various British currency commissions considered how to align Indian currency with the British gold standard without, in the process, destroying an Indian economy that was heavily dependent on exports and in need of large amounts of liquidity.

From one perspective, the gold standard was a logical choice for Indian currency. Three-quarters of Indian trade was with gold standard countries—primarily Britain. India also owed considerable foreign debts in gold—again, primarily in London. But this was looking only at India's external relations. English colonists who relied on export income favored silver. Colonial officials who had to pay taxes and debts denominated in gold, favored gold. Indian Office officials in London favored gold as well, believing trade benefits to India by staying on silver were outweighed by trade losses to the rest of the empire.

Domestically, the value of gold was considerably more ambiguous. Between the prohibition on minting silver in 1893 and the introduction of British currency in 1898, British currency policy in India was a disaster. Simultaneously, with the decision to stop minting silver, the Indian government moved to contract the money supply. Then an earthquake struck, credit tightened more than planned, prices fell, credit tightened even more, and the result was an almost complete lack of liquidity.

The decision to stop minting silver affected not only India but also every other country that was considering changing its currency in the 1890s. India's size, and the huge amount of silver it used, meant that the 1893 end to coining silver had repercussions on the worldwide silver market similar to those when Germany abandoned silver for gold in 1873. Silver once again began to depreciate after leveling off due to U.S. silver purchases under the 1890 Sherman Silver Purchase Act. The Indian action increased official calls in Japan and Russia for adopting a gold standard, even as merchants that competed with Indian textile exports saw an opportunity to undercut Indian prices. In the United States, the Indian decision resulted in the almost immediate repeal of the Sherman Silver Purchase Act.

India was large enough to significantly influence world financial markets. Smaller countries such as Chile had no such influence, and their currency problems remained their own. Notably, Chile was the rare country that sought to adopt a gold standard irrespective of its economic condition and monetary needs. It also took English theory seriously. In essence, the

Chilean government sought to adopt the gold standard for the sake of adopting a gold standard, believing that its mere adoption was a solution to monetary woes.

Chile enacted gold conversion in 1892 and 1893 to combat depreciating paper. As earlier in Argentina, Japan, and the United States, the primary cause of depreciating paper was warfare—Chile's 1891 civil war and the huge government expenses associated with it. But instead of studying the actual causes of the currency depreciation, gold standard advocates jumped on conversion as a one-size-fits-all solution. Specifically, as numerous countries sought to do in the 1920s, they attempted to impose conversion at a rate notably different from the market rate.[14] The experiment ended disastrously, with Chile finding itself in the anomalous position of having to pay higher rates for foreign loans when they were on the gold standard than when their money was unbacked paper.[15]

The Chilean disaster received prominent play in Argentina, where the Argentine government in the 1890s was having its own currency problems and considering its own move to the gold standard. But if the Chilean case was one of poorly thought out imitation, the same problem did not plague Argentina. Argentines had a far more ambitious conception of their nation and its future in the world than that allowed for by mere surface mimicry.

The Argentine move to the gold standard in 1899 was predicated not on mimicry of English institutions, or any attempt to appeal to English ideas or interests, but on nationalism, protectionism, and currency devaluation. In short, the Argentine government took the English institutional form of the gold standard and reshaped it to fit the second nineteenth-century model of Listian developmentalism. In so doing, it produced the seeming paradox of the most fervent advocates of English liberalism, cosmopolitanism, and hard money opposing what on its surface appeared to be adoption of an English-based gold standard, and advocates of protectionism, nationalism, and inflationary finance pushing for its adoption.

PART TWO

Industry and Argentine Money

4

Gold and
Industrial Developmentalism

The neoliberal Pax Britannica tale of the late nineteenth century has tended to turn Argentina into an informal adjunct—even an informal colony—of the British Empire. But contemporary Argentines were far more selective in their use of market principles and British ideas and institutions than this image implies.

Like the United States, Argentina emerged in the nineteenth century as a self-consciously new nation with a particular vision of its role in the Western Hemisphere, its roots in Europe, and an ostensibly limitless future. Residents of what would become Argentina rebelled against the Spanish Empire in the first decade of the nineteenth century and then spent the next seventy years attempting to establish an Argentine nation—institutionally, geographically, and intellectually. In the 1880s they turned to promoting the political, cultural, and economic advance (or progress, in the language of the age) of their new nation.[1] In doing so, they turned economically not to English theory, but to the ideas of List and Hamilton and the historical examples of the United States and continental Europe.

The New Nation

Argentina emerged out of the 1810 overthrow of Spanish rule in the colony of Río de la Plata.[2] Although de facto political independence became official in 1816, decades of civil and regional wars followed. Internal rebellions challenged both specific governments and the broader idea of a national government. The first task for the national government was to guarantee the physical existence of a state incorporating Buenos Aires and the surrounding area. The second task was to populate the nation with European descendants. The final task consisted of constructing the institutional, social, and ideological accoutrements of a nineteenth-century nation-state: public army, public education, flag, history, and political and financial institutions. All of these institutions formed part of the obsessive concern of nineteenth-century Argentines to replace indigenous "barbarism" with European "civilization."

In 1853 most of the provinces that now make up Argentina accepted a constitution. But the wealthiest and largest, Buenos Aires, insisted on its independence and refused to be part of a national union until the 1860s. Even then, Buenos Aires served as the center of opposition to national governments not controlled by *bonaerenses*. Not to be outdone, various regional caudillos claimed autonomous rule in their own regions.

Not until the presidency of Julio Roca (1880–86) is Argentina generally considered as an established state, with accepted, centralized political power.[3] This did not mean that all disputes vanished. The members of the political class retained sharp differences in their points of view, particularly over economic questions. These divisions reflected the interests of those who sought to develop Argentina as a manufacturing power versus those who preferred to act as a supplier of primary products to the British Empire.

The fiercest debates, which involved commercial policy and tariffs, culminated in congressional debates over tariff laws in 1876, 1895, and 1899, as well as the debate over the gold standard in 1899. The tariff debates revolved around the advantages of free trade or protectionism for various classes and interest groups: merchants, farmers, bankers, exporters, and importers. The gold standard debate effectively served as a proxy for the free trade versus protectionism disputes, with each side seeking a currency system most beneficial to its interests. Protectionists, inflationists, and industrial promoters led the charge to enact the gold standard in Argentina. They shaped the gold standard institutionally to reflect their particular business interests and their belief in industrial promotion and national development.

Ideas of industrial promotion and national development came in two institutional and ideological forms. These two models reflected the dominant ideas in Europe and the Americas: British liberalism and free trade, and German and North American Listian developmentalism.

Two Models

British abandonment of protectionism in 1846 left Argentina with a choice of two economic models: English liberalism or Listian developmentalism. In Argentina, the first model emphasized integration within the British system of trade and finance, forgoing "artificial" manufacturing in favor of the "natural" industries of cattle and agriculture, which would be exported primarily to Britain.[4] The second model aimed not only at developing cattle and agriculture but also at developing national manufacturing industries.[5] These industries were meant to reduce not only the uncertainty of crop cycles and primary product prices but also the number of imported goods.

Britain's abandonment of protectionism meant concentrating British production in manufacturing and importing food and primary products. For Argentina, with its ample supplies of land for grazing and farming, the possibility of exporting what Britain needed and importing what Britain produced proved extremely attractive.

But this was not the only choice nor even the most logical one. When Argentines looked at the United States and Germany, they saw protectionism and industrial promotion. The distinction between the industrial model and the agricultural model became still more pronounced after the defeat of the agricultural, free trade South in the U.S. Civil War. Whereas the South had centered its economy on supplying Britain with agricultural products, the North, with its history of industrial development and protectionism, seemed to offer the ascendant, and safer, model. To Argentines who wished to develop their country into the "United States of the South" the Hamilton-List model offered advantages that the plantation model of agricultural supplier could not.

In both models the need for populating the country and attracting foreign capital was accepted as a given.[6] But the particular uses to which these two arrangements were to be put differed. In the first model, Argentines would concentrate on the open land of the Pampas and develop the nation as an exporter of beef and grains. Immigrants would work as farm labor. Foreign capital would be used to build railroads, ports, and other basic infrastructure that would transport Argentine primary products overseas. Alternatively, Argentines could develop not only agriculture but, as in the United States, industry as well.

If foreign capital proved relatively easy for Argentines to acquire, immigration was another matter. Late nineteenth-century Argentines obsessed over how to attract Europeans, how to construct a society around those immigrants, and how to turn them into Argentines.[7] Immigration was meant to be European and supplant indigenous "barbarism." But this did not mean that all European immigrants were created equal. Although most immigrants came from Spain and Italy, a significant number of people emphasized the need to "refresh" the "Latin race"—in presumptive decline since the fall of the Roman and Spanish empires—with an influx of settlers from "ascendant" northern European countries.[8]

The ability to create an Argentine people, and with it an Argentine nation, was hampered because many immigrants traveled between Europe and Argentina in line with the harvest season. This ability was further hampered by the tendency of even long-term immigrants to forgo Argentine citizenship. Those concerned with anglicizing Argentine society attempted to promote English culture and family units through which Spaniards and Italians would become anglicized Argentines.[9] These efforts met with little success as Spanish and Italian immigrants preferred to remain Spanish and Italian.

English influence did not extend to economic ideas or to government policy either. Argentina's trade and financial relations with Britain never evolved into a political alliance. Even as producers of Argentine wool and beef readily supplied the needs of British armies, Argentina never became a diplomatic or military ally of Britain. Argentina neither cut off trade with Germany during World War I, nor did it agree to join the League of Nations after the war, which the Argentine government viewed as victor's justice.[10] Argentines widely condemned British imperialism in general and the Boer War in particular.

Ideological and political resistance to Argentine anglicization appeared particularly in Argentina's adoption of the gold standard. This would at first seem odd given that the nineteenth-century gold standard was centered in

Britain and its adoption has traditionally been considered a sign of adherence to British ideas, institutions, and an English-dominated world order. But Argentina's gold standard emerged out of a desire to protect industry and exports from the effects of appreciating currency.[11] It rested on ideas of infant-industry protection, export promotion, and industrial developmentalism dominant during the age. In this, it reflected the protectionist, industrial, and devaluationist model of Argentine economic development that had competed against the alternative model of free trade and metallic currency since the 1860s. It reflected an acceptance of Friedrich List rather than Adam Smith.

The architect of Argentina's gold standard, Carlos Pellegrini, was a lifelong advocate of the industrial development model. He supported protectionism, government monopolies to develop key industries, and expansionary monetary policy. He designed Argentina's gold standard currency system to promote the goals of this model. A former president and the leader of the protectionist forces in a Senate dominated by protectionists, Pellegrini advocated a brand of developmentalism typical of the age. Both Pellegrini and the system he designed reflected ideas advanced by various U.S. politicians and writers, such as Alexander Hamilton, Henry Clay, and the economist Henry Carey, and by Friedrich List and other members of the German historical school.[12]

It was natural for a new, late nineteenth-century nation to seek to foster industry in ways opposed to midcentury English ideas of free trade and industrial laissez-faire. This was the case in the United States and Germany. It was also the case in Argentina. By the 1890s classic English theory of free trade and industrial laissez-faire had passed its midcentury peak in Argentina, as it had on the European continent.[13]

Classic English theory still carried weight in Argentine academic debates and among a handful of politicians and their affiliated newspapers. But as a practical doctrine it gave way from the 1880s to List and industrial promotion and protection. When developmental nationalists cited English economists, it was not to invoke the universality of mid-nineteenth-century English precepts but to point out their inapplicability to developing countries, be they England in the past or Argentina in the present.[14] Nor were these ideas limited to the 1890s. As late as 1912 a leading magazine ran a series of articles discussing how List's ideas were still dominant in Argentina.[15]

Listian nationalism carried the greatest weight within the ruling Partido Autonomista Nacional (PAN), which monopolized Argentine politics

from the 1880s to World War I.[16] PAN's support for protective tariffs as
a means of infant-industry promotion was shared by the dominant Argentine writers and speakers on economic affairs. Typical of the era in
Argentina, these individuals were politicians and government officials
rather than academics. Leading PAN figures such as Pellegrini, Vicente
Fidel López, José Terry, Emilio Berduc, and José María Rosa all shared a
preference for moderate protectionism and industrial promotion. It was
completely unremarkable that a PAN representative in 1913 attacked free
trade as being against "national solidarity" and "lacking in the very concept of nationality."[17] It was similarly unremarkable that a major daily in
1899 attacked support for lowering tariffs as "economic nihilism" and "industrial retrocession."[18]

The free trade model competed equally with protectionism in Argentina in the 1860s and 1870s. But by the late 1890s, trade debates meant not
protectionism versus free trade but how much protectionism would best
promote Argentine industry.[19] For advocates of industrial development,
the role of the government was to meet the needs of producers, who were
seen as the central movers of progress, as opposed to consumers who were
considered unproductive.[20] Pellegrini and other industrial developmentalists dismissed aversion to protectionism as an illness. This reversal of cosmopolitan English economic thought informed the economic perspective
of industrial developmentalists and underlay Argentina's adoption of the
gold standard.

Industrial developmentalists considered protectionism, and a fondness
for expansionary monetary policies, as pragmatic and practical. To their
critics it was inconsistent, faddish, and prone to favoritism. Their economic views reflected an inductive approach to the world that emphasized
changeable conditions of time and place over universal, deductive theory.
This reflected the dominant, nationalist late nineteenth-century economic
point of view, in which countries shaped their economic theories to suit
their particular conditions.

This did not mean that protectionism went unchallenged. The strongest
adherents of free trade doctrines existed among Buenos Aires' foreign merchant and banking communities. These interests supported a bilateral, An-
glo-Argentine relationship in which Argentine wheat and beef were traded
for British manufactures, and improvements in domestic infrastructure
were financed through borrowing in London.[21] Equally committed to free
trade and hard-money doctrines were immigrant workers for whom unfet-

tered agricultural exports meant demand for their labor and unimpeded imports of British manufactures meant low-priced consumer goods.

More generally, regional interests broke down along protectionist and free trade lines.[22] The interior provinces were generally protectionist, and the coastal Pampas near Buenos Aires mostly free trade.[23] Some protectionists, such as Pellegrini and Vicente Fidel López, came from Buenos Aires and the Pampas. But they saw their roles less as regional representatives than national figures intent on developing Argentina into a world power. In the 1880s the interior provinces were under the administrations of Julio Roca and Miguel Juárez Celman. They saw regional interests and what they viewed as Argentina's national interest in industrialization as aligned in opposition to the free trade interests of Buenos Aires' commercial establishment.

In emphasizing historical particulars over universal principles, industrial developmentalists in Argentina admired not only Friedrich List but also Richard Cobden, the English free trader and founder of the Manchester League. They viewed both men as protectionists because they advocated for policies aimed at protecting and promoting their respective national industries. Argentina's industrial developmentalists advocated neither protectionism nor free trade per se. Instead, they advocated whichever policy seemed best suited to furthering what they saw as the nation's interests. To the extent that industrial developmentalists viewed economic, military, and political strength as tied to industry and exports, infant-industry protection was a natural and logical doctrine that could be viewed as functionally equivalent to British free trade rather than its opposite. If one considers historical specifics and goals rather than general theory and means, the two policies were, indeed, functionally equivalent. They each gave priority to industrial promotion, choosing means best suited in each country to attain that end.

The late nineteenth-century Argentine state relied primarily on import duties for government revenue. This made a minimum level of protectionism a given. It also led inevitably to favoring some industries over others as long as import duties were not equal for all products. This raised the question of whether favoring specific industries with greater tariff barriers would remain tacit, limited, and ad hoc or be adopted explicitly, strategically, and aggressively as Pellegrini, Vicente Fidel López, Ernesto Tornquist, and other enthusiasts of industrial developmentalism urged.[24] In particular, the support of López, who was Argentina's most aggressive advocate of industrial and protectionist ideas, reinforced the contemporary association of Argentina's gold standard with infant-industry protection and a vision of state-supported industrial promotion. Reports that López had helped draft Pellegrini's gold standard plan further increased this association with protectionism and industrial promotion.[25]

Appreciation and the Currency Question

Prior to the 1880s Argentina's currency system was a mass of national and provincial bills and coins reflecting the lack of unified central authority and the tenuous state of government finances.[26] In the 1880s, after the recalcitrant province of Buenos Aires was brought under federal control, the central government moved to establish a unified national currency. In 1883 the government of President Julio Roca established gold conversion at a rate of one paper peso to one gold peso (100) in an exercise that lasted a scant seventeen months due to a lack of gold reserves.[27]

This nominal 100 rate as expressed on the face of the bills served as the starting point for subsequent market fluctuations in the value of paper. The market exchange rate gradually declined to 189 by 1889 before dropping rapidly due to the 1890 financial crisis.[28] At the height of the crisis, paper fell briefly to 500 (although registering an average of 258 for the year). By the mid-1890s this depreciated rate aided not only manufacturing but also agricultural products, which benefited due to the price advantage that inconvertible paper gave to Argentine agriculture over that of the United States.[29]

Paper's appreciation from the mid-1890s gradually whittled away the export advantage of the early 1890s. After slipping to 344 in 1895, paper gradually appreciated to 296 in 1896 and 291 in 1897.[30] Although the economy expanded after the early 1890s, the 1890s themselves were typified not only by currency appreciation but also by deflation. This process accelerated from 1895 despite the countervailing effects of interest rate declines from worldwide gold discoveries. From 1892 to 1894 the exchange rate appreciated 3.1% annually while domestic prices fell by 9.3% annually. From 1895 to 1899 paper appreciated by 37.1% while prices declined by 12.8%.[31] By mid-1899 appreciation had become acute, with paper appreciating from 280 in November 1898 to 204 in early summer before recovering slightly to 220 by July 1, only to fall back to 210 the following week.[32] This sudden

Table 4.1

Rate of Exchange, Paper to Gold, 1882–1914

Year(s)	Average Exchange Rate (100 paper pesos per 100 gold pesos)
1882	100
1883	100
1884	100
1885	136
1886	139
1887	135
1888	147
1889	183
1890	258
1891	375
1892	332
1893	324
1894	357
1895	344
1896	296
1897	291
1898	258
1899	225
1900	231
1901	232
1902	236
1903–14	227

Source: Rocchi 2006: 44; Alvarez 1929: 113.

appreciation prompted concern about exchange rate instability in general and more particularly about the effects on industry.

The problem of paper's appreciation—euphemistically called the "currency question"—led to numerous theories of causes and meanings. Some observers saw appreciation as a validation of the country's moral health. Most, however, emphasized a shortage of money to keep pace with rapid domestic growth and increased exports.[33] Supporters of appreciation argued that appreciating currency made little difference since prices would adjust to the new currency level, producing no underlying change in the economy. For opponents, this view overlooked the time needed for these adjustments to occur, differences in the speed and degree of adjustment among prices, and the effects on creditors and debtors. Appreciation hit debtors particularly hard since they were repaying loans in currency worth more than when borrowed.[34] Those concerned with appreciation argued that it blocked the "development of national labor," decreased immigration, increased emigration, depressed industry, and even discouraged cultural pursuits necessary for Argentina's continued transformation from indigenous barbarity to European-style civilization.[35]

Devaluation and Protectionism

President Julio Roca appointed his sometimes ally, sometimes rival Pellegrini to devise a plan to deal with the peso's appreciation.[36] In order to stop the peso's appreciation and aid industry, Pellegrini proposed adopting the gold standard at an exchange rate that would permanently devalue the currency from the nominal 100 rate established in 1883 to 227, which was meant to be equivalent to the current market rate. The gist of the plan was to promote and protect industry. This did not mean that all proponents of industrial promotion favored the 227 rate, making devaluation permanent, or Pellegrini's use of the gold standard in order to accomplish these goals. But for industrial developmentalists the issues were technical disputes rather than fundamental differences in goals or outlook. The most vociferous opposition came from those who viewed industrial promotion, infant-industry protection, and devaluation in and of themselves as harmful and unnatural.

Creditors, who profited when repaid in appreciated currency, and merchants who benefited from handling imports and feared foreign retaliation in response to Argentine protectionism viewed the peso's rising value favorably, interpreting it as a "sign of confidence, stability, credit, and restoration."[37] They virulently opposed any attempt to stop its appreciation. They did not dispute that industry fared better with the exchange rate at 200 or above than it did at lower rates. But they argued that it was possible for industry to survive at rates of 110, 130, or 150 as it had in the late 1880s.[38] More generally, they argued that a one-to-one relationship between gold and paper was a natural, scientific relationship and that industries incapable of surviving at that rate were "artificial" and should be allowed to fail.

Not all supporters of the currency proposals shared Pellegrini's enthusiasm for infant-industry protection. But they universally argued that currency rates were based on social laws, not natural laws, and could and should be changed when necessary. Whether this amounted to a fundamental difference with the projects' opponents was another question, however, as many of the same people who condemned currency intervention as being outside the bounds of appropriate government power in the case of appreciation had, in the early 1890s, urged just such an intervention to stop the peso's depreciation.

Despite the arguments about general stability, the primary divide over the currency proposals remained a difference of opinion regarding infant-industry protection and industrial development. Since the gold standard proposal rested on protectionism and Listian developmentalism, the first line of attack inevitably became an attack on protectionism.

Theoretical opposition to protectionism centered on the idea that protectionism and devaluation could only aid "artificial industries" inherently unable to exist without perpetual protection. Opponents of industrial developmentalism believed that only those industries that could survive without state assistance, at any stage of development, were natural and were worthy enough to survive. In this view, natural industries would survive at any exchange rate, thus making the actual rate moot for industrial purposes.[39] The narrowest rendering of the natural versus artificial industry idea held that the only natural industries were agriculture and cattle, with any protection aimed at other industries merely aiding "speculators."[40]

The natural versus artificial distinction produced two responses from supporters of a devalued gold standard. The first argued that "industrial autonomy" was "the most constant and legitimate aspirations of peoples," and looked to examples in Europe and the United States of protected industries.[41] The second response contended that the natural versus artificial distinction itself was false. As Pellegrini put it, "Industries . . . cannot be classified as natural or artificial: they are industries that are all in the same state, and some flourish in one part and others in another due to varied conditions, according to the requirements and necessities of each industry."[42]

In addition to the nature of industries, a second current in the debate over Pellegrini's gold standard plan divided supporters of industrial promotion from their opponents. Here the question was not the legitimacy of industrial promotion or protectionism per se, but rather the legitimacy of using a devalued currency and monetary expansion to advance those goals. This was fundamentally a divide between those who benefited under inflation and those who benefited under deflation; it echoed similar arguments at the time in Japan, the United States, and other countries.[43]

Much time was spent discussing the attributes of *moneda sana* (literally, "healthy money"), which for its proponents generally meant appreciated currency.[44] The various arguments aligned less according to scientific or philosophical beliefs than they did with the specific economic interests at play. Creditors and importers favored appreciation, while debtors and manufacturers who stood to gain from the increased exports and decreased imports a depreciated currency implied, favored depreciation. In addition, in Argentina a large number of immigrant workers provided a popular base of support for appreciated currency lacking in, for example, the United States.

Inflationary *papelistas* who favored unbacked paper currency and whose interests ran contrary to appreciation provided the strongest support for Pellegrini's gold standard plan. First among the papelistas were rural landowners and producers whose expenses and costs were denominated in paper, but whose agricultural and cattle products were priced in gold. When paper depreciated they needed to spend less of their gold-denominated income to pay for their paper expenses. With appreciation, the situation was reversed. Wheat, with gold at a market rate of 230 pesos, per bushel would sell for the paper equivalent of close to 6 pesos while at the old gold rate of 100 it would sell for only 2.30 pesos paper. An export calf would bring 35 gold pesos, equivalent to 80 pesos in paper at the 230 rate, while at the old rate it would bring only 35 paper pesos.[45]

Farmers and ranchers who borrowed capital in the off-season had their debts denominated in paper as well. What was important to them was how much paper a given gold peso could buy. With the 230 rate, when wheat sold at 6 paper pesos and cattle at 80 paper pesos per head, they would have adequate funds to pay off their debts. With paper tied to gold at a 1:1 (100) rate their revenue—based on the gold rate—would decline in terms of paper, while their paper debts would remain constant producing a situation where they would have less paper revenue to pay off their constant paper debts.

Next among the papelistas were manufacturers. They favored depreciated paper for its help in promoting exports and impeding imports. They demanded additional tariff protection as the market exchange rate with gold moved from 250 to 200 during the first part of 1899. They fiercely opposed returning to the old nominal parity of 100 that supporters of metallic currency argued must be preserved. Whether one viewed these industries as artificial or not, industrial developmentalists were quick to argue that these industries employed more than 150,000 people, supported an additional 250,000 in the form of families, and represented capital investments of 400 million pesos. All of this gave them political influence and counterarguments for opponents who said they represented only a few artificial industries versus a multitude of consumers and workers.[46]

Although landowners, farmers, ranchers, and manufacturers had their individual reasons for opposing paper's appreciation, they all coalesced in support of Pellegrini's devaluation proposals, organizing meetings around the country and sending telegrams to newspapers and Congress.[47] But even when nominally expressing support for Pellegrini's plan, industrial groups more often than not pushed for greater devaluation than simply locking in the current market rate as Pellegrini proposed.[48] They also cared little about metallic currency or Pellegrini's insistence on tying devaluation to a gold standard. The important point for agriculture, cattle, and manufacturing was paper's depreciation, whether accomplished by official devaluation (with or without actual gold conversion) or some other means.

In opposition to the papelistas, and likewise to Pellegrini's gold standard, were Argentina's traditional gold standard advocates—or *metalistas* as they were known—who supported appreciated metallic money. Metalistas benefited from the peso's appreciation, supported moving to a gold-based currency at the old 100 rate as soon as possible, and fervently opposed any paper issues and government intervention in currency markets that reduced the value of paper. They consisted primarily of foreign merchants and creditors, whether living in Argentina or overseas, importers handling British goods, and investors who had used foreign currency to purchase assets denominated in paper. As the foreign currency value of paper increased, so too did the foreign currency value of assets denominated in paper.

Foreign workers also favored metalista ideas since appreciated paper allowed them to send back to relatives in Europe the equivalent of more European currency. Appreciated currency also allowed them to purchase more and cheaper imported goods. These, of course, were the same people who favored free trade over protectionism—and natural industries over artificial industries—giving them two reasons to oppose Pellegrini's currency proposals: protectionism and devaluation.

It is hardly surprising that foreign merchants—and their Argentine trading partners and intermediaries—favored foreign imports and opposed protective measures. These merchants borrowed the language of "artificial industries" to oppose state action, contending that Pellegrini's currency proposals amounted to "tampering" with the natural laws of markets for the benefit of a few, unnatural industries.[49]

Worker and immigrant groups argued somewhat differently both in terms of protectionism in general and devaluation in particular. These groups combined attacks on artificial industries more tightly with attacks on Pellegrini's plans for a "pseudo conversion." They saw Pellegrini's monetary plan as an inflationary, loose-money policy harmful to consumers and immigrants disguised in the institutional form of a hard-money gold standard.[50] If worker and immigrant groups belonged strongly to the metalista camp, it was not only as metalistas that they mattered. Protectionists and free traders—papelistas and metalistas—all regarded immigration as essential for national progress. All argued that their particular policies would most effectively promote it.[51]

The dominant view in Argentina held that population was a prerequisite to establishing the nation, promoting progress, and advancing civilization. Or, in the perennially cited aphorism from the politician and writer Juan Bautista Alberdi, "to govern is to populate [*gobernar es poblar*]." It was thus a matter of course that the 1853 constitution would enshrine both a governmental obligation to foster European immigration (article 24) and full rights for noncitizens within Argentina (article 20). As the Roca newspaper *La Tribuna* put it in 1899, what the nation lacked was "people, more, much more population, that indispensable complement that we urgently need to conquer and at all cost . . . we must . . . administrate, populate, produce, and enlarge through labor, source of all progress and all civilization."[52] The ardent free trader and metalista Lorenzo Anadón shared this sentiment, declaring, "Where are we as a nation in the universal concert of civilized peoples with little more than four million inhabitants? What will we be in 1910 with little more than six million, if we do not dedicate ourselves to attracting and spreading immigration?"[53]

It was natural, even indispensable, that supporters present Pellegrini's gold standard proposals as aiding not only industry but also population growth. Proponents argued that workers were leaving Argentina due to the appreciation of paper.[54] Supporters agreed that appreciation would increase the value of immigrant savings in gold. But they argued that the negative effects on agriculture and industry would increase the number of workers without jobs and place immigrants in a position of choosing between emigration or misery.

Opponents argued that Pellegrini's proposals would backfire by decreasing the value of real wages in an attempt to mimic the low wages that aided Japanese industry.[55] This, they argued, was objectionable in principle and unrealistic in practice given Argentina's relatively high cost of living and the fact that workers could be squeezed only so far. If wages were pushed down far enough, workers would simply return to Europe. The immigrant press argued that rather than promoting immigration, Pellegrini's proposals were aimed at preventing emigration. In this rendering, the currency proposals sought to lock the door by decreasing the value of immigrant savings in gold so that immigrants could not return to Europe.[56]

If immigration could be argued both in support of and opposition to devaluing the currency, the free trade versus protectionism and metalista versus papelista divisions were clearer. The near perfect overlapping of free trade and hard-money supporters meant that the most vociferous attacks combined antiprotection arguments with antidevaluation arguments to attack, as one, Pellegrini's industrial and monetary ideas. In the forefront were foreign business interests, Argentine merchants involved in banking and the import trade, and their press organs.[57] These arguments received their widest audience in the two dailies with the largest circulation, *La Prensa* and the *La Nación*, which led the attacks on Pellegrini and his "protectionist" plans of monetary "robbery."[58]

The satirical magazines *Don Quijote* and *Caras y Caretas* launched attacks portraying Pellegrini, in a series of disguises, as killing commerce and issuing a flood of paper money. The arguments were based on the same combination of merchant, immigrant, and creditor concerns as those aired in the daily press—Pellegrini's plans were aimed at helping a few industries at the expense of the mass of consumers, were financially irresponsible, and would result in enormous amounts of paper money.[59] In the magazines Pellegrini's currency proposals were depicted in the form of the bubonic plague—"Death" with traditional black cape and scythe—and various versions of Pellegrini impaling, throttling, and otherwise murdering an angel-winged "Commerce" and sending immigrants back to Europe.[60] Pellegrini's currency proposals were a "Pandora's box" and "Columbus egg" meant to deceive and pervert. They were a product of Pellegrini's pet protectionist obsessions, all overseen by a teary-eyed Pellegrini in various costumes and animal shapes.[61]

But quite aside from the image of Pellegrini wearing a wedding gown, decked out in gladiator gear, or transformed into a giraffe, Pellegrini was a special case among traditional metalistas and papelistas. He supported using the means of the metalistas (a gold standard) to achieve the ends of the papelistas (depreciated currency and promotion of exports and industry). The mixing of these ends and means produced inflationary papelistas supporting a gold standard, with gold standard enthusiasts as their harshest critics. It also resulted in a strange alliance of free traders and protectionists—and metalistas and papelistas—in the parliamentary adoption of Argentina's gold standard.

5

Strange Bedfellows

The surface incongruity of paper currency enthusiasts rallying to the gold standard, and gold enthusiasts attacking it, was not the only oddity in the lineup of supporters and opponents of the Argentine gold standard.

The breakdown reflected competition between the two main economic models of the time: free trade and inclusion as a primary products supplier within the British trading system versus protectionism and industrial promotion. British dominions such as Canada and Australia followed the first model. Formal and informal colonies followed this model as well, though rarely by choice. Countries such as the United States and Germany that sought to challenge British industrial predominance followed the second model. But the special dependence of the Argentine economy on exports made currency appreciation of particular concern even for individuals otherwise disposed to free trade doctrines and views that money could only be gold.

Once the Partido Autonomista Nacional (PAN) government endorsed Pellegrini's currency proposals, their passage was assured since the party had majorities in both houses of Congress. But the combination of gold, industrial promotion, and devaluation made for as strange a mix of supporters and opponents in Congress as it did in society at large. The most vocal opposition came from opponents of devaluation, protectionism, and industrial developmentalism, and supporters of hard money and free trade doctrines. But not all supporters of industrial developmentalism agreed with Pellegrini's proposal to make devaluation permanent. And not all free traders opposed devaluation as an interim solution.

Supporters of the industrialist Ernesto Tornquist favored greater devaluation than was provided in Pellegrini's currency proposals.[1] The metalista Eduardo Olivera defended the currency proposals because he feared that both paper's rapid appreciation and the old gold exchange rate would destroy commerce and industry.[2] Most notably, the minority correspondents for the Finance Committees in the Senate and Cámara de Diputados, Francisco Uriburu and Santiago O'Farrell, took positions that were theoretically fluid, pragmatic, and reflected a majority strain of opinion more concerned with practicalities than theoretical consistency.

Francisco Uriburu, a self-described industrialist and supporter of infant-industry protection, attacked Pellegrini's currency proposals from both papelista and metalista perspectives. From the papelista side, he attacked the proposals for not devaluing the peso enough in the short term. From the metalista side, he criticized the proposals for ignoring the long-term possibility of a less devalued standard. Uriburu criticized Pellegrini for attempting to establish a gold standard without gold reserves. He also argued that, even if a gold reserve could be funded, those funds would be better used to provide capital to industry, agriculture, and immigrants. This placed Uriburu's views in favor of temporary devaluation close to those of the otherwise free trade opponent of industrial promotion Santiago O'Farrell. O'Farrell accepted a need for temporary devaluation to deal with what he saw as the economic crisis that would result from paper's continued appreciation. Like Olivera, however, O'Farrell favored eventually returning the peso to the nominal 100 rate with gold, believing such a rate the only natural one possible between paper and gold.

Establishing the Argentine Gold Standard

This strange bedfellows aspect of Pellegrini's currency proposals stemmed directly from the proposals' idiosyncratic mix of devaluation, protectionism, and gold, which cut across the traditional economic divisions in Congress and in society as a whole.

In Congress, there were two economic conflicts apparent not only in the debates over Pellegrini's currency proposals but also in debates over other issues. The first was free trade versus protectionism, which tracked the two dominant economic models of the age. Free trade versus protectionism also served as a catch all for the conflict between primary products and industry, and loose money versus hard money.

The second was theory versus practice. This placed a deductive preference for theory against an inductive belief in the value of contemporary and historical examples. Advocates of deductive theory looked to England and English liberalism. Advocates of inductive reasoning looked to Germany and North America and took their academic cues from the German historical school.

Concern with free trade, a predisposition toward English theory, and a preference for deductive reasoning went hand in hand. The protectionist stance more often than not emphasized practice, historical examples, and inductive reasoning. These tendencies were not entirely exclusive given the dominance of practical arguments in general and the wildly different states of the Argentine and English economies. For example, Santiago O'Farrell cut and shaped his free trade doctrines to respond, as he saw fit, to circumstances. But for those most committed to free trade and hard money ideas, English theory was the ultimate frame of reference—a frame in which Pellegrini's gold standard proposal did not fit.

Given the developmentalist dominance in the Senate and, to a lesser extent, the Cámara de Diputados, the debates in those chambers rested less on the revealed truths of English theory and more on cataloging historical examples. Proponents and opponents of the currency proposals were well aware of the monetary experiments in other countries and referred to those examples to support their arguments.[3] Chile was held up as the example to be avoided: its disastrous adoption of the gold standard at an overvalued exchange rate and with inadequate reserves had led to recession and a financial crisis. Opponents of Pellegrini's currency proposals wielded the Chilean example as a club. Proponents dismissed the Chilean example as inapplicable and quickly invoked the United States as counterweight.[4] Proponents and opponents of conversion also sought to make the Russian example their own even if it meant erasing wars and other inconvenient occurrences from the picture.[5]

Uriburu and O'Farrell shared this tendency to favor practice and historical particulars over theory and claims to universality. Both opposed the currency proposals even while believing in a need to intervene to stop the peso's appreciation. And they both voted for Pellegrini's plan once their own counterproposals were defeated. But they started from radically different stances. Uriburu opposed Pellegrini's currency proposals from the standpoint of a self-described industrialist sympathetic to the needs of industry, in favor of infant-industry protection and willing to accept devaluation both in practice and principle. O'Farrell took the free trade position in attacking all measures which he believed favored artificial industries even while believing that the peso's appreciation had reached a crisis point requiring state intervention.

The gold standard proposals, and the message of President Julio Roca introducing them in the Senate, emphasized two points that echoed arguments for gold advanced in Japan: devaluation and stability.[6] Roca first outlined the precedents for devaluation. He then argued for the need to avoid disrupting the economy by trying to force an outdated exchange rate on a long-since depreciated currency.[7] Roca also addressed the criticism that devaluation amounted to robbery by arguing that debts contracted over the years in depreciated currency provided an unbargained for windfall to creditors if paid back in currency stronger than what had been loaned. Finally, Roca stressed the need for currency stability in order to promote commerce, industry, and progress.

This emphasis on commerce, industry, and progress reflected the industrial preferences dominant in the Senate. The bill itself went beyond devaluation and gold currency to provide for reorganization of the Banco de La Nación in order to provide low-cost capital to industry. The banking provisions were relatively uncontroversial and attracted little of the attention showered on the currency proposals. They did, however, reflect the dominant industrial mindset of the currency plan.

More questionable than the emphasis on industry was how the proposals were to be financed. In the Senate Finance Committee, Uriburu argued that the government could avoid unnecessary expenditures by intervening periodically in the exchange market. In this way it could sustain the desired rate without a commitment to establish the gold reserves necessary for a gold standard.[8]

The Senate debate centered on Pellegrini for the Finance Committee majority, Uriburu for the minority, and Senator Lorenzo Anadón in opposition to both the majority and minority reports. Anadón's speech was the outlier in the Senate debate in its focus on English political economy and theoretical concerns. In this, it more closely matched the free trade arguments of O'Farrell and the free trade forces in the Cámara de Diputados, although with far greater regard for theory as a guide for state policy. Pellegrini and Uriburu typified the Senate's industrial inclinations. Pellegrini reiterated his industrial and devaluationist concerns in a speech that centered the debate and was much lauded for its rhetoric even by the otherwise hostile opposition press.[9]

Pellegrini touted the dangers of currency appreciation and its effects on industry. The first problem for Pellegrini was the lack of stability from the sudden change in values associated with appreciation. Currency appreciation meant changing the value of all wages, prices, and salaries "so as to make life impossible." Pellegrini believed appreciation more harmful than depreciation because "appreciation is more rapid, and . . . produces more upheaval than depreciation." Notably, he rejected a moving scale for the peso's value under which the new exchange rate could be revised to adapt to changing conditions. He believed a permanent exchange rate should be locked in, thereby removing the dangers of instability and speculation.[10]

Uriburu embraced Pellegrini's general industrial goals and beliefs, while splitting the linkage between industrial promotion and gold conversion.[11] Like Pellegrini he argued for the need to prevent the peso's appreciation in order to assist industry, but unlike Pellegrini, he maintained that there was insufficient gold to accomplish conversion. This was true. Whereas Pellegrini sought to fudge the issue by leaving the date for conversion unspecified, Uriburu favored not even addressing conversion as long as it was a practical impossibility. Pellegrini and Uriburu also differed with regard to the particular exchange rate to be established—whether to devalue to 227 as Pellegrini proposed or to devalue to 250 as Uriburu proposed in a nod to the industrialist Ernesto Tornquist who had been advocating such a rate for months.[12]

In the Cámara de Diputados the dissenting member of the Diputados Finance Committee, Santiago O'Farrell—like Pellegrini and Uriburu—believed the peso's appreciation threatened to spark a crisis and needed to be halted. O'Farrell did not share Pellegrini's and Uriburu's views on industrial development. Instead he attacked "exaggerated protectionism" and "artificial industries" and called for a commitment to English free trade doctrines. His willingness to intervene to stop the peso's appreciation separated him from die-hard opponents of the currency proposals, who saw appreciation as a positive good and any attempt to prevent it an illegitimate use of state power.

THE PRACTICAL PROTECTIONIST

If Uriburu supported Pellegrini's basic industrial focus, he parted company with Pellegrini in the details and Pellegrini's insistence on proclaiming gold conversion without gold reserves. Uriburu was primarily concerned with what was practically possible and with producing minimum disruption. He disagreed with Pellegrini's more grandiose desire for proclaiming permanent conversion even where that was a practical impossibility. Just as Pellegrini did, Uriburu denounced the evils of speculation. This put both men within the dominant PAN majority and at odds with those like Lorenzo Anadón, the senator from Santa Fe, who viewed speculation as a natural expression of economic laws.[13]

For Uriburu, the borderline unreality of the currency proposals risked promoting speculation in their attempt to enact gold conversion without the required resources. He thought that the question of gold conversion and a gold standard was moot because the government had no gold reserves. He favored devaluation but without the fiction that the currency proposals had any direct or immediate connection to gold conversion or a gold standard. Uriburu could never support conversion as Pellegrini was proposing because it was a plan that "had neither a solid base nor any of the elements necessary in order to put it into practice."[14] Uriburu believed that the gold conversion aspects of Pellegrini's proposals would "fail fatally." In Uriburu's view conversion would mean maintaining gold reserves worth 60 to 70 million pesos, but with the level of existing government debt that scenario was, for the foreseeable future, a practical impossibility.

Uriburu felt that avoiding gold conversion was the logical and necessary consequence of being a new and poor country: "A poor country such as our own, because we have only recently been founded, how is it possible that we can provide a treasury of 60 or 70 million gold pesos? Who would believe that such a wonder was true?" When gold conversion was tried in the 1880s, it had proved "inconvenient and ineffective, because when it was put into practice any contingency would obstruct it."[15] For Uriburu, the same defect with gold conversion remained in 1899 and was underlined by the lack of gold reserves. With reserves shaky at best, other uses in need of the same funds, and extensive outstanding debt, trying to force gold conversion would be inherently unstable and do more harm than good.

Uriburu found himself forced to conclude that paper was the obvious and only choice regardless of what economic theory in other countries, and in different circumstances, might advise. Argentina was too undeveloped industrially and too lacking in financial reserves. As Uriburu argued, "I know what almost all the ancient masters of science say: paper is fatal, it is a disgrace; but I, with eyes that do not look abroad but merely at what is our own, say: in paper there is a mystery necessary for us to define—there is an unquestionable truth: when the Pampa has gold money, we are unable to buy anything, and when this money is removed we obtain all that is necessary in order to live. This proves that paper is not so ignoble, that there is in it something true, that there is something we should study before removing it from our body because we will perhaps remove with it a great strength."[16]

Uriburu argued the need for a system that would be "reactive and practical," "comprehensive and expansive" so that it could "moderate or restrain the violent appreciation of paper or its depreciation" and avoid "dangerous oscillations."[17] He believed the state should react flexibly to paper's appreciation or depreciation bearing in mind that the amount of money in circulation needed to increase as economic activity increased and that adjusting the money supply was a sovereign function of governments. Uriburu agreed with Pellegrini regarding the objective dangers of currency appreciation, arguing that Pellegrini "was entirely correct" in saying that "the harm from rapid appreciation is infinitely worse" than from depreciation.[18] For, "with currency appreciation, foreign producers dominate the national producer. The national producer must pay more in salaries, for its own consumption, and . . . must produce at higher cost than the foreigner whose money provides him with cheaper production. It is the excessive appreciation of money that causes a loss of compensation and also capital and, in the end, the result is poverty." Appreciation meant "consumption declines" and "public rents decline." In short, depreciation increased wealth, whereas appreciation decreased it. And depreciation risked causing less harm because of the built-in brake on it applied by the constant need for additional currency as economic activity increased.

Quoting the former British chancellor of the exchequer George Goschen, Uriburu criticized appreciation for its negative effects on producers, workers, industry, and commerce. In this, Uriburu was in complete accord with those nineteenth-century economists who had emphasized industrial promotion such as J. B. Say, Laveleye, [Henry] Carey, and Dana Horton, all of whom were "in complete agreement on the fatal effects that a violent appreciation of money produces in the economic order of a country."[19] This argument was entirely compatible with Pellegrini's interest, shared by Uriburu, in infant-industry protection. It was, however, the exact opposite of those who regarded industries without "solid bases" as "artificial" and those who would later advocate deflationary, liquidationist arguments in the 1920s.

Uriburu's primary disagreement with Pellegrini's plan was its attempt to lock in a permanent exchange rate. Although Uriburu preferred a rate of 250 compared to Pellegrini's 227, he most objected to the idea that the 227 rate would be permanent. In Uriburu's view, it was entirely possible that in five or ten years, the rate chosen might very well no longer match the needs of the economy as it had evolved over that period. Accordingly, there needed to be room to revise the exchange rate to adapt to these changing circumstances.

Uriburu's counterproposal aimed to stop the peso's appreciation as a temporary measure without locking in decisions that would not, and could not, go into effect for several years. Uriburu believed that "the most prudent move would be to establish . . . an exchange rate that for the time being prevents the excessive appreciation of paper, and [to] limit the Government's action to this. If at some point it is necessary to change this rate, the harm this would produce for contracts and the country would never be equal to the harm that currently comes from the disturbance of paper money. Why can we not fix a regular term of ten, fifteen or thirty years for this business? If the country can do conversion at a greater rate, what reason is there to decree it now?"[20]

Since Uriburu intended to make the new exchange rate temporary he had no problems arguing for greater devaluation than Pellegrini. Uriburu intended to establish a different rate once there were enough gold reserves to put conversion into practice. His current concern was not the long-term exchange rate but rather the most effective immediate response to a short-term crisis. Uriburu regarded both his proposed rate of 250 and Pellegrini's 227 rate as equally arbitrary. And since they were both arbitrary—and both, he believed, should be temporary and subject to change—he proposed using the rate that seemed the most useful for spurring industry and economic activity, and avoiding an economic crisis.

Uriburu did not in principle prefer depreciation to appreciation. He did not oppose appreciation that was gradual and allowed time for prices to adjust. Instead, he sought to avoid the destruction of wealth associated with sudden and rapid appreciation. He proposed devaluing the exchange rate only for so long as it took prices to adjust. In short, Uriburu criticized Pellegrini for not devaluing enough in the short-term and then attempting to establish a permanent system without sufficient reserves—and with what reserves there were being diverted from more pressing uses—at an undisclosed future date by which time circumstances could well have changed.

THE INDUCTIVE FREE TRADER

The minority member from the Finance Committee in the Cámara de Diputados, Santiago O'Farrell, could not have been more different from Uriburu in his opposition to protectionism, his emphasis on natural versus artificial industries, and his belief that free trade held the key to industrial growth. In his basic economic outlook, O'Farrell had far more in common with opponents of the currency proposals than he did with Uriburu or Pellegrini. And, yet, his counterproposals—and his criticisms of Pellegrini's plan—were remarkably similar to Uriburu's. Like Pellegrini and Uriburu, O'Farrell believed paper's appreciation represented an immediate danger to industry and the economy that, unchecked, would lead to a national crisis. Where O'Farrell differed from Pellegrini was in arguing, as Uriburu did, that the government should not set a permanent devalued exchange rate. Uriburu's ideas were more open-ended, making clear that the rate of 227, or in Uriburu's case 250, was merely temporary. But they did not specify what would come after this temporary phase. O'Farrell proposed a specific timetable under which the 227 rate would gradually return to its original 100 rate from the 1880s.

O'Farrell, like opponents of the currency proposals, divided industries into natural industries—or, as O'Farrell phrased it, real industries—and artificial ones. For O'Farrell, real industries were "those that the country truly needs and that work with the materials the country produces." Impermissible was support for what O'Farrell criticized as industries "that live off the country's calamities, its high taxes." O'Farrell was not indifferent to the needs of what he viewed as real industries. But he believed the growth of real industry depended not on currency devaluation, protective tariffs, and state subsidies, but instead on free—or at least freer—trade, in the form of lower tariff barriers and multi- and bilateral trade treaties. O'Farrell did not concern himself with the question of whether to promote industry. Instead, he worried about how to promote it. He believed that permanently devaluing the exchange rate as Pellegrini proposed would temporarily aid industry by controlling the peso's appreciation. But he also believed that it would ultimately damage industry through "establishing the discredit of the country."[21]

This view of the nation's "discredit" rested on the argument that devaluation meant "fraud" or "robbery" by having the government "change the legends on the notes" by paying out less than one peso gold for one peso paper as established on the face of those notes. At a broader level, O'Farrell objected to protectionism not only because he believed it less effective in promoting industry than free trade but also as a matter of democracy. For O'Farrell, protectionism was inherently undemocratic in favoring the few over the many: "For whom should the Argentine Congress legislate? Should it legislate exclusively in order to protect A, B or C however noble they may be? Or, perhaps should not the object of all laws, of the aspirations of all of us, be the general welfare of society, the well-being of the greatest number wherever they are?"[22] O'Farrell argued that Congress should, indeed, legislate for the "general welfare of society" and avoid "laws that establish exaggerated privileges." Pellegrini's currency proposals established just such exaggerated privileges through setting a permanently devalued exchange rate, which O'Farrell viewed not only as an exaggerated privilege but also as "exaggerated protection."

Yet O'Farrell agreed with Pellegrini's currency proposals regarding the need to stop the peso's appreciation. In his Diputados speech, O'Farrell argued that he was in agreement with the currency proposals "in all things with the exception of that regarding setting the exchange rate, conversion, and the power of the executive to set the value of money." In this, O'Farrell was essentially objecting to the bulk of the proposals, but his objections were a mixture of Uriburu's concerns and those of the most ardent free traders and metalistas. None of these individuals, O'Farrell included, accepted Pellegrini's claims to conversion. As O'Farrell argued in criticizing the currency proposals' claims to gold conversion, "It will be what they want, but it will not be conversion; they will prevent paper fluctuations, but, I repeat, it will not be conversion."[23]

O'Farrell sided with the metalistas about the state's power to set the value of money—which both O'Farrell and the metalistas, in opposition to

Uriburu and Pellegrini, denied it possessed. As O'Farrell argued, "It is necessary that we not let ourselves be deceived by the theory of government omnipotence, that could sanction, if one so wanted, an iniquity, but could never convert it into something just."[24] What this essentially meant was that the government could set any number of devalued exchange rates, if there were a pressing need, so long as the government ultimately returned to an official, "natural" rate of one gold peso to one paper peso.

This commitment to an ultimate 1:1 exchange rate led O'Farrell to propose a plan temporarily setting the exchange rate at 220. Even if such a rate were currently impossible due both to its destructive effects on industry and the government's lack of gold reserves, O'Farrell believed the 1:1 rate needed to be preserved. Despite the difference with Uriburu's rate of 250, O'Farrell's reasoning was the same as Uriburu's: that the peso's value should temporarily be fixed, but no move should be made to make that devalued rate permanent. O'Farrell was clear that "the only goal of this project is to prevent money's rapid appreciation."[25]

Thereafter, O'Farrell proposed that the government "convert" this "iniquity" "into something just" by gradually returning to the nominal 1:1 exchange rate over the course of twelve years. Where Pellegrini proposed "a single and definitive exchange rate" of 44 centavos gold for each paper peso, O'Farrell planned to arrive, over twelve years, from 220 to "par" through 5 points of appreciation biannually, such that the end result would be "the conversion of circulating currency at its nominal value."[26] O'Farrell set forth a descending scale for the exchange rate with the government converting paper to gold through March 31, 1900, at the rate of 20 centavos in paper for each gold peso; from April 1, 1900, through September 30, 1900, at the rate of 2 pesos for 15 centavos; from October 1, 1900, through March 31, 1901, at 2 pesos for 10 centavos; and so on. In this way the price of gold in paper bills would gradually decline by 5 centavos every six months until it reached a level where 1 gold peso equaled 1 paper peso.[27] Although O'Farrell ultimately wanted the exchange to return to the 1:1 rate on the face of the bills, he believed allowing any rapid or sudden currency change would be disastrous. As O'Farrell put it, echoing Uriburu, "I believe that rapid appreciation, like violent depreciation of money, will bring ruin, but not slow and gradual appreciation or depreciation of like manner."[28]

Despite his objections to Pellegrini's attempt to make the devalued exchange rate permanent—and to tie emergency steps to stop paper's appreciation to gold conversion for which there were no gold reserves—O'Farrell's

objections did not prevent him from voting in favor of Pellegrini's currency proposals.[29] O'Farrell believed paper's rapid appreciation was dangerous enough to warrant voting for Pellegrini's proposals. In this, O'Farrell
resembled Uriburu, who also voted for the currency proposals once his
own proposals were defeated.

But what were Uriburu and O'Farrell voting for? If Pellegrini's currency
proposals later came to be viewed as a gold standard in the standard English
political economy meaning of the age, this was not how they were viewed at
the time. This was, again, the incongruity of a gold standard supported by
papelistas, opposed by metalistas, and producing a mix-and-match collection of supporters and opponents cutting across traditional lines of support
and opposition to free trade, hard money, and English political economy.
Linked by their own political and economic interests, these strange bedfellows represented that part of the late nineteenth-century world for which
specific interests—individual, group, and national—took precedence over
ideological consistency.

Ideological consistency was easier for those representing a narrower
range of interests, those with a clear long-term personal stake, and those
with little personal stake at all. It was here—among importers and creditors, representatives of British interests, and those most committed to
English theory as science—that English political economy and English
ideas of gold currency received their fullest support.

And for those most committed to English political economy and English
ideas of gold currency, Pellegrini's currency proposals were not simply flawed
and mistaken. They were antithetical to the natural workings of the economy as they came to understand them through the workings of English theory. If Pellegrini, Uriburu, and O'Farrell, in their own particular ways, agreed
about the danger from the peso's appreciation, the most fervent supporters
of English political economy did not. The most ideologically inclined free
trade and metalista followers of the former president and opposition leader
Bartolemé Mitre, the senator Lorenzo Anadón, and the journalist Augustín
de Vedia worried little about the practical matter of paper's appreciation or
the interests that appreciation threatened. Their concern was the deviation
from English theory—and the certainty and scientific truth it was believed
to embody—that Pellegrini's proposals represented.

6

Law 3871
and the Gold Standard

After World War I Pellegrini's currency plan was commonly described as Argentina's adoption of the gold standard, with "gold standard" carrying the meaning assigned to it in nineteenth-century Britain and classic English liberal theory.

This meant the full collection of free trade, free capital flows, automatic adjustment, laissez-faire, hard money, anti-inflation, procreditor, and probanker policies revolving around a set exchange rate presumably immutable to change and free from government devaluation. This was the image the gold standard acquired in the market fervor of the 1920s. This was also the image of the gold standard in the years before World War I that privatizers and market enthusiasts in Argentina in the 1990s invoked to support their own policies.

This was not, however, what the turn-of-the-century Argentine currency system was. This was not what the Argentine economy was. The architects and advocates of what came to be called the Argentine gold standard were neither enthusiasts of privatization and laissez-faire nor were they reticent about using state power for economic purposes. Enthusiasts of laissez-faire and English political economy opposed the Argentine gold standard. They opposed that system because they believed it was not "the gold standard" in any sense that they knew. For them, the Argentine gold standard had nothing to do with English political economy, English liberalism, and the scientific truths they believed underpinned them.

In this, they were correct. During the final decade before World War I, Argentina paper currency was convertible into gold. But this was not the gold standard of English theory. It was certainly not recognized as such in Britain, where the Argentine system was sharply criticized for its lack of English input and roots in industrial protection.[1]

For the first three years little changed from the previous system of unbacked paper currency. Thereafter, there was simply de facto conversion—a fixed exchange rate under which the government traded paper for gold when and if it had the funds. This was the skeleton of the British gold standard, but it did not include the ideological hard money, free trade trappings that nineteenth-century Englishmen and twentieth-century deflationists described as forming part of that system. Instead, industry's call for protection from appreciating paper and Pellegrini's lifelong enthusiasm for infant-industry protection and industrial promotion provided the driving force behind Argentina's currency system.

In Pellegrini's case, the devaluation aspects of his currency plans were clear. Less clear was the part about conversion. This led to much debate up to 1914 when conversion was suspended due to World War I. There was little agreement over what Pellegrini and the government had actually intended with the references to gold conversion in the currency law. In fact, those references were so intentionally ambiguous as to mean different things to different people, including those meant to enforce it.[2]

Law 3871 and the Two Utopias

Pellegrini's economic beliefs rested on two pillars: protectionism and the gold standard. Together they made up Pellegrini's "two utopias," around which he believed the Argentine economy should be constructed.[3] But this was not a reflection of Pellegrini's fealty to English political economy. Rather, it was an attempt to use an institution taken from English political economy for the ends of Listian developmentalism.

As of 1899 the government lacked the gold reserves necessary to allow conversion of paper to gold. But this did not mean that Pellegrini simply addressed the problem of appreciating currency as industry and others in Congress such as Francisco Uriburu demanded. Rather, in full pursuit of his two utopias, Pellegrini developed a plan that would immediately devalue the peso under the guise of implementing conversion of paper to gold.

Although devaluation took effect immediately, Pellegrini put off enacting legal conversion into the indefinite future. This resulted in a law intended to stop paper's appreciation, enacted in response to pressure from industry and Pellegrini's own industrial concerns, but which was placed within a wrapping of gold conversion that gave no date, timetable, or other indication of when convertibility might ultimately occur. It was, in short, a law advertised as conversion, but in which the only element specifically decided on was a devalued exchange rate. It was, in the words of opponents, "pseudo conversion."[4]

Referred to contemporaneously as the "monetary law"—and only after the fact as the "convertibility law" or "conversion law"—the official name of Pellegrini's currency proposals became simply Law 3871. Law 3871 consisted of a mix of devaluation, potential future conversion, and institutional reorganization. In practice, the conversion provisions added nothing new. They acknowledged the existing status quo operations of the Caja de Conversión and its lack of gold reserves, while stating that the government would enact legal conversion at some point in the unspecified future, but not obligating it to do so. Devaluation and reorganizing the Banco de La Nación were more straightforward efforts to develop industry: stopping paper's appreciation and providing credit to agriculture and industry.[5]

Initially, the government announced a series of measures to establish conversion.[6] These measures attempted to cobble together a conversion fund through spending cuts, selling off government assets, and additional tariffs. But most of this involved shuffling budget items or one-shot cash infusions that did little to provide a sustainable conversion fund.[7] The government dropped a proposal for contributing one hundred thousand gold pesos monthly until reaching a total of 5 million gold pesos due to a lack of financial resources. The government ultimately also put aside promised sales of the state-owned Andino railroad and various bank properties. To the extent the Caja had funds for conversion prior to 1903 this was due to borrowing from the Banco de La Nación and from standard arbitrage (or speculative, as they were inevitably known) inflows and outflows. Gold flowed in when the market price fell below the 227 parity and flowed out when it went above.[8]

The Caja de Conversión's role and the interplay between articles 2 and 7 represented the key ambiguity in Law 3871. Article 2 referred to a decree to be issued at an unspecified future time fixing the date and means for commencing conversion. Article 7 stated that, as long as the decree set forth in article 2 had not been issued, the Caja de Conversión would issue gold in exchange for paper at the 227 rate using gold that the Caja had already received through exchange operations under article 7.[9] In other words, if the Caja had received funds through the conversion of gold to paper, it could pay those funds back out. It was not otherwise obligated to convert paper to gold.[10]

Articles 2 and 7 differed in terms of de jure and de facto conversion. Article 2 specified a decree that would legally commit the government to exchanging paper for gold at the new 227 rate and, in turn, would define legal tender as gold. The exchange mechanism set up by article 7 merely stated that the Caja would use whatever funds it had already received from exchange operations to exchange paper for gold. Legal currency itself still remained paper until whenever the decree referred to in article 2 might issue. In fact, the decree was never issued in the years before World War I. From 1903 only de facto conversion under article 7 continued in place, not the official conversion system of article 2. The year 1903 only mattered because it was from that time that the Caja consistently had enough reserves to pay out gold on demand—an occurrence aided by the declining demands on the Caja for gold conversion in the final years before World War I.

For those such as Ernesto Tornquist and other industrial advocates who had pushed for the government to act to protect industry, the legal laxity of the conversion provisions made no difference. For them, it only mattered that Law 3871 stopped the appreciation of paper currency. Whether this came through gold conversion, Uriburu's proposal for the government to buy and sell paper at the new 227 rate, or some other means mattered little to them.

For Pellegrini, the means did matter. Committed as he was to his two utopias of industrial protection and gold conversion, Pellegrini preferred to proclaim conversion while fudging the practical details. Thus he nominally declared conversion in article 2 only to pull back in article 7 in the face of a lack of funds. This caused a problem for those more precise in their definitions of conversion and a gold standard. For supporters of classic laissez-faire theory, Pellegrini's conversion plan acted as a Trojan horse to promote devaluation and industrial protection. For them, it was a "poorly named conversion," "a delirium of protectionist speculation," and an "economic coup d'etat."[11]

Even for some nominal supporters of the currency proposals, this loose definition of conversion caused problems and confusion. Some claimed Law 3871 amounted to conversion. Others claimed it did not. Pellegrini described the currency plan as conversion. Finance Minister José María Rosa—in whose name the plan was presented—contended that it was not. As Rosa argued in the Diputados debate, "what [the currency plans] in reality propose are preparatory measures tending to lead to a future conversion. Above all they attempt to give stability to the currency and obtain for means of de facto convertibility the benefits that we would receive from legal conversion."[12] Rosa did not even consider conversion to be the purpose of Law 3871. For him, the law aimed simply to stabilize the exchange rate.[13]

Conversion Without a Conversion Fund

The sleight of hand regarding conversion reflected the government's lack of funds. Taxes and import tariffs were already high enough to prompt demonstrations by merchants demanding reductions. But any reduction meant further shortfalls in government revenue. Spending cuts routinely failed to pass a Congress intent on providing funding for their home constituencies.[14] Debt service on foreign borrowing and provincial debts taken over by the national government further limited the government's financial options. This left the only reliable source of conversion funding the gold that arrived at the Caja de Conversión directly through exchange transactions.

Expenditures for railroads, ports, and other infrastructure, military expenses, and the funding proposals of industrial development advocates meant a steady stream of government expenditures. Limited population meant a limited tax base. Together these two factors produced comparatively high levels of both per capita government spending and government debt.

Table 6.1

Government Expenditures, 1899

Country	Population (in millions)	Expenditures (gold pesos, in millions,)	Expenditures per capita (gold pesos)
Argentina	4.5	70	15
Brazil	14	65	4.5
Chile	3	32	10
France	38.5	700	18
Germany	55	350	6
Italy	32	340	11
Mexico	13	52	4
Spain	18	160	9
United Kingdom	40	515	13
United States	72	440	6

Source: "Tribuna libre, Cuestiones conexas con los proyectos monetarios," *La Tribuna*, October 6, 1899, 1.

Table 6.2

Interest on the National Debt, 1899

Country	Population (in millions)	Interest on the national debt (gold pesos, in millions)	Interest per capita (gold pesos)
Argentina	4.5	24	5.33
Brazil	14	20	1.5
Chile	3	6	2
France	38.5	200	5
Germany	55	54	1
Italy	32	126	4
Mexico	13	11	1
Spain	18	75	4
United Kingdom	40	100	2.5
United States	72	33	0.5

Source: "Tribuna libre, Cuestiones conexas con los proyectos monetarios," *La Tribuna*, October 7, 1899, 1.

The population shortage also set a ceiling on the possible level of production and exports due to the limited supply of labor. This also pushed up the per capita figures. Thus the immense concern with immigration and the perceived need to rapidly increase Argentina's working age population.

At the root of the state's funding problems lay Argentina's limited population. The government spent huge sums on relatively fixed-cost development activities in a country with substantially less population than other countries making roughly the same types of expenditures. Contemporaries worried that this limited population—and the inevitably high per capita

Table 6.3
Worldwide Exports, 1899

Country	Population (in millions)	Exports (gold pesos, in millions,)	Exports per capita (gold pesos)
Argentina	4.5	140	31
Brazil	14	135	10
Chile	3	25	8
France	38.5	950	25
Germany	55	920	17
Italy	32	220	7
Mexico	13	128	10
Spain	18	170	9
United Kingdom	40	1,200	30
United States	72	1,200	17

Source: "Tribuna libre, Cuestiones conexas con los proyectos monetarios," *La Tribuna*, October 5, 1899, 1.

Table 6.4
Argentine Population and Exports, 1870–99

Year	Population (in millions)	Exports (gold pesos, in millions)	Exports per capita (gold pesos)
1870	1.9	30	16
1875	2.2	52	23
1880	2.5	58	23
1885	3.0	84	28
1890	3.4	100	29
1895	4.0	120	30
1899	4.5	140	31

Source: "Tribuna libre, Cuestiones conexas con los proyectos monetarios," *La Tribuna*, October 5, 1899, 1.

figures resulting from it—meant a fundamental limit on production, exports, and growth.[15] That, in the years after World War II, these same per capita figures would become a basis for ideas of an Argentine climacteric in which a turn-of-the-century Argentine economic powerhouse went astray from an established path of glory would have struck observers at the time as puzzling given their obsession with the limits on growth posed by scarce population. For Argentines at the turn of the century, their high per capita rates represented economic weakness, not strength.[16]

Contemporaries also worried about how large a conversion fund needed to be in relation to the paper money supply. This did not particularly matter to Pellegrini given the de facto only conversion obligations in article

Table 6.5

Population by Country

	1850 (in thousands)	1900 (in thousands)
Argentina	1,100	4,693
Brazil	7,234	17,984
Chile	1,443	2,974
China	412,000	400,000
France	36,350	40,598
Germany	19,952	31,666
India	187,657	235,729
Japan	32,000	44,103
Mexico	7,662	13,607
United Kingdom	25,601	38,426
United States	23,352	76,391

Source: Maddison 2003.

7. If the Caja had gold, it would it pay it out; if not, it wouldn't. The size of the conversion fund only mattered if the government made conversion a legal obligation rather than a discretionary practice based on the availability of funds. If conversion were made a legal obligation, the simplest answer to the "how large should the conversion fund be?" question was whatever amount was needed to cover anticipated withdrawals. This was not, however, the only possible answer.

For conversion advocates, such as former president Bartolomé Mitre and the Mitre newspaper *La Nación*, the only theoretically possible gold to paper coverage ratio was 100%. They criticized devaluation as robbery and saw any coverage ratio less than 100% as unnatural and illegitimate. This belief in 100% coverage was not limited to opponents of Pellegrini's currency proposals. Even some supporters, such as the newspaper *El Tiempo*, believed that conversion could only mean 100% coverage. This stemmed ultimately from a belief that only metal could be money. Paper was either a debt owed by governments to paper holders or a symbol of money that circulated for purposes of convenience. It was not, in this view, money itself.

The ambiguity afforded by the interplay of articles 2 and 7 allowed supporters such as *El Tiempo* and José María Rosa to remain committed to

100% coverage even when other supporters pushed for permanent devaluation. Whereas opponents claimed that Law 3871 bastardized conversion and sanctioned government robbery, those who sought to reconcile Law 3871 with 100% conversion argued that Law 3871 did not in fact establish conversion at all. For them, Law 3871 merely established the preparations for a future conversion that inevitably must provide 100% coverage.

Supporters thus used the ambiguity of articles 2 and 7 as a shield to counter the attacks of opponents who used that ambiguity as a sword. This allowed those who saw an impending crisis from the peso's appreciation to avoid abandoning the idea of 100% coverage. Those predisposed to support Pellegrini's currency proposals out of fear of paper's appreciation could thus retain their views about the meaning of conversion even as Pellegrini stated clearly that his projects were already conversion. Leaving the time limit for legal conversion open ended also removed pressure for reaching a given level of reserves within a fixed time period. This mattered in particular since even the 50% figure being circulated was questionable given the government's budget constraints and new plans to cut taxes in response to commercial protests.[17]

While José María Rosa emphasized the de jure versus de facto distinction between articles 2 and 7, Senate Finance Committee member Francisco Uriburu had less patience with Pellegrini's drafting sleight of hand. Uriburu argued that publicly claiming the government was enacting conversion made no sense when it was patently obvious there were no funds.[18] Other supporters took a different tack and dismissed the need for a conversion fund entirely. They argued that gold reserves were unnecessary as people were used to using paper for daily transactions and would continue to do so.[19] In this view, exchange requests at the Caja would be for paper rather than gold, removing any need to worry about gold reserves.

Others argued that the more paper the government issued the more gold would flow into the Caja.[20] According to this argument, because paper was needed for domestic transactions—and the Argentine economy would continue to grow—there would be a continual demand for paper on the part of gold holders seeking to conduct transactions within Argentina. Given this demand, any increase in the amount of paper available at the Caja would result in an increase in the amount of gold being exchanged for that paper. This argument left aside the possibility that demand for paper might be less steady and more limited than its proponents believed. It also ignored the possibility that more paper being printed might decrease paper's market value below the official rate, thereby causing gold outflows from the Caja.

The argument did, however, touch a nerve with opponents of Law 3871 who suspected that Pellegrini's conversion machinations were intended to fuel paper issues. Pellegrini's reputation as a rampant inflationist and issuer of paper currency increased the suspicion.[21] For opponents, Law 3871 had built into it a mechanism for ongoing paper issues that would "drown the people in a mass of paper currency."[22]

This concern with paper issues rested on domestic transactions being conducted entirely in paper. It also resulted from the provision in article 7 that conversion from paper to gold would occur only if the Caja had a net gold surplus from prior exchange transactions. Article 7 said nothing about the source of paper for conversion. This meant that the government could potentially be obligated, or might simply choose, to print paper money to be exchanged for gold presented at the Caja. There would thus be an asymmetry built into the Caja's operations under which the Caja might always exchange paper for gold and print paper if need be to enable that exchange, but would only exchange gold for paper under limited circumstances.

In addition, the circumstances under which the Caja would exchange gold for paper—that is, when the Caja had accumulated gold reserves available from prior exchange transactions—implied trade surpluses and gold inflows. This was precisely when requests for conversion from paper to gold were least likely to occur. This all led to the suspicion that Pellegrini had intentionally set up a system that would not only permanently devalue the exchange rate but also provide an institutional mechanism to continually expand inflationary paper issues.[23]

Opponents believed this was all intended to protect industry, promote exports, and lower wages.[24] These suspicions only increased when the president of the Caja notified the Finance Ministry that without more paper issues there would be insufficient paper to exchange for the level of gold inflows he expected to the Caja.[25] For opponents, this only confirmed that article 7 was intended to be a disguised means of producing unlimited paper issues.

If the suspicions of unlimited paper issues painted Pellegrini in a somewhat flattering light—at least from the perspective of technical skill in rigging a system as he wished—there was another issue that flipped not only the fear of paper issues but also the image of a Machiavellian Pellegrini on its head. This was the question of how much control the government had over the exchange market given that the Caja lacked reserves and a suddenly depreciating market rate would produce gold rather than paper outflows from the Caja.

The government's primary purpose had been to stop paper's appreciation. But it had done so in a general attempt to stabilize exchange rates at a fixed level—227 pesos paper per 100 pesos gold. But, after enactment, market exchange rates continued to fluctuate, as they would until 1903 when the Caja had enough reserves to commence de facto conversion. The difference after Law 3871's enactment was that paper was depreciating beyond the 227 level rather than appreciating. Although this served to protect industry, it simultaneously undercut government finances by reducing the real value of government revenue and made balancing those finances effectively impossible no matter how austere the budget might be.[26]

Pellegrini's plan rested on 227 being a sustainable exchange rate or, at the very least, one that would undervalue paper and produce inflows of gold into the Caja as new paper issues flowed out into the economy. But this overlooked the consideration that the peso's market rate might decline further either in response to anticipated government action or other causes.[27] Neither Pellegrini nor opponents had anticipated that the peso's market price would depreciate enough to cause gold outflows from the Caja. Given that the Caja had no obligation to pay out gold, the practical effect of the peso's depreciation was merely to prolong de jure and de facto inconversion. Pellegrini and industry had been focused on paper continuing to appreciate rather than depreciate. Pellegrini's opponents worried about paper money issues flooding out from the Caja, not the supply of gold.

Pellegrini assumed that announcing conversion at the 227 rate would stabilize the market rate while gold flowed into the Caja in exchange for paper to be used for domestic transactions.[28] Pellegrini wanted the Caja to absorb gold and issue paper in line with the economy's growth. He did not see requests for conversion from paper to gold as likely to form a substantial number of transactions. The increase in gold's market price to greater than 227, however, left even de facto conversion under article 7 a practical impossibility. The Caja almost immediately ran out of all gold reserves as the minimal gold it had held flowed out to be exchanged at the higher market rate. This left a Caja de Conversión that, in the words of its critics, was "neither caja nor conversión."[29]

Even many of those who had supported Law 3871 out of a belief that something needed to be done to control appreciating paper came to question their decision. This included Finance Minster Rosa. In particular, they came to doubt Pellegrini's competence, the institutional mechanisms Law 3871 had set up, and the wisdom of nominally announcing a conversion that was factually impossible.[30] In Rosa's case this reflected ongoing ambivalence about the proposals and their claims to conversion. But it also reflected an ex post facto flowering of criticisms tracking almost exactly those that Uriburu had made before the proposals' enactment into law.[31]

Critics attacked on two fronts. First, although one might have supported temporary measures to stop the peso's appreciation, it was another thing entirely to establish a permanent devalued exchange rate with its shift in wealth from creditors to debtors—with the biggest debtor being the state. Second, even with the peso's devaluation, the government still lacked the gold necessary to exchange paper for gold. Trying to guess how many years it might take for that to happen—if ever—simply increased uncertainty and speculation. Yet by announcing that the government would implement legal conversion, Law 3871 applied pressure to divert to a conversion fund revenue otherwise needed to balance the state budget and fund the great works of infrastructure and industrial development needed for national progress.

There remained one option legally in play. Despite Pellegrini's insistence on setting a permanent and definitive exchange rate, the government could devalue the exchange rate further. Virtually simultaneously with Law 3871, Congress passed a new tariff law—supported by Pellegrini as well—that reserved the government's right to adjust the official exchange rate without additional congressional approval.[32] This was primarily a reactive move to the government's limited capacity to accomplish conversion. In this it resembled the fudging of legal and practical conversion in articles 2 and 7. Whether one acknowledged that limitation explicitly, as Uriburu did, or attempted more obliquely through legislative drafting to fudge the issue, as Pellegrini preferred, the bottom line was that a lack of funds made conversion a practical impossibility for the immediate future. Thereafter, it remained questionable without a change in external conditions or in the underlying structure of the Argentine economy.

In short, Argentina's lack of capital, industry, and population—combined with the self-conscious pursuit of national development that defined Argentina in the last quarter of the nineteenth century—required continuous borrowing from abroad. Pellegrini's emphasis on industrial development was in part meant to solve this problem. But it inevitably rested on imports of foreign capital. Pellegrini's second utopia of conversion, meanwhile, did nothing to solve the problem, as it had to be constructed on loopholes necessitated by a lack of gold. Lacking the sort of rent-bearing investments overseas and large capital stocks that propped up the British Empire, the Argentine government had to pay for goods bought from abroad in credit borrowed from abroad. Domestic transactions depended on the government printing paper money whose value depended on a combination of market forces and government fiat, with the government lacking the resources to back up its proclamations.[33]

That Pellegrini would resort to a cobbled together arrangement of nominal conversion, paper issues, devaluation, and protective tariffs is not itself especially surprising given Argentina's economic conditions and the not all that different combinations in countries such as the United States, Japan, and Germany. This combination, however, fit awkwardly with English economic theory and the English image of the gold standard. It was thus among adherents of English political economy and English ideas of the supremacy of gold currency that Pellegrini's currency proposals and Law 3871 had their fiercest critics. And it was this opposition that underlined the considerable distance between Law 3871 and what its hard money and laissez-faire critics regarded as the only "true and universal money"—gold.

"True and Universal Money"

The fact that Pellegrini's currency proposals and Law 3871 were predicated on the state's intervening in currency markets (and devaluing paper to prevent it from appreciating toward its nominal parity) made support from advocates of English political economy unthinkable. Add in the motives of protectionism and industrial promotion and there remained virtually no common ground uniting Pellegrini and his free trade, laissez-faire opponents. Hard core metalistas and critics of "artificial industries" had nothing in common with Pellegrini and his currency law.

Even more galling for supporters of English political economy was Pellegrini's insistence on describing his projects as gold "conversion" when they failed to require the government to exchange paper for gold and when the government clearly lacked the resources and the intention to pay out gold at any time in the foreseeable future. For those who most wanted Argentina to adopt the gold standard, Pellegrini's currency proposals were anything but.

English ideas of the gold standard had their strongest support politically among the family interests of former president Bartolomé Mitre (or *mitristas* as they were known)—the Mitre political party the Unión Cívica Nacional, and the Mitre newspaper *La Nación*—and Senator Lorenzo Anadón. Anadón belonged to PAN (Partido Autonomista Nacional) but was from the agricultural export region of Santa Fe and perpetually at odds with PAN's protectionist and inflationary tilt.[34] In Congress, Anadón and the Mitre family scion Emilio led the attack on Pellegrini's currency proposals for their deviation from English currency views and their failure to adopt a "true" gold standard. Meanwhile, in the press, the most noted individual gold standard advocate was Augustín de Vedia, the former editor of the Roca daily *La Tribuna*, who left the paper rather than support Pellegrini's currency proposals.[35]

Given that their concern with English theory placed them among the mainstream of English academics and, rhetorically, among the practical men of British finance, commerce, and liberal politics, the arguments made by Mitre, Anadón, and Vedia reflected the views of most English observers who attacked Law 3871 for being a protectionist, inflationary folly far from the English ideal. That this ideal only partially reflected contemporary British practice and was worlds away from historical British practice was an inconvenience left unconsidered by gold standard enthusiasts. Mitre, Anadón, and Vedia wanted a "real" gold standard, not the smoke-and-mirrors protectionism and loose money policy they believed Pellegrini was creating.[36]

THE MITRISTAS

If Uriburu essentially shared Pellegrini's views of industrial development, the debate in the Cámara de Diputados proceeded from different bases. First, the opposition came almost exclusively from the mitrista Union Cívica Nacional, which had greater representation in Diputados than in the Senate. The debate thus became in large part an expression of mitrista ideas and mitrista political maneuvering. Second, the Cámara de Diputados was considerably less protectionist than the Senate even with its PAN majority and even excluding the mitristas. This was reflected in the free trade views of Santiago O'Farrell. But where O'Farrell, even in arguing from free trade and English bases, believed the state had to intervene to prevent what he regarded as an impending crisis from paper's appreciation, the mitristas opposed even this concession to Pellegrini's currency proposals. Speaking for the Union Cívica Nacional in the Diputados debate, Emilio Mitre attacked not only Pellegrini's industrial views but also the basic premises that rapid currency appreciation was a danger and that it was the state's role to remedy it.[37]

Like Santiago O'Farrell, Emilio Mitre argued classic English political economy and the interests of trade and commerce.[38] He went further than O'Farrell, however, in opposing all special efforts to support industry and all government intervention meant to stop paper's appreciation in furtherance of that goal. The mitristas based their opposition to Pellegrini's currency proposals primarily on the argument that currency devaluation equaled robbery. Rather than devaluation, the mitristas urged fiscal retrenchment and a monetary policy in which paper could only act as a temporary substitute for gold, with one paper peso always to equal one gold peso and never to be subject to the "criminal" act of devaluation.[39] This fundamental stance placed the mitristas diametrically opposite Pellegrini regarding the devaluation and industrial promotion aspects of the projects—not to mention Pellegrini's underlying protectionist beliefs. It was thus hardly a surprise that Pellegrini's currency proposals ultimately led to the break up of the political alliance between PAN and Mitre.[40]

The mitristas favored foreign capital and merchant activity centered in the Mitre political stronghold of Buenos Aires. But they were not opposed to industry per se. Instead, they opposed industrial protection and promotion that sought to impede free trade or devalue the currency. The mitristas placed particular emphasis on finance, emphasizing that, rather than being a danger, paper's appreciation offered benefits in making foreign debt payments cheaper in paper. This, for Mitre, was essential given that "we work in large part with borrowed capital."[41]

Although accused by their opponents of being protectors of "foreign interests" against national industry, the mitristas did not view foreign ownership of Argentine industry as a benefit. But the solution for the mitristas rested with paper's appreciation. They argued that appreciation would allow Argentine industries to lessen their foreign debt burdens. As Emilio Mitre put it, "There are, it is said, 1000 million in English gold in the country, whose product must be remitted to London, a sum that increases as each industry increases, such that each new industry that produces income is converted immediately into an English company, and we have a case where everything that finds itself in similar conditions will pass to foreign hands, and as the dividends must be remitted in gold, paper's appreciation is beneficial."[42]

In contrast to Pellegrini and Uriburu who argued for industrial promotion through promoting exports and blocking imports, the mitristas argued that currency balance could only be regained—and foreign capital inflows controlled—by reducing exports and increasing imports. The mitristas, in particular, argued that exports in and of themselves were not a sign of economic health. As Emilio Mitre argued, "If from what occurs with us, that exports are greater than imports, one deduces that this difference is a benefit for the country, they are making a mistake." In the mitrista view the most advanced economic state was a situation analogous to England or Germany where "what occurs . . . is that exports are less than imports."[43] The key to economic health for the mitristas was not exports, industrial promotion, and import protection, but rather a stable currency.

For the mitristas Argentina's economic "backwardness" rested not on a lack of industry as Pellegrini believed, but rather on the failure to have a stable, inalterable currency. As Emilio Mitre argued, "The lack of stable money is the cause of our arrears. We have a need for real, invariable money."[44] This real, invariable money, however, could only be metal because, Mitre argued, it had become the world standard and people had come to psychologically associate the currency's metallic value with economic health. As Mitre put it, "Civilized countries have adopted units of measure for time, and the necessity for uniformity is no less when one works with time than when works with values. The people have become accustomed to see in its metallic value a sign of good times or bad, an infallible barometer of the circumstances in which the nation finds itself." The mitristas viewed Pellegrini's currency proposals as anathema to this goal of stable, invariable, and "real" money. For them, Pellegrini's plan produced "disillusionment" about the state of the nation, perpetrated a "fraud" on holders of paper currency, and was "in combat with the country's interests."

Mitre argued that the defenders of the currency proposals had fallen into "many contradictions and many errors" in their understanding of paper money, confusing paper with "real money," which could only be metal. He argued that they were seeking to destroy the true one-to-one relationship between metal and paper by seeking to devalue paper's exchange rate with gold. For Mitre, the only national money that existed was "a disc of gold or silver whose unit for different transactions is one peso." As Mitre explained, "In the Republic there is no other national money than this and there is no more national money, in consequence, than the gold peso and paper." By changing the relationship between "real" metallic money and its paper representation, however, Pellegrini's currency proposals had, in the mitrista view, destroyed the very foundations of monetary "truth." As Mitre argued, "In the projects presented the relation between the gold peso and paper are changed. If we cannot achieve conversion without altering these things, these principles, these relations, we will sacrifice and not do it, rather than to disdain the truth and economic fundamentals."

Like Uriburu, Mitre believed that the government acted "precipitously" in announcing conversion "as long as we do not have the necessary resources in order to realize conversion."[45] But Mitre's objections went further than Uriburu's in that Uriburu did not object in principle to devaluation—although he cautioned against devaluing more than necessary and for longer than necessary. Mitre believed that "true" conversion could never be accompanied by devaluation and argued that the currency projects mimicked the form of an English gold standard without the substance. As Mitre argued, "The financial projects that are currently being discussed appear similar to those put into practice by England, in that they tend toward conversion, but they are completely different in the means to realize that." As Mitre put it, "Conversion is not the same thing as depreciation; it is necessary not to confuse the words. Conversion is the well-being of the national economy, which is obtained through monetary stability, and depreciation means upheaval of the economy, harm for the country."[46] For "to depreciate paper is to increase the state of monetary inconstancy in which we find ourselves." The mitristas sought to "combat the projects" because "although they pretend to give stability to money, they contribute to devaluation."

Mitre believed that the government could not, as a matter of logic and fact, establish a given exchange rate. The only rate at which the state could exchange paper for metal was one peso of metal to one peso of paper. This was a matter of "truth and economic fundamentals." No other rate could logically or factually be conversion. If the government could not accomplish true conversion, then the only other option was to "sacrifice" and do without metal currency. In this case only currency markets, through the natural effects of commercial transactions, could set paper's value. The government's attempt to establish nominal conversion at a rate of its own choosing was "a completely negative act" that applied the label of conversion to something that lacked the requirements of conversion.[47] In Mitre's view Pellegrini's currency proposals were merely selecting an arbitrary rate with no logical or natural basis and pretending, fraudulently, that this amounted to conversion.

The mitristas believed that conversion of paper money to metal was a natural process that would happen of its own accord through commercial transactions once the market exchange rate had reached the true level of one paper peso to one metal peso. This was a process over which the government could have no control. As Emilio Mitre put it, "Conversion is not even in the hand of government, that is to say, it cannot do it although it is a fair aspiration, and I believe that the Congress should not become involved in this matter, and should not set the relation between paper money and gold, because this will come to [instill] distrust in the people who fear . . . that they want to give an exaggerated scope to the legislative functions, attributing to them rights that do not correspond to them." Instead, for the mitristas, Pellegrini's currency proposals—both by cutting the 1:1 exchange rate of paper to gold in half and in providing for no actual conversion fund—"in reality do not propose anything but the substitution of one inconvertible currency for another currency equally inconvertible."[48]

ANADÓN

Although committed to free trade and opposed to devaluation, the mitristas were still not as committed to English political theory itself—as opposed to the interests aided thereby—as the senator from Santa Fe, Lorenzo Anadón. Upon his election in 1892 Anadón had become the one and only no-holds-barred supporter of English political economy in a Senate divided between moderate protectionists and extreme protectionists.[49] Given his minority status, Anadón had little effect on the outcome of legislation. He was, however, a perpetually vocal advocate for English doctrine in a Senate that was otherwise allied with industrial developmentalism and infant-industry protection. Due to his fondness for citing English theory, Lorenzo Anadón invited considerable criticism that he should focus less on theory and more on practical examples.[50] But Anadón's fondness for theory was a matter of degree. Anadón did not divorce himself entirely from practical concerns, acknowledging that Argentina, due to its particular history and circumstances, neither was nor could be a carbon copy of England.

Still, Anadón's approach fundamentally differed from both Pellegrini's and Uriburu's. Although Uriburu argued that conversion would be a waste of funds better spent on providing low-cost capital to industry, he shared Pellegrini's basic concern with national development and industrial promotion and had no essential objection to devaluing the exchange rate. Anadón's emphasis on the preexisting legal parity and free trade ran directly counter to Pellegrini's combination of devaluation and protectionism. If Uriburu, and even O'Farrell, shared points of agreement with Pellegrini, there were not enough spans in the world to bridge the gap between Pellegrini's economic views and Anadón's. Anadón advocated "gold and free trade" ideas "diametrically opposed to those of the monetary project arguing the illegitimacy of the measure being rushed through as well as its unsuitability for the general economy of the country."[51]

Above all, Anadón objected to Pellegrini's use of devaluation and approached the issue "from the side of the rights of those holding bills to demand their reimbursement at par with gold."[52] Pellegrini viewed the currency question fundamentally in terms of his two utopias of protectionism and conversion—and most immediately in terms of stopping the peso's appreciation. Anadón saw the currency question as one part of a larger imbalance in government finances, "nothing more than one incidence of the problem with which we are concerned."[53] Where Pellegrini focused almost exclusively on devaluing the exchange rate, conversion, and reorganizing the Banco de La Nación to provide industrial credit, Anadón was more concerned with what he saw as excessive wages, prices, and government expenditures.

For Anadón the principal issues were "the questions of wages, salaries, the value of land, public administration and its expenditures, the floating debt, and transport."[54]Anadón accepted that there was an economic crisis, but he did not believe that currency appreciation was at the root of that crisis. Despite the continuing calls from industry for the government to stop the peso's appreciation, Anadón did not believe those groups and individuals affected by the economic crisis actually saw a fixed exchange rate as a solution. In effect, Anadón was challenging not only Pellegrini's solution—which Uriburu and O'Farrell had done as well—but the entire understanding of the economic crisis held by Pellegrini and industrial advocates who were calling for measures to stop the peso's appreciation. It was this sort of argument—that those industrialists calling for depreciation did not really mean what they said—that most frustrated Anadón's critics and that led to claims that he was more comfortable with theory than reality.

In other ways Anadón was not all that far from Uriburu. Like Uriburu, Anadón believed Congress was rushing into projects without sufficient study.[55] As Anadón argued, "There is not in the entire country a single man, not a single one, truly prepared about these questions. Our [country's] statistics do not deserve our trust. There is the most complete anarchy of opinions about facts perfectly in dispute. Merchants, builders, settlers, farmers—all of them should have been called upon to study these economic matters." Anadón also agreed with Uriburu in arguing the incongruity of claiming to be enacting conversion for which there were no conversion funds. Like Uriburu, Anadón believed the state had no business declaring even nominal conversion when it lacked the necessary resources.[56] Attempting to do so would simply damage Argentina's image overseas.[57]

Anadón and Uriburu's agreement, however, ended there. Not only did Anadón differ from Uriburu in arguing that Pellegrini's belief that "the remedy for the situation that the country is passing through lies in fixing the currency" was something rooted entirely in Pellegrini's own obsessions rather than a measure that overlapped with industrial calls for stopping the peso's appreciation, he also came at the issue from a radically different theoretical conception about the economy and a radically different set of nineteenth-century ideas.[58]

In terms of the two nineteenth centuries, Anadón belonged to the first, the nineteenth century of free trade, English political economy, and cosmopolitan consumerism, which had reached its peak in the 1850s and 1860s (see chapter 1). Pellegrini and Uriburu belonged to the second nineteenth century of protectionism, industrial promotion, nationalism, and imperial warfare dominant in the 1890s.

In this sense, the dominant state consensus in Argentina in the 1890s was less Smith and Ricardo than it was List and Hamilton, less cosmopolitan than national, less centered on individuals and consumers than the nation as a collective unit and producers. In this view, protectionism would not harm consumers because all consumers were also producers. Aiding producers would thus also aid consumers. The counterargument to this was that, if the goal was to aid everyone, then no industry should be favored above any other.[59] But for great power advocates and developmental nationalist thinkers, all industries were very much not created equal, just as not all people were created equal.

Fundamentally, supporters of Pellegrini's currency proposals and Law 3871 were developmental nationalists and protectionists in the vein of List, Hamilton, and the conservative leaders of the age: Bismarck, Jules Méline, and other mid-1890s French protectionists who reversed Napoleon III's free trade policies of the 1860s, and the Republican Party in the United States.[60] Their opponents were the opposition parties who drew an earlier heritage of English liberalism—or, as often as not in the Argentine case, English liberalism as translated through French thinkers such as Jean-Baptiste Say.

In the context of late nineteenth-century Argentina, these latter views put Anadón in a clear minority. Not until the election of Roque Sáenz Peña in 1910—with Anadón as finance minister and the free trader Victorino de la Plaza as vice president—did a move away from protectionism begin to emerge.[61] This essentially coincided with the suspension of Law 3871 at the outbreak of World War I.

In the 1990s President Carlos Menem described his combination of a currency board, deregulation, and privatization as analogous to Pellegrini's plans in the 1890s. But whatever the benefits and losses of those distinctly 1990s proposals may have been, they had nothing to do with Pellegrini or the dominant ideas and practices of the 1890s. They would have pleased Anadón. But Argentina's turn-of-the-century gold standard was Pellegrini's, not Anadón's.

VEDIA

Where Anadón-style views carried more weight was in the press, particularly under the influence of the Mitre-run *La Nación*. But where *La Nación* tempered its positions to match the not always consistent political incarnations and alignments of the Mitre family, the most doctrinaire expression of English currency views came from the former *La Tribuna* editor Augustín de Vedia, who argued that there could be no "true and universal money" other than gold. For Vedia, Argentina's existing silver and paper currencies could at best be symbolic representations of money. They could never themselves be actual money.[62]

Vedia's views on the supremacy of metallic currency—similar to, but more rigid than, those of the mitristas—belonged squarely to the classic debate about the nature of money, which was only slowly receding in the late nineteenth century. That is, was money, in essence, something approaching a Platonic form—a natural artifact that existed of its own accord and had an intrinsic value separate from any action of the state. In this view, metal by definition was, as Vedia put it, "the only money that exists." Taken to the extreme, this view could mean that any debate about the specific exchange rate between paper and gold was, itself, meaningless. As Vedia argued, paper was "nothing more than a representation, better or worse, of gold" and any decline in the value of that paper itself made no difference to the actual value of the underlying metallic money.[63]

In this view, nominally changing paper's value—and pretending that this could change the actual value of money—simply made the government a party to fraud. Or as Vedia argued, in enacting the devaluation provisions in Law 3871, "the sovereign commits counterfeit in giving to money a value separate from its intrinsic value."[64] Vedia saw paper currency not as money but as a loan from the holders of paper to the government. This loan had to be repaid in metal at the face value printed on the notes. Vedia argued that devalued currency meant the state was committing robbery on behalf of debtors. The state's devaluing paper meant it was unilaterally repudiating its own debts.[65]

The opposing view held that money was whatever people believed it was. If they accepted it as money, then it was. It might be metal or it might be paper notes, bank drafts, checks, or some other material or device, none of which were inherently more or less legitimate than any other item. For supporters of Pellegrini's currency proposals, money was a creation of the state with its value assigned by the state. It was "nothing more than a disc carrying a seal, on which the State sets forth the weight and metallic law establishing it, assigning it a market value."[66] For monetary relativists such as Pellegrini, even metal could not embody a perfect relationship between intrinsic and nominal value. For monetary relativists, that the value of metal itself changed daily due to the laws of supply and demand proved that there was no intrinsic value to metal and thus no immutable value of money.

If Anadón and Vedia were more theoretically inclined in their opposition to Pellegrini's currency proposals, the opposition in London was more
practical. The first problem was that it was obvious to observers in London
that Pellegrini's currency proposals were aimed primarily at devaluing the
peso.[67] This, coupled with Pellegrini's reputation as a protectionist, led the
Times of London to argue—much as Anadón did—that Pellegrini's increasing influence had tarnished the government's reputation overseas.[68]

This, in turn, prompted arguments that the Argentine government
should avoid intervening, and instead allow the peso to appreciate naturally.[69] The *Times*, echoing the arguments of opponents in Argentina,
contended that Pellegrini's projects were an attempt to protect artificial
industries at the expense of agriculture, which, it averred would result in
the destruction of commerce. The general thrust was that the Argentine
government should refrain from "artificially" forcing conversion by changing the exchange rate or by any other measure that would interfere with
"the law of supply and demand" finding a "true equilibrium."[70]

Despite this uniform opposition to Pellegrini's currency proposals from
English and Argentine proponents of English political economy, a case
of historical amnesia occurred in Argentina in the 1920s with the prewar
"gold standard" morphing into an ex post facto replica of the English
model. Most notably, preserving "parity" in Argentina would become a
question of national honor even though parity by the 1920s had come to
mean not the 1:1 (100) rate it meant before World War I but Pellegrini's
devalued 227 rate.[71] This obsession with preserving parity as a matter of
national honor, in turn, would extend to scorning such previous models of
civilization as Germany and France for devaluing their own currencies.[72]

But here the argument of those in Argentina intuitively concerned with
honoring an unchanging exchange rate ran up against the problem that
Law 3871 itself had been based on devaluing the peso. This reimagining of
the gold standard in the 1920s, however, did not apply to Argentina alone.
More dramatically, it replayed itself in Japan, where a system founded on
export promotion and imperial expansion was presented as a model of
theoretically pure, deflationary English political economy.

PART THREE

The Meiji Gold Standard

7

The Meiji Gold Standards

Currency in Meiji Japan (1868–1912) was not only a matter of commerce and state-guided industrialization as it was in Argentina. It was also an issue of military might. In Meiji Japan, as in Argentina, progress and civilization became matters of state concern. But in Japan this concern carried diplomatic and military meaning absent in Argentina.[1] In Japan, government policy from the 1870s concerned itself with the concept of "rich nation, strong army" (*fukoku kyōhei*)—industrial promotion and military expansion. Acting within an age of empire, Japanese leaders aimed first at preventing colonization by the West and, then, from the mid-1890s at establishing Japan itself as a colonizing great power.

The arrival of U.S. gunboats in 1853 forced Japan open economically to the United States and Europe and shaped Japanese domestic politics and foreign affairs into the twentieth century. The efforts of the Americans Matthew Perry and Townsend Harris and their European counterparts resulted in Japan signing trade treaties with the United States and various European countries. These treaties came to be known as the unequal treaties for the semicolonial state in which they placed Japan.[2] They also precipitated a political crisis that ended with the overthrow of the 250-year-old Tokugawa regime and its replacement in 1868 with the new Meiji regime.

The treaties established ports in which U.S. and European citizens were allowed to live and trade, immune from Japanese laws. The treaties also established the currency to be used in those treaty ports and took away the Japanese government's power to set tariffs. The treaty ports were, in short, colonial outposts modeled on the system of semicolonial rule established in China after Britain waged the Opium War in the 1840s. Under military threat from the West, the Tokugawa government signed away political and economic control of the treaty ports and of U.S. and European citizens within Japan.

Unlike Argentina, Japan had no primary products like cattle and grains that suited the British economic model. Without such products—and with the option of protective tariffs removed by force—there existed in Japan little of the controversy over free trade versus protectionism that occupied contemporary Argentines.

Merchants and industrialists concerned themselves with locking in the most depreciated, export-friendly exchange rate. But the prime movers for adopting the gold standard in Japan linked industry and finance to political and military power. At times, their views diverged into impressionistic arguments about gold and its supposed symbolism of an advanced stage of civilization.[3] But even this was symbolism in the pursuit of political power and military strength, not symbolism as an end in itself.

The actual result was similar to that in Argentina: conversion at a devalued exchange rate. But this came without the legal fudging and vitriol of the Argentine debate. In part this resulted from Japan having enough money to implement conversion. In part it came from there being virtually no opposition to devaluation either in theory or practice.

More fundamentally, the debate over adopting the gold standard in Japan produced little of the vitriol it did in Argentina because the debate was split into three discrete areas, consisting of three separate bases of support that reinforced each other in their ultimate conclusions in favor of the gold standard without ever interacting or dealing with their mutually conflicting goals and assumptions. In their very different rationales for the gold standard, these three bases of support imagined three different sorts of gold standards and three different contexts in which they would apply.

As discussed in chapter 8, merchants and industrialists wanted the most depreciated currency possible. They formed the first base of support for the gold standard, and their views differed little from industrialists in Argentina. In Argentina, the importance of trade with Britain, and Argentina's reliance on manufactured imports, left substantial numbers of Argentine merchants favoring appreciation over depreciation. But in Japan support for gold or silver among merchants tracked the views of industrialists. Both supported the metal most likely to depreciate and promote exports and industry.

Few contemporary Japanese doubted that trade benefits went to industries operating with depreciated currency. Fluctuating silver and gold values were, for some, a concern due to the instability this produced. But of wider concern was the yen's potential appreciation. What opposition there was from merchants and industrialists to the gold standard rested on speculative guesses about whether gold might appreciate. This meant that the gold standard debates in Japan lacked the clear division of financial interests and the appeals to ideological rights and wrongs that drove the Argentine debate.

The desire of the finance minister Matsukata Masayoshi and his supporters for diplomatic and military advantage formed the second base of support for the gold standard. Chapter 9 discusses their use of the gold standard as a component of military strategy and power politics. For Matsukata, the gold standard served as an adjunct to military and diplomatic planning. He and his supporters saw it as providing access to foreign loans to fund a war treasury for use against Russia and other potential great power adversaries.

In contrast to Carlos Pellegrini in Argentina, Matsukata concerned himself only secondarily with commerce and industry. He saw industry primarily as a means toward developing the political and military prerequisites to nineteenth-century great powerdom. He did not see industry as an end unto itself. Industry had military uses as well as economic ones, and it was the military uses that most attracted Matsukata.

Matsukata's support for the gold standard meant a radical break with the past in aiming to open access to foreign financial markets. But this was as much a political as an economic break. Matsukata and Meiji state policy opposed foreign loans in the 1870s and 1880s due to national security concerns. They feared that foreign loans would provide an excuse for military intervention in support of foreign creditors as had occurred elsewhere in Asia and in Latin America and the Middle East.

But after victory in the Sino-Japanese War (1894–95) Matsukata sought to increase industrial and military spending, as well as access to foreign funding. This came in anticipation of a coming conflict with Russia over Japan's newly expanded political power in Korea, and conflicting claims to influence in Manchuria. With Japan's military victory over China, foreign capital became for Matsukata not a security risk but a necessary component of great power politics, warfare, and empire building.

Finally, the third base of support for the gold standard, discussed in this chapter, came from those who emphasized stability. This, in general, meant a desire to avoid fluctuating currency values regardless of their direction. In Japan stability arguments were more complicated than in Argentina due to the fact that Japanese trade, unlike Argentine, was split between silver and gold countries.

In Argentina trade meant trade with countries on gold standards or countries with paper quoted in terms of gold. Trade stability thus meant stabilizing the currency's value relative to gold. In Japan, however, trade stability meant stabilizing the currency's value relative to both silver and gold. Since silver and gold fluctuated relative to each other, it was essentially impossible to stabilize both silver-country trade and gold-country trade. This meant that the gold standard in Japan could only partially stabilize trade and potentially carried with it as many trade disadvantages as advantages.

Matsukata and Finance Ministry officials recognized these disadvantages and reacted with an array of compensatory measures relative to silver countries such as China. Most notably, they opted to devalue the exchange rate out of fear of the effects on industry and commerce of an appreciating currency.

In practice these three different bases of support produced a strange, parallel track to adopting the gold standard in Japan. Matsukata pushed through proposals largely aimed at the political and military aspects. Industry, commerce, and the daily press meanwhile emphasized the commercial issues of stability and trade. This disconnect between the commercial and political bases continued in other areas as well. The politics of Matsukata's adopting the gold standard meant a break with the past in terms of foreign funding, government expenditures, and an expansive new militarism. But the economics rested on the rhetoric of conservatism—of preserving past gains. This was as true of the depreciation and industrial promotion arguments as it was of the stability arguments.

These various paths—the export and industrial promotion views of merchants and industrialists discussed in chapter 8, the empire-building path of Matsukata discussed in chapter 9, and the stability arguments discussed in this chapter—presented very different conceptions of what the gold standard meant. Each came with its own idea of the purpose and effects of adopting the gold standard. But they mixed and matched means taken from one another while moving toward the same end of adopting the gold standard. In this, the process resembled the strange bedfellows aspect of support for the gold standard in Argentina. Both pulled together a diverse collection of institutions, interests, and ideas. But in Argentina the terms of the debate and the likely economic effects were clear: appreciation versus depreciation, imports versus exports, and free trade versus protectionism. In Japan they were not.

The Early Meiji Gold Standard

As the gold standard evolved in the nineteenth century, Japanese governments attempted periodically to fit Japan into this emerging world system. But it was only from the late 1890s that the gold standard became sustainable in Japan. Interest rates declined worldwide easing finance; gold production increased; and a conversion fund emerged in the form of China's war indemnity from the Sino-Japanese War.[4]

A variety of gold, silver, and paper had circulated in Japan throughout the first half of the nineteenth century. The forced expansion of foreign trade in the 1850s pushed the currency system into crisis due to the different exchange rates for gold and silver that existed between Japan and Europe and America.[5]

Since the 1770s the Tokugawa government had issued token (or fiduciary) silver coins valued not by their weight in silver but by a separate face value that overvalued silver in terms of its market value. These new silver coins circulated jointly with older silver coins valued per the market value of the silver they contained. The market rate for the silver-by-weight coins was roughly 1:10 as of 1858. The rate for the token silver coins would have been approximately 1:5 if they had been intended to be valued per their silver content, which they were not.

The 1858 commercial treaty with the United States, and similar commercial treaties with European powers thereafter, destroyed this two-tier system. Specifically, the treaties required that all foreign coins be accepted in Japan according to the weight of the silver or other precious metal they contained. They also required the Tokugawa government to lift all restrictions on export of Japanese coins.

With the silver to gold ratio outside of Japan being roughly 1:15, European and American traders hastily converted their silver coins into Japanese silver coins according to the amount of silver they contained when the treaty came into effect in 1859. They then exchanged the token Japanese silver coins for Japanese gold coins at the official face value and shipped the gold overseas. Very quickly, gold coins flowed overseas with an estimated 4 million ryō (the Japanese accounting unit) flowing overseas in 1860 alone.

Thereafter, currency remained a decentralized mass of notes and coins. After coming to power, the Meiji government printed large amounts of paper currency as it sought to consolidate its political hold.[6] Foreign pressure for currency consolidation to aid foreign merchants coalesced after 1868 with the new Meiji government's desire to centralize currency both for financial reasons and as a matter of political control. In 1869 the Meiji government established a new currency law setting a silver standard, with copper and gold as subsidiary currencies. The system itself was a deliberate break from the past, being modeled on the system established by Britain in Hong Kong rather than earlier Japanese systems.

This desire to follow selected European forms did not stop with Britain. It encompassed a broader concept of the "West" and world standards. In 1871 the first Meiji attempt at the gold standard combined explicit imitation of European forms with an appreciation of the advantages of adopting a world standard. The system resulted from the efforts of Itō Hirobumi, the future prime minister and drafter of the Meiji constitution. Itō wrote from the United States in 1870 that Japan should adopt the same currency system as the United States. He raised the issue at the end of a discussion about the U.S. banking system and weights and measures, all of which he saw as part of a unification of world standards. It was in this context that Itō argued for adopting the gold standard as part of putting Japan in line with emerging standards worldwide.[7]

But attempting to find world standards in the United States or elsewhere was not without its problems. The unequal treaties mandated silver as treaty port currency to match silver's use in the China trade. This in turn made a unified gold standard impossible. In practice, silver from the China trade seeped into the domestic economy making a unified gold standard even outside the treaty ports impossible.[8] In seeking to adopt what he saw as Western trends, Itō put himself in opposition to the silver standard used in East Asian trade—a trade standard accepted by the same Western countries Itō sought to mimic and required by those same countries for use in the treaty ports.

On one level, the expansion of the gold standard in the late nineteenth century reflected the influence of the British Empire. The appeal of gold stemmed in part from its use in the British Empire. For countries that wanted to increase trade and financial ties with Britain, it was natural to use the same form of money as Britain. Silver in Asia, however, rested on a previous imperial age. Silver's use owed a heavy debt, even in Asia, to Spain's fifteenth-century conquests in the Americas. Since Spaniards had begun mining silver in the Western Hemisphere, silver coins from Mexico and Peru regularly circulated throughout Asia as well as Latin America and Europe.[9] Only after the decline of the Spanish Empire in the early nineteenth century did Spanish imperial coins disappear.[10]

The decline of Spanish imperial coins did not, however, mean the end of Latin American silver circulating in Asia. The newly independent Mexican Republic began producing silver dollars in the 1820s—almost 1.5 billion of which were coined between 1824 and 1903. These Mexican silver dollars circulated freely throughout Asia and later served as a model not only for the Japanese silver yen but also for the Hong Kong dollar (1866), American trade dollar (1878), French *piastre de commerce* (1885, 1895), Canton dollar (1889), American-Philippine peso (1903), and Chinese yuan (1911).[11]

As with other de facto or de jure bimetallic countries, problems developed when market exchange rates differed from official rates. The undervalued metal vanished from circulation as described by Thomas Gresham in his famous formulation of "good money" (undervalued currency) being chased from circulation by "bad" (overvalued currency). With world silver prices declining from the 1870s, Japan's official exchange rate once again overvalued silver, as it had in the 1850s. This prompted increased amounts of Mexican silver to flow into Japan. Silver was exchanged for gold, and that gold flowed overseas.

In an attempt to force out Mexican silver, the Meiji government devalued the silver yen in 1875 and 1876 to keep pace with the market rate. But the plan failed. In May 1878 the government repealed its previous restriction on silver coins circulating only in the treaty ports. Legally, Japan was now on a bimetallic system to match its de facto status from the early 1870s. But with gold having flowed overseas, the system now became de facto a silver standard.

Even this de facto silver standard proved unsustainable. As in Argentina, the government lacked specie reserves to convert paper currency. The Meiji government launched various nation-building projects at home—telegraphs, railroads, and other infrastructure—that resembled similar efforts that were so burdensome for Argentine state finances. These were all standard for countries in the late nineteenth century seeking progress and civilization. In addition, the Meiji state pursued industrial promotion more aggressively than did the Argentine state, even given Carlos Pellegrini's perpetual trumpeting of industrial promotion ideas. All of these efforts cost money and left no funds for currency reserves.

Under industrialization policies pushed by Finance Minister Ōkuma Shigenobu in the 1870s, the government pursued a four-pronged strategy based on industrial protection, industrial subsidies, leasing and transferring new machinery, and establishing and eventually transferring ownership of state-owned model factories.[12] The government aimed to promote industries, most notably textile, through government support and model factories.

In addition to infrastructure and industrial promotion, the government also spent heavily on expanding the new national military and consolidating central political control. All this spending meant chronic import surpluses. This, in turn, meant additional specie outflows that led, as in Argentina, to the only remaining option of the age: inconvertible paper money.

Adding to the negative side of these nation-building expenditures, the main funding source—land tax revenue—proved insufficient to cover costs. To extricate itself from this financial bind, the Meiji government issued still more paper currency. These paper issues increased further after war broke out in the late 1870s between the government and former members who had gone into opposition. By 1880 the amount of inconvertible paper currency in circulation dwarfed the number of gold and silver coins.[13] For all intents and purposes specie coins vanished from circulation while paper currency had increased threefold since 1871.

The subsequent increase in inflation prompted the government to ratchet up the exchange rate for silver. But this undervalued silver, just as gold had been undervalued in the 1850s and early 1870s, and ended up producing the same result. Silver flowed overseas leaving Japan with a currency system of inconvertible paper.

In 1880 Ōkuma began to retire paper from circulation, retrench government expenditures, and revise taxes in order to increase revenue in an attempt to revalue the currency and reduce inflation. This general line of policies continued for another year until Ōkuma was expelled from the Meiji government in October 1881 and Matsukata took his place as finance minister. Ōkuma's expulsion resulted in part from political and personality conflicts and in part from Ōkuma's proposal to adopt the gold standard by taking out loans in London.[14]

After Ōkuma's dismissal, Matsukata continued to cut government expenditures and restructured the banking system. He established the Bank of Japan and abandoned the decentralized U.S. banking system set up under Ōkuma.[15] Finally, Matsukata radically reduced the amount of paper currency in circulation. This contraction went far beyond Ōkuma's measures and fundamentally reshaped the Japanese economy by inducing mass deflation—the "Matsukata deflation"—on a scale unsurpassed until the Depression of the early 1930s.[16]

From 1885 Matsukata had the Bank of Japan issue notes fully convertible into silver. But this did not mean an end to currency instability. Fluctuations in world silver values now controlled the value of the yen. As silver depreciated in the 1880s, the yen did as well, prompting an industrial boom between 1886 and 1890.[17] Between 1885 and 1890, the relative values of gold and silver fell from approximately 1:16 to 1:30. This boosted Japanese exports, which were now cheaper than products from gold standard countries. Increased exports promoted greater industrial activity within Japan. Between 1885 and 1897 exports increased at an average rate of 11% per year in yen and 7% per year in real terms.[18] As of 1885 there were 1,269 companies registered in Japan. By 1900 there were 4,296. Total corporate capital increased from 50 million yen to 220 million yen in the same period.

Silver's depreciation also caused a mild increase in prices within Japan, improving business conditions and spurring economic activity. As prices increased, real interest rates and real wages declined, promoting industrial expansion. Rising prices also led to an increase in public expenditures.

But memories of the inflation of the late 1870s were still fresh and there were concerns about renewed inflation. In addition, the exchange rate became difficult to predict, making business decisions difficult. Although silver's decline had been relatively steady since 1873, weekly and monthly fluctuations could still be substantial. These events coalesced in the 1890s into a push by Matsukata to adopt the gold standard. It was a push that ran counter to commercial and industrial views more than it reflected them.

Silver to Gold

In Japan, as in Argentina, currency appreciation stood out as the primary industrial and commercial concern of the late 1890s. Contemporary Japanese feared that silver would appreciate relative to gold, forcing up the yen's value and harming exports.

Silver had depreciated consistently on world markets since 1873. But it also appreciated briefly in the early 1890s in response to gold discoveries in South Africa and silver purchases by the U.S. government. This uptick in silver's value caused doubt about whether silver or gold would be the weaker currency in the future.[19] If silver continued to appreciate, prices for Japanese products would become increasingly expensive in terms of foreign currency (thereby damaging exports) and foreign products would become increasingly cheap in yen (thereby increasing imports). In response to these concerns, the Minister of Finance Watanabe Kuniaki in 1893 named a Currency Inquiry Commission to examine the benefits and costs of the existing silver system.[20]

As was apparent from the final version of the commission's report issued in 1895, opinion was split concerning what, if any, changes to make to the currency system. Keeping silver or adopting bimetallism had more support than adopting the gold standard, particularly among those like the industrialist Shibusawa Eiichi who sought to promote industry and exports. Among the commission's other members, the economists Kanai Noboru and Taguchi Ukichi were influential supporters of bimetallism. Seven of the committees' members, including Shibusawa, favored silver. They saw no reason to change the existing currency system. Only six members on the commission favored the gold standard. Watanabe also had no particular interest in the gold standard. He preferred to delay any action until the future outlook for gold and silver prices was clearer.[21]

The commission first voted 10 to 5 to avoid any currency change.[22] A minority then moved to have the vote retaken to count members who believed a currency change might be advisable at some later time in the future but did not at present favor a currency change. The new tally recorded was 8 votes in favor of a change and 7 opposing. The final question was what change the currency should be. This third vote removed silver as an option, and gold garnered more votes than bimetallism. Convinced that world trends could no long support a silver or bimetallic standard, Matsukata took the commission's report and used it as support for adopting the gold standard.

The commission's support was not, however, the only prerequisite. As in Argentina, gold reserves posed a practical obstacle. Here the late nineteenth-century great power penchant for warfare proved indispensable. After its victory in the Sino-Japanese War, Japan received a war indemnity from China. This resembled the war indemnity Germany had received from France after the Franco-Prussian War, which Bismarck used to fund Germany's move to gold in 1873.

The indemnity became an argument in and of itself for adopting the gold standard. Funds were now available, so why not use them for the gold standard? To gold standard opponents this sort of argument was fundamentally backward. It argued not for any inherent benefits of gold but merely the technical feasibility.[23] Following this latter tack, Watanabe Kuniaki opposed rushing into the gold standard and instructed the Bank of Japan to have half the Chinese indemnity paid in silver and half in gold, believing it was unclear in which direction silver and gold prices would move in the future and thus unclear what Japan should do with its currency system.

This view was not shared by Matsukata. Matsukata saw the gold standard as necessary for great power priorities and the Chinese indemnity as the means to achieve it. Once Matsukata returned to the Finance Ministry in September 1896 he arranged for the indemnity to be paid in British pounds and deposited in London.[24] This too mirrored the Franco-Prussian War indemnity, of which only 5% was paid in specie, the rest in commercial paper drawable in various financial centers.[25] Given the pound's conversion into gold this was functionally equivalent to specifying gold. But it offered the advantages of greater ease of use and the ability to earn interest on those funds. Simultaneously, Matsukata pushed his gold standard Currency Law through the Diet, with that law being publicly proclaimed law March 26, 1897, and the start of the system set for October 1897.

The Sino-Japanese War indemnity in and of itself did not guarantee the system's durability or stability, nor was it viewed as such. Just as in the 1850s and 1870s, the issue was silver: its future value and its future need as circulating currency in Japan even under the gold standard. Both these points became tied to devaluation of the existing exchange rate and the desire for currency stability and the certainty that entailed.

Certainty and Stability

As in Argentina, the "currency question" or "currency problem" (*kahei mondai*) in Japan was tied to broader issues of certainty and stability. Substantively, the economic debate in both Japan and Argentina rested on a desire to obtain the trade benefits of depreciating currency. But there was also a secondary concern about changes in currency values, whatever the direction. Fluctuating exchange rates produced instability and uncertainty.

This meant instability in terms of effects on both trade and domestic prices. Matsukata and his aides believed in the need for stability. They distrusted large economic fluctuations in prices or exchange rates.[26]

In Argentina the desire for depreciated currency worked hand in hand with the desire for stability. Calls to stop currency instability were calls to stop appreciation and the two arguments supported and reinforced each other. In Japan calls for stability most always meant arguing that silver should be jettisoned in favor of gold.[27] This meant trade stability by controlling currency fluctuations with gold standard countries. This meant price stability by controlling inflation caused by depreciation. Finally, this also meant devaluation as a defensive means to prevent the choice of gold from causing an economic downturn and damaging industry and commerce.

TRADE STABILITY

Trade stability formed the first type of stability concern. This resembled trade stability arguments in Argentina in that fluctuating exchange rates made it difficult to calculate prices and costs in advance. There was a significant difference, however, between Japanese and Argentine trade. Argentina's trade was exclusively with gold standard countries—or those with unbacked paper—and thus unaffected by changes in relative gold and silver prices. In Argentina, currency and trade stability were a matter of fluctuating, unbacked paper currency or fixed exchange rates relative to gold. There was no issue of favoring trade with one set of countries at the expense of another.

Japan's trade, however, was split between European gold standard countries and Asian silver countries with their trade centered on China. Fluctuations in gold and silver values thus led to fluctuations in exchange rates with one or the other group of countries. This added a constant speculative element to trade transactions between silver and gold countries.[28] Using gold currency would stabilize exchange rates with Europe and North America while subjecting Asian trade to exchange rate fluctuations. Using silver currency would do the reverse.

Two-thirds of Japan's total trade was with gold standard countries and only one-third with silver countries. This presumably meant that adopting gold would remove currency fluctuations for two-thirds of Japan's trade and increase them for one-third.[29]

But two related factors muddied the picture: whether gold- or silver-country trade was more likely to increase in the future and whether trade was likely to involve a Japanese export surplus or an import surplus. In trade directly between Japan and East Asian silver countries, silver's depreciation would make Asian products cheaper and Japanese products more expensive. Japanese exports to those countries would decrease and imports would increase. It would also make planning for Asian trade more difficult.

As long as trade remained weighted toward gold standard countries, the potential losses from Asian trade could presumably be outweighed by gains in trade with the United States and Europe.[30] But exports to Asian countries had increased in the 1890s, leading merchants to believe they would continue to increase in the future. For many of them, there was more financial advantage in increasing less-developed trade with East Asia than there was in emphasizing the United States, where trade was already more developed and, arguably, had less possibility to grow in the future.[31]

Asian trade had increased through the 1890s. But Japan's trade with gold standard countries had stagnated since the late 1880s despite retaining a larger overall share.[32] Although the nominal value of trade with gold standard countries had doubled since 1887, this was almost entirely a statistical quirk reflecting silver's depreciation. Once values were converted to gold, nearly all the increase in gold-country trade vanished. This did not answer the question of why real trade with gold standard countries had stagnated—whether it was due to the inconvenience and uncertainty of fluctuating exchange rates or due to some more basic reason. If the former, adopting the gold standard conceivably could aid trade overall. If not, the advantages of the gold standard became far more questionable.

The tradeoff thus became stable exchange rates for Euro-U.S. trade versus stable exchange rates for Asian trade. Gold might solve one form of instability, but it would increase another. And this was unavoidable as long as there was no single world standard.[33] Because stability arguments in Japan generally favored adopting the gold standard, they inevitably ended up arguing for greater trade with Europe and the United States. They assigned Asian trade either a secondary position or argued for a colonial policy in which the gold standard would gradually be established first in Taiwan and thereafter throughout Asia.[34] In this latter vision, Japan would act as Asia's gold-based financial center.

Shifting of trade from Asia to Europe and North America can be seen in Asian trade figures from the 1880s to World War I as the formerly solid Asian silver block became a mix of countries on either silver or gold standards. Intra-Asian trade continued to increase more rapidly than Asian-Western trade, but the gap lessened as a common gold currency encouraged trade with Europe and the United States.

If one favored imports—as Matsukata did in favoring imports of warships, munitions, and heavy machinery from Britain and other gold standard countries—gold provided a benefit.[35] Nor did it necessarily mean losses to Japanese industry if the products being imported were not also produced in Japan. It did, however, raise the question of government finances and how increased imports would be paid for. It was logical to assume that adopting the gold standard would result in a significant increase in Japanese imports since trade with gold standard countries would be easier. It was also believed that the major portion of that increase would be due to heavy industries involved in military production.[36]

There were doubts at the time whether exports to Europe and the United States would expand significantly even if Japan adopted the gold standard. Although the total volume of trade might not appreciably change under the gold standard, the composition of that trade very much would. Silver meant increased exports. Gold meant increased imports. And in particular gold meant that machinery and industrial goods needed for Japan's rapidly expanding military industries could be purchased more cheaply than if Japan stayed on a silver standard. Militarily, the choice was in gold's favor.

Similar to Argentina, Japan's exports to gold standard countries consisted primarily of raw materials and semimanufactured goods for which demand was relatively fixed. Even the outlook for by far the most valuable export product, silk thread, was questioned by gold opponents who worried whether the rapid increase over the previous ten years in the U.S. and European silk market could be sustained. This was particularly so since that growth had been driven by lower Japanese thread prices based both on low wages and depreciating silver.

From the viewpoint of trade stability the gold standard was at best a mixed bag, particularly if one concentrated on growing export markets in Asia. With gold standard countries Japan could expect an increase in imports but no increase in exports. With silver countries, however, if Japan kept a silver standard, Japan's exports would almost certainly continue to increase. But, if Japan adopted gold, the "natural development of trade" with silver countries would be blocked and the future exports for which Japanese merchants had such high hopes would be damaged. From the position of Japanese trade as a whole then, the shift would be to increase imports and decrease exports, while routing trade from Asia to Europe.

Given the split of Japanese trade between gold and silver countries it was hard to accept arguments that the gold standard meant trade stability at face value. Were all of Japan's trade with gold standard countries—and all of its trade competitors on the gold standard—the balance would have been different and more straightforward. But that was not the case. For Japanese trade, and Japanese economic interests, effectively straddled both gold and silver currency systems. Given that basic fact, overall trade stability was impossible. The best that could be hoped for was that the benefits to gold-country trade would outweigh the losses to Asia trade and the losses to silver countries in gold standard markets.

PRICE STABILITY

Stability meant more than controlling exchange rate fluctuations and their effects on trade. It also meant price stability. As Matsukata wrote, "The chief economic advantage lies in the freedom from fluctuations in the price of commodities. By the adoption of gold as our monetary basis, the variability of the standard to which the price of commodities is referable will be lessened, and consequently we shall become exempt from the present constant fluctuations."[37]

Forced to address Japan's comparative prosperity under silver, Matsukata covered all bases, arguing the evils of inflation, deflation, and sudden shifts between the two: "An unrestricted appreciation [of commodity prices], it is true, may for a time cause an apparently prosperous state of things; but as the prices of raw materials and wages will be gradually affected thereby, the result will be crippled production and reduced export. A sudden fall of price, on the other hand, will prove injurious to both commerce and monetary circulation. At any rate freedom from sudden fluctuations is most desirable; but such fluctuations are inevitable with the silver standard and can be, it seems, to me, avoided only by the adoption of the gold standard."[38]

A number of European studies appeared in the 1880s and 1890s looking at the relative differences in gold and silver currency purchasing power. Predominant in these studies was the view that rather than silver depreciating, gold was appreciating, with silver's value staying relatively constant. In Britain, Germany, France, and other European countries that were de facto or de jure gold standard countries during the so-called Great Depression of 1873–96, it was logical to see a connection between an economic slump and appreciating currency. The British Royal Commission on the Depression of Trade and Industry in its 1886 report identified price declines as a primary factor in Britain's slump.[39] The most frequent explanation given, within Europe, for these price declines was a shortage of gold, causing currencies to appreciate in gold standard countries.

In Europe, the answer was a return to bimetallism or, for monometallic gold advocates, discovering more gold as had happened in the 1850s with substantial new gold discoveries in California and Australia. Similarly, bimetallic theorists in Japan assigned the increasing gap between gold and silver values to an increase in gold's value rather than a decrease in the value of silver.[40] If anything, though, the view that gold standards could be deflationary appeared more often in comments from Europeans or Americans such as the American economist Garrett Droppers, whose comments appeared regularly in the Japanese press.[41]

Reflecting a common view in the United States and Europe, Droppers argued that declining prices and sluggish commercial and industrial activity, and the social distress that produced, resulted from the gold standard. In Droppers' view, over the course of the 1890s only Japan—"to a truly surprising degree"—had experienced "developmental progress," which he attributed to its use of silver rather than gold. Droppers believed currency was the cause of both Japan's development and the downturns in Europe and the United States. That is, gold's appreciation had caused prices to fall in Europe and the United States, in turn causing those economies to slump.[42]

In contrast, Droppers believed that silver's relative depreciation had spurred Japanese exports, profits, and industrial development. Nor, for Droppers, was silver's relative depreciation a sign of silver's instability. Rather, as silver's value had fallen only in terms of gold, Droppers argued that the problem was not silver's instability, but gold's. Japan adopting the gold standard would invite currency appreciation, deflation, an economic downturn, and debtor unrest. Far from stabilizing the economy, it would destabilize it.

Prices increased after 1897 when Matsukata pushed through the gold standard. This, however, was as much a reflection of government spending as it was a question of currency types. Gold proponents and classic theory argued that gold would bring domestic prices into line with world levels. After 1897, however, prices continued above world levels. Osaka wholesale prices increased 4.6% between 1885 and 1897 and 3.1% between 1897 and 1913. Though prices increased more under silver, the price deflator under gold was actually higher than under silver (2.8% to 2.5%).[43] Japan's export prices moved noticeably higher than world export prices in the years after the Russo-Japanese War. Continued inflation reflected the new fiscal expansion.

Military spending had always been the one expansionary element in Matsukata's fiscal policy, even in the 1880s. From 1873–77 military spending had totaled 16.3% of all government spending. It stayed relatively steady from 1878–82 at 16.6% and then moved upward to 21.3% for 1883–87 and 29.3% for 1888–92. After the Sino-Japanese War, however, the Meiji government pushed a dramatic increase in military spending. Military spending absorbed 63.2% of government expenditures for 1893–97 (including the Sino-Japanese War in 1894–95). From 1898–1902 military expenditures continued to absorb 41.4% of government spending. In absolute terms aggregate military spending increased from 16.3 million yen for 1883–87 to 23.6 million for 1888–92, 137.4 million for 1893–97, 109.6 million for 1898–1900, and 620.7 million for 1903–7.[44] From the late 1890s through the early 1900s annual military expenditures exceeded Sino-Japanese War levels.[45]

The Meiji government also increased spending on infrastructure and military-related industries such as transport, shipbuilding, steel production, railways, waterways, and roads. The massive state-run Yawata Steel Works, which would produce the bulk of Japan's steel through World War II, opened in 1901 as part of this infrastructure spending spree. Total government spending increased from 76.7 million yen for 1883–87 to 80.7 million yen for 1888–92, 217.3 million for 1893–97, 264.6 million for 1898–1902, and 927.8 million for 1903–7.[46] Though inflation continued, growth slowed. Gross national expenditure, which had grown at an annual average rate of 3.21% for 1887–97, dropped to 1.83% for 1897–1904 after the gold standard was adopted.[47] A slowdown in exports had begun to show up as a slowdown in growth.

DEVALUATION

Despite concerns about a deflationary gold standard, the gold standard did not necessarily need to be deflationary. Whether the gold standard was deflationary depended on at least two factors. In the long term it depended on the amount of gold production or expansion of the money supply through the use of paper or non-gold supplemental currency. In the immediate term it depended on the exchange rate established and the potential for altering that rate if necessary to adapt to changing circumstances.

As in Argentina, the gold exchange rate prompted considerable debate. But in Argentina the argument was not only about the specific rate to be applied but also, more fundamentally, about the legitimacy of changing the exchange rate in the first place. In Japan the question was more a matter of choosing the most advantageous rate. In Japan, currency rates were accepted as tools to other ends much as Pellegrini, Uriburu, and even O'Farrell argued in Argentina. No one with any influence in Japan argued—as the mitristas, Anadón, and Vedia did in Argentina—that currency had an innate, natural value that existed outside the control of governments and could only be expressed in terms of gold. In this view, any government attempt to alter the exchange rate from an exact substitute of one unit of paper to one unit of gold was both against nature and an illegitimate exercise of government power.

None of these "nature of money" arguments carried weight in Japan. This made setting the exchange rate a practical matter of weighing the costs and benefits of various potential rates without the more metaphysical Argentine concern about devalued currency not being true and universal money. In Japan this meant, in practice, deciding whether the exchange rate would be at the still legally existing rate from the 1871 Currency Law or whether the gold rate would be devalued to compensate for two and a half decades of falling silver prices relative to gold. If one adopted the dominant view taken in the 1920s that the preexisting exchange rate was sacrosanct and should be retained if at all possible, the answer would be to keep the 1871 rate and induce a depression in order to force the economy to deflate down to the old exchange rate. Why someone would want to do this was another question entirely. But unlike in the years after World War I, the most recent point of reference for most governments was deflation, not inflation, and governments in both Japan and Argentina in the 1890s were more concerned with promoting industrial expansion than they were with the cult of induced deflation that developed around the gold standard after World War I.

A state orientation toward industry and economic expansion did not mean that devaluation was a given. As in Argentina, there existed a range of opinions regarding the specific exchange rate that should be set even if those arguments lacked the vitriol of the Argentine debates. The economist and Diet member Taguchi Ukichi argued for keeping the 1871 rate of 1 gold to 16 silver. This, however, would mean a drop of 50% in the general price level, which while beneficial for creditors would be disastrous for debtors, including farmers and manufacturers.[48] Britain and Italy generally valued at 1:14 versus the current Japanese market rate of 1:28, prompting proposals that one or another of these rates be used.[49] Various banking groups proposed rates ranging from 1:24 to 1:21, which would still cause the yen to appreciate though not to European levels. Similarly, devaluating the exchange in the event of adopting the gold standard enjoyed considerable support among members of the 1895 Currency Commission.[50]

The question of what exchange rate to adopt was also complicated by renewed declines in silver's price relative to gold while Matsukata's Currency Law was being debated.[51] The potential problem with silver's decline and adopting the gold standard lay in the possibility that the market price would fall below the official rate leading to an increase in exchanges from silver to gold, Bank of Japan losses, and then gold outflows as in the 1850s and 1870s.[52] Throughout the 1890s there had been periods when silver had declined only to recover its losses. The 1897 decline, however, was somewhat different. First, investors in the United States were preemptively selling off silver in anticipation of Japan moving to the gold standard. Second, the new McKinley administration in the United States was moving to sell off US$150 million in silver. Third, Russia and Germany were increasing their efforts to obtain gold reserves in order to build up war treasuries, which in turn pushed up gold's price relative to silver. The main cause for silver's renewed decline in 1897, however, was India, which had stopped absorbing silver and was now releasing excess silver onto world markets.[53] This was primarily due to famine that had decreased India's demand for silver. India had also sold off silver supplies to buy food and other supplies from abroad, which put further downward pressure on silver.[54]

Although Matsukata did not go as far as Pellegrini, who had used conversion as a means to achieve devaluation, Matsukata did use devaluation as a means to gold conversion. Matsukata ultimately devalued the gold exchange rate in article 2 of the Currency Law 50% from what it had been under the 1871 currency law.[55] The 1 gold equals 32.3 silver rate that Matsukata ultimately established in the Currency Law was meant to reflect the existing 1:28 Japanese market rate—as opposed to the 1:16 rate in the 1871 law—thereby leaving the price level and debt relations unchanged, plus an extra margin to allow for potential silver depreciation in the future be it from India or some other source.

Matsukata was not, of course, the only advocate of devaluation in the 1890s, be it in Japan, Argentina, the United States, or elsewhere.[56] Carlos Pellegrini's currency projects in Argentina were predicated on devaluation. In the United States, William Jennings Bryan and the silverites' calls for free silver were in effect calls to devalue the currency. Above all, Matsukata emphasized the need to avoid larger economic and social changes as a result of currency changes. The point was to avoid unnecessary shocks to the economy and to prevent changes in the relative economic positions of different groups merely through currency changes.

Silver's renewed depreciation quickly passed through this extra margin. Although the Currency Law passed the Diet in March it was not set to go into effect until October. By August, however, silver's market rate had dropped below the 1:32 level set in the Currency Law, falling to 1:36.62.[57] There was still the matter of the gold points—the cost of actually shipping gold overseas, melting it down and selling it—but if silver's market price declined further below the official Japanese government exchange rate, sooner or later one could expect that silver would be imported into Japan and exchanged for gold, and gold would accordingly flow overseas, as it had in the 1850s and 1870s, making the gold standard unsustainable.

This continuing possibility of silver inflows and gold outflows in Japan was far more acute than it was in Argentina and other gold standard countries for one reason: Japan had effectively set itself up as a gold standard island within a larger silver region. The adoption of the gold standard, though, did not mean a complete turn away from Asia—and certainly not from Japan's new colony, Taiwan.[58] Rather, it meant a reordering of relations with Asia, Europe, and the United States. If trade and finance would now be eased with Europe and the United States and downgraded with Asia, this was in large part to gain the funding and heavy industrial equipment necessary for consolidating Japanese influence in Korea and Manchuria and engaging in the almost inevitable military conflict with Russia that this would entail. Visions of Japan as an East Asian gold financial center taking the place of silver-based Hong Kong and Shanghai, in turn, raised the prospect of Japanese financial dominance in Asia, with Taiwan either as a silver reservoir linking Japan to China or as a first step toward a yen bloc encompassing not only Taiwan but also Korea, Manchuria, and potentially the rest of China.[59]

These, however, were issues of imperial management that arose in the late 1890s, after the gold standard was enacted in 1897. Before then there was the matter of industry and commerce, whose interests potentially ran counter to the adoption of the gold standard. That the desire of merchants and industrialists for depreciated currency would in hindsight seem to have put them at odds with the imperial and military concerns of Matsukata and the Meiji government did not prevent any number of industrialists and merchants from supporting the gold standard. This support rested on the assumption that silver would soon appreciate relative to gold. That this view ultimately proved to be incorrect neither lessened its influence in the debate over the gold standard nor undercut its effectiveness in limiting industrial and commercial opposition to Matsukata's entirely distinct gold standard motivations.

8

Industry and the
Economic Uses of Gold

Although part of the economic appeal of the gold standard in Japan rested on the idea that gold was more stable than silver, this idea coexisted with two other arguments. The first argument emphasized gold's instability rather than its stability. The second argument had nothing to do with inherent stability at all; instead, it concerned institutional context.

The first argument sought to lock in the trade benefits of a depreciating currency: export promotion and import substitution. This differed little from the goals of industrial promoters in Argentina. Japanese merchants and industrialists sought to adopt gold in the belief that gold would depreciate. For them the trade advantages of depreciating currency, which had belonged to silver through most of the 1880s and 1890s, would soon switch to gold. If so, products from silver countries would become more expensive in foreign currency than their gold standard competitors.[1]

The second argument remained agnostic on the inherent benefits of silver and gold and ignored their future price movements. Instead, it emphasized the benefits of adhering to an emerging world standard. In this view the advantage of gold lay not in anything having to do with gold per se, but instead on the advantages of adhering to a dominant currency standard. The intrinsic pluses or minuses of the particular currency system mattered little in this argument. What mattered was how widely that system was adopted. This argument rested on the idea that once a certain number of countries adopted a particular currency system, the system would naturally expand to other countries as well.[2]

Fears of silver appreciation dominated the first half of the 1890s. U.S. government silver purchases from 1890 caused silver to appreciate.[3] This prompted an outpouring of opinions and studies on the costs and benefits of moving from silver to gold.[4] The world-standards argument remained a constant throughout the 1890s as international practice shifted from silver to gold and various attempts at international conferences to establish bimetallism failed. The appreciation argument differed little from concerns about appreciating currency in Argentina. But the world-standards argument was absent in Argentina, where trade was centered on gold standard Britain. Both of these arguments focused on what was best for developing Japanese industry and commerce as opposed to the political and military concerns that so preoccupied the Japanese government.

The Uses of Depreciation

There is nothing surprising about exporters and industrialists in Japan and Argentina favoring depreciated currency. In Japan, as in Argentina, depreciation worked to promote and protect industry. It made exports cheaper and imports more expensive, simultaneously promoting and protecting domestic industry. In Argentina this preference for depreciating currency took the form of seeking government intervention to devalue the exchange rate relative to gold. In Japan it appeared as a guessing game to figure out which of gold or silver appeared most likely to depreciate. The ultimate goal, however, was the same.

The appeal of gold for Japanese exporters and industrialists in the 1890s rested on the belief that silver's price had reached bottom and would soon begin appreciating. This meant that divisions among industrialists were not so much based on goals as on predictions of future international events. This meant, however, that gold standard critics such as the industrialists Shibusawa Eiichi, Asabuki Eiji, and Nakamigawa Hikojirō; economists like Wadagaki Kenzō and Taguchi Ukichi; financial officials such as Sōma Nagatani; and most notably, the textile industry as a whole were unable to mount effective opposition to Matsukata's gold standard plans. Differing predictions of future events left little room for united opposition.

Neither gold nor silver supporters disputed the export and industrial promotion effects that depreciating silver had produced in Japan.[5] From 1882 to 1887 chronic trade deficits reversed, yielding a surplus of 52.910 million yen on exports of 246.280 million yen and imports of 193.370 million yen.[6] Between 1889 and 1895 exports increased from 70.176 million yen to 136.000 million yen.[7] The economy slumped briefly in 1890 as American silver purchases pushed up silver's value but recovered thereafter as silver once again depreciated. As exports expanded, specie reserves increased: from 47.840 million yen in 1890 to 82.160 million yen in 1893.[8] Even with depreciating silver, however, Japan tended toward trade deficits. Gold opponents feared that Japan's tendency toward deficits would become uncontrollable under an appreciated gold standard.

Depreciation particularly helped the silk industry, which relied on exports for most of its growth and revenue. No other export came close to the importance of raw silk for exports. In the 1870s tea exports accounted for 29% of all exports compared to raw silk with 33%. In the 1880s this dropped to 19% compared to 38% for raw silk. By the 1890s tea had fallen to 8% of all Japanese exports while raw silk took 36%, and processed silk and cotton fabrics, which had been virtually nonexistent as exports in the 1870s and 1880s, accounted for approximately 6%. Silk thread production increased from 1.36 million kilograms in 1878 to 3.46 million in 1890, 6.41 million in 1895, 7.1 million in 1900, 11.9 million in 1910, and 15.17 million in 1915.[9]

Depreciating silver also helped cotton textiles. In the 1870s cotton textiles made up 20% of Japanese *imports*, second only to wool textiles at 21%.[10] By 1910 Japan was the world's second largest *exporter* of cotton textiles—well behind Britain, but ahead of Italy, France, and the United States.[11]

Since Britain prohibited the free coinage of silver in India in 1893, Indian cotton textiles had been at a significant price disadvantage relative to Japanese and Chinese cotton textiles. As a result Indian producers had abandoned the Japanese market and were faltering in the Chinese market as well.[12] Japanese silk manufacturers worried that adopting the gold standard would damage Japanese industry, as they believed it had damaged Indian industry.

While India seemed to be increasingly weak, China appeared to be a growing threat. Little competition existed between Japanese and Chinese textiles during the first half of the 1890s due to the inferior quality of Chinese silk thread. Silk merchants and manufacturers in Japan, however, worried that continued improvements in Chinese silk would make Chinese textiles a competitor in foreign markets. In fact, Chinese silk did not develop into a major competitor. But this did not change the contemporary concern among silk manufacturers that Japan's adoption of the gold standard would create a Chinese industrial giant. Those fearful of Chinese competition went so far as to argue that Chinese silk would entirely drive out Japanese silk from the U.S. market.

For those who believed silver would appreciate, the obvious response was to support Matsukata's Currency Law. For those merchants and industrialists who believed gold would appreciate, the response was different. First, they opposed Matsukata's Currency Law. Then they turned to figuring out how to ameliorate the negative effects of appreciating gold once it became apparent that Matsukata would push through his plan with or without industry support. Even as Matsukata announced his currency plan, various textile groups were already mobilizing to oppose that plan.[13] Concern that the government was ill prepared to adopt the gold standard added to worries about potential appreciation.

Disagreement over whether gold would appreciate—and how to counteract the effects if it did—led to divisions across and within industries. These divisions undercut efforts to formulate a unified response whether in support of or opposition to Matsukata's proposals. In Osaka, silk and cotton manufacturers and merchants opposed gold. Other industries that relied less on exports and more on imports and low-cost capital favored gold. The strength of textile opposition in Osaka was enough for the Osaka Chamber of Commerce to present a united front in opposition to Matsukata's Currency Law.[14] But Osaka merchants failed to reach a united position with merchants in the other dominant silk trading center, Yokohama. In Yokohama, silk merchants split over both the substance of Matsukata's currency plan and the speed with which he seemed set on enacting it.[15] Pro-silver merchants assumed that gold would continue to appreciate and urged uniting with Osaka merchants in common opposition to Matsukata's plans. These merchants also argued that the very act of Japan's abandoning silver would cause silver to depreciate, thus making any belief in the potential depreciation of gold misplaced.

Yokohama silk merchants did not dispute that gold would most likely appreciate in value. But they subscribed to the trade stability argument.

They argued that gold would reduce exchange-rate fluctuations with Europe and the United States, thus allowing silk merchants more stability in pursuing Euro-U.S. markets. Pro-gold merchants in Yokohama accepted the argument that Japan's adopting the gold standard would itself cause a decrease in demand for silver and a fall in silver's price.[16] But this, they argued, would be offset by gold's appreciation, allowing silk manufacturers to buy raw materials from China at cheaper prices.[17] But this shifting of raw silk purchases to China would mean that Japanese silk growers would suffer as the textile industry switched from purchasing Japanese silk thread to purchasing silk thread from China. This increased the opposition of silk thread producers.

Many saw the gold standard as a temporary hedge in a fluid world economy. They believed that gold would protect against Russia and the United States purchasing silver and a worldwide move to bimetallism.[18] Gold supporters feared that Russia might start purchasing silver as a part of a longer-term move to gold or a more immediate move to bimetallism. Gold supporters also worried about proposals in the United States calling for the McKinley administration to convene an international bimetallism conference that could result in additional silver purchases. Gold supporters also believed that, regardless of any movement to bimetallism, support in the United States for silver would continue to grow. They believed this even after William Jennings Bryan's defeat in the 1896 presidential race.[19] Gold supporters who were convinced silver would appreciate based their arguments on a belief that the official U.S. gold to silver ratio of 1:16, valuing silver significantly higher than market rates, would still have an effect, even with expiration of the Sherman Act.[20] In this view, as long as gold depreciated, the trade benefits of stable exchange rates with Europe and the United States, and the export benefits of abandoning an appreciating currency, would make up for any resulting difficulties for Japan's Asia trade.

There were others who wanted to retain the export and industrial benefits of depreciation until the final moment before the world moved en masse to bimetallism. As one country after another adopted bimetallism, silver would appreciate thus offering trade benefits to gold standard countries.[21] If Japan stayed on silver during this process, gold supporters argued, it would experience a contraction in exports, decline in prices, and the assorted results of stagnation and recession. Thus, they argued, it was in Japan's interest to adopt the gold standard in anticipation of silver appreciating as bimetallism was adopted worldwide.

Alternatively, others, such as the Yokohama Specie Bank's director Sōma Nagatani, opposed gold because they believed neither an international agreement on bimetallism nor a return to U.S. silver purchases was likely.[22] Bimetallism and U.S. silver purchases were crucial to depreciationist support for gold because if silver production held steady there would still need to be an increase in demand for silver to appreciate. That, in turn, meant either a worldwide move to bimetallism or a conscious effort by a large government to buy silver.

This uncertainty about international developments made mobilizing support or opposition to Matsukata's gold standard plan from merchants and industrialists difficult. Despite their agreement on goals, they remained divided regarding the future international outlook for gold and silver. If the most common position among Japanese merchants and industrialists was to support gold or silver on the assumption that one or the other was more likely to depreciate, the alternative was simply to wait and see how events developed. The former finance minister Watanabe Kuniaki and the textile industrialist Asabuki Eiji followed this approach.[23] In this Watanabe and Asabuki most resembled Francisco Uriburu in Argentina in cautioning against locking in changes that might ultimately prove harmful.

Matsukata emphasized the stability that the gold standard would provide for trade with gold standard countries. He also stressed the ability of a central bank to finesse any negative effects of gold. Under the presumed rules of the gold standard, if exports did not expand, gold would flow overseas and equilibrium could only come from domestic price deflation. Matsukata, however, saw central banks as a key means to short-circuit this principle of classic English political economy. As Matsukata put it, "The influx and efflux of currency take place according to the condition of the foreign trade of a country. When the imports exceed the exports, if no special efforts are made to prevent it, the specie will tend to leave the country, which may bring about a scarcity of money and a consequent distress among the people. No individual merchant can afford, even if he wished, to try to remedy this kind of evil."[24]

A central bank could, in the event of temporary surpluses, intervene to compensate current account deficits by purchasing "foreign bills, or gold and silver bullion, with the object of increasing the influx of specie."[25] While Matsukata struggled to show that gold would increase exports, other proponents of gold acknowledged silver's favorable impact on exports but dismissed its importance. Instead, echoing arguments that would be taken up in the 1920s by those who urged a return to the gold standard at the, by then, overvalued prewar exchange rate, they argued that trade deficits resulted from "unhealthy over-expenditure" that could be controlled by limiting domestic consumption, and inducing deflation.[26]

These deflationary arguments reflected classic English economic thought and stemmed from David Hume's eighteenth-century idea of a price specie flow mechanism. They did not, however, reflect the realities of late-Meiji politics and international relations when the government was rapidly increasing industrial and military expenses.

Increased trade deficits were compounded by the fact that gold continued to appreciate. As silver proponents had predicted, export prices increased relative to Chinese wholesale prices once Japan adopted gold. Although gold proponents had argued that exports would increase under gold, they did not. Though the consequences failed to reach the levels predicted by silver advocates, export growth began to stagnate and dropped further in the recession of 1900. Merchandise trade balances went from minor surpluses of 0.3 million yen in 1885 and 8.7 million in 1886 to deficits of 3.3 million yen in 1895, 68.5 million in 1896, and 73.1 million in 1897. After 1897 deficits jumped to 142.1 million in 1898 before settling back to 74.6 million in 1899 and 1900.[27]

The uses of depreciation was not the last of the economic arguments. There was one other argument, which might be called the QWERTY argument—that is, there are advantages to subscribing to an emerging world standard for the simple reason that it is the emerging world standard regardless of the particular form it may take or even the particular advantages and disadvantages that standard may embody. In other words, it is an argument about the economic benefits of world standards.[28]

The Benefits of World Standards

Despite the concern among merchants and industrialists about predicting whether silver or gold would appreciate, there was a third possibility for those who had not already decided to adopt the gold standard for other reasons: that neither silver nor gold would appreciate but simply retain their present values. If so, then the argument moved to a different basis entirely. Advocates of the view that silver was inherently unstable argued that exchange-rate fluctuations were due to unstable silver depreciating relative to stable, or relatively more stable, gold. They did not consider that gold might be the unstable metal appreciating against silver.

The nothing appreciates view held something different even in reaching the same conclusion that Japan should adopt the gold standard. In this view all countries were likely to move to the gold standard, it being inevitable that a single currency system would come to dominate throughout the world. As long as there were no benefits from depreciation at play, then adopting the majority standard would aid domestic industry not only through reduced exchange-rate fluctuations with Europe and the United States but also through the reduced interest rates proponents of this argument believed would result.[29]

If it turned out that the ultimate worldwide standard became bimetallism, gold would still be preferable in the short term. As more countries switched to bimetallism silver would appreciate and Japan could take advantage of gold's declining value until finally switching to bimetallism. If, however, silver simply retained its present value, then the best course would be to align with "the world's civilized countries" and immediately adopt the emerging world financial standard, which by default if not bimetallism, would, it was believed, be gold.[30] In either event, the immediate choice was to adopt gold, either to join the emerging world standard or as a temporary measure to take advantage of gold's depreciation in advance of a final move to a bimetallic world standard.

If gold really were the emerging world standard, and if silver were not ultimately to depreciate as that trend developed, then the world-standards argument was a clear winner. It did away with the fuzziness of trying to balance the benefits of depreciating currency against stable exchange rates with gold or silver countries versus the benefits of belonging to the dominant, or even unitary, world standard. In fact, things did not work out so cleanly. The United States did ultimately adopt gold, but Asia remained on silver, and silver itself continued to depreciate. In practice the world-standards argument did nothing to solve the confusion over predicting depreciation that so bothered its most enthusiastic supporters.

Still, just as there is no great mystery about the appeal of depreciation for exports and infant industries, there is also no surprise in the comfort of numbers and the benefits of mass standards. The more people who adopt a particular standard—be it weights and measures, computer operating systems, DVD codes, or whatever—the fewer the compatibility and exchange problems and the easier it is to interact with one another. The same principle applies to currency. It is a major reason that countries, since the emergence of nation-states in the mid-nineteenth century, have in general done away with multiple currencies.

But this concept, too, failed to provide a clear answer to what currency system Japan should adopt. Proponents of the world-standards argument either took depreciation off the board even before the game began or assumed it would be only temporary. While theoretically and aesthetically pleasing in removing the guesswork about gold and silver prices, this move did not, however, actually provide an answer once the simplifying assumptions proved mistaken. For in the late 1890s, when not only Japan and Argentina but also India, Russia, the United States, and a range of other countries were debating their currency systems, it was not yet clear that the emerging world standard would in fact be gold. By the early 1900s all of these states had indeed adopted gold standards, but that did not change the uncertainty in the 1890s.

Although the gold standard was the only currency standard in the late nineteenth century that came with ideological claims as an "eternal and immutable system"—or in the words of the Argentine Augustín de Vedia, the only "true and universal money"—this sort of "gold standard absolutism" was not unchallenged.[31]

Gold standard critics focused either on the international bimetallism movement or the increasing acceptance of paper and other metal substitutes. They believed the world was undergoing a gradual, yet inevitable, move away from gold. Gold standard absolutism rested on two assumptions: that gold was inherently the best-suited material for currency, and, second, that European countries would support the gold standard indefinitely. For critics who saw those two bases challenged in Europe there was little purpose in switching to the gold standard in order to match world trends if those trends were already moving away from gold.

That there were benefits to trade in adopting the currency system of one's most important trading partners was undisputed. The problem was what happened if one's trade, present and potential, was split between two different currency systems and at least the theoretical possibility of a third. Silver dominated in Asia, gold in Europe, and a question mark hung over the United States that merged into a larger question over a possible worldwide move to bimetallism.

Bimetallism, however, was not something Japan, or most countries, could adopt unilaterally. Without all countries agreeing to fixed exchange rates between gold and silver, one country attempting to do so on its own would merely invite outflows of one or the other metal if its own exchange rates came to vary from those in other parts of the world. This was what had happened to Japan in the 1850s and 1870s as undervalued gold had flowed out to the rest of the world. There were, however, significant numbers of people in Japan, as elsewhere, who believed that bimetallism would ultimately be adopted worldwide. They, in turn, believed Japan should accept bimetallism as the world standard but should do so only after all other countries had moved to bimetallism. The question, then, became what to do in the meantime.

Ōkuma Shigenobu, the former finance minister and future prime minister, belonged to the camp placing greatest emphasis on world standards, without specifically knowing what that meant in practice.[32] This left Ōkuma uncommitted in the long run between the gold standard—his support for which, and more specifically his support for massive foreign loans to fund it with, had contributed to his ouster in 1881—and bimetallism as Ōkuma believed it was still unclear which would become the world standard. In the short-term Ōkuma favored gold as he focused primarily on Europe rather than Asia.

Until such time as a single world system emerged, Ōkuma favored a two-track approach. First, he wanted unilaterally to adopt the currency system of those countries with whom Japan most traded, which, for the moment, meant gold. At the same time he wanted to follow developments in Europe in anticipation of any moves to bimetallism. This initial preference for gold was understandable given that Ōkuma had been a long-time advocate of the gold standard. Despite his support for world standards, Ōkuma had clearly invested himself in gold and proclaimed its adoption the "fulfillment of a hundred year great plan."[33]

Despite the relatively effusive rhetoric, Ōkuma did not divorce gold from what he saw as its emerging role as a world standard. It was this role, rather than the particular properties of gold itself, that attracted most gold supporters who were not exclusively focused on depreciation or, like Matsukata, simultaneously concerned with military and great power aspirations. This largely pragmatic attempt to read future developments produced a certain ambivalence and contingency in almost all arguments in favor of or opposed to gold. As Yokohama Specie Bank director Sōma Nagatani put it, he was not inherently "pro or anti gold, silver, bimetallism or any other currency system."[34] There was simply an advantage in "following the general world trends rather than attempting to go it alone."

Even those who supported bimetallism warned against Japan moving to adopt bimetallism on its own.[35] The permutations surrounding when, or if, the world's nations would agree to a bimetallic system, and the fact that, as a major silver country, any move by Japan to abandon or revise its silver standard would itself affect the price of silver, led bimetallic supporters most often to support keeping the existing silver while waiting for bimetallism to make headway internationally. Most observers who believed bimetallism would become the world standard urged staying with the current silver system, seeing no particular benefit in moving quickly to adopt the gold standard, which in turn would need to be replaced with bimetallism.[36] That move to bimetallism could not be made alone.

This, of course, was the fundamental reason why bimetallism needed to be adopted by all countries at once and depended on a formal, international agreement regarding the respective values to be assigned to gold and silver. Bimetallism required the sort of agreement that established the Bretton Woods system after World War II. But the occasional Hague Conference aside, the late nineteenth-century world did not favor international agreements and multilateral institutions. The primary point of reference—politically, economically, and philosophically—was discrete nation-states presumed to be in inevitable and unavoidable competition with one another.

The opinion of the economic journal *Tōyō keizai shinpō* echoed the uncertainty as to whether to support gold or bimetallism until it became clear which would become the world standard.[37] Like other world-standards proponents, *Tōyō keizai* believed the world's currency systems would converge into a single standard, although only in the distant future of fifty or a hundred years.[38] If gold production continued to increase, and absent a shortage of gold from producing countries, *Tōyō keizai* expected the future world standard to be gold rather than bimetallism. In the event gold production failed to keep pace with demand, however, they expected a move to bimetallism and would support that system as well.

Tōyō keizai's concern with world standards took precedence over the trade and industrial benefits of depreciating currency and drew on world-standards and stability arguments. As *Tōyō keizai* put it, "To buck the tides of general world trends in currency systems and take temporary advantage of fluctuations in relative silver and gold values in order to gain a temporary benefit from imports or exports not only violates the basic tenets of international commerce, but would also entail losses for export-import businesses as a result of currency fluctuations, and would impede foreign trade."[39]

Despite this somewhat tacked-on concern with "basic tenets of international commerce" added to an otherwise standard trade stability argument, *Tōyō keizai* promptly moved back into the depreciation camp. They conceded they would be perfectly happy to stay on silver—and obtain the export advantages from silver's declining value—if it were clear that silver really was going to depreciate in the future. But the editors of *Tōyō keizai* were convinced that gold or bimetallism—not silver—would be the eventual world standard.

Saying that Japan should adopt the world standard did not solve the question of what that standard in fact was—or would be. *Tōyō keizai*'s choice thus became a matter of waiting for indications from the rest of the world regarding future trends. Like Watanabe Kuniaki, *Tōyō keizai*'s editors favored denominating the Sino-Japanese War indemnity in equal parts silver and gold so that it could be used for adopting either the gold standard or bimetallism. In this they readily acknowledged that the position was one of "currency opportunism" (*heiseijō no kikaitō*)—although they did not explain why this would not "violate the basic tenets of international commerce" with which they were at least rhetorically concerned.[40]

Pointedly, the editors' choice of currency systems was only between gold and bimetallism. They excluded silver monometallism because they believed it impossible to have a world standard that did not use gold in some form given the number of countries that had adopted gold. They also could not imagine a global standard that was not based on metal. It was silver, in this view, that would signify isolation and mean that Japan would be left "alone in the world"—assuming, implicitly, that China and the rest of Asia abandoned silver as well. It was silver, and silver alone, that would invite "great loss" (*dai sonshitsu*) and "great difficulties" (*dai konnan*).[41]

This belief that staying on silver would invite great loss and great difficulties stemmed from *Tōyō keizai*'s long-term emphasis on developments over fifty or a hundred years. Although silver supporters—and the depreciationist block of gold supporters—sought to take advantage of depreciating silver or gold in order to spur exports and domestic industry, *Tōyō keizai* nominally objected because that benefit would last only so long as silver (or gold) continued to depreciate and then only for a few years thereafter. This was unacceptable because it was "not long term."[42] And, yet, for all the focus on world standards, century-long chunks of time, and elusive "basic tenets of international commerce," *Tōyō keizai* could still not bring itself to oppose silver if it were clear that silver would continue to depreciate. This uncertainty came down once again to predicting gold and silver price movements.

If the world-standards argument could not entirely escape the depreciation argument, it also risked embracing passing fads with no other substantive advantage than the fact they were embraced by other countries as well. The banker and manufacturer Morimura Ichizaemon embodied this danger. He moved from advocating the gold standard for most of the 1890s for stability reasons to a full embrace of the world-standards argument once it became apparent that Japanese trade and industry had actually benefited from depreciating silver.[43]

Although Morimura remained convinced of silver's inherent inferiority to gold, by 1897 he had tacked on the world-standards argument as evidence that the world had, at last, recognized gold's inherent superiority. For Morimura, gold had become the obvious currency system, with European countries and "even small countries like Chile" adopting gold standards. Putting aside, apparently unknown to Morimura, that Chile's adoption of the gold standard had been a short-lived disaster, Morimura saw a movement "even among common people" to value gold and devalue silver. Women were "tossing aside their silver jewelry in favor of gold," which, in Morimura's view, attested to gold's innate superiority.

Morimura believed adopting the gold standard would be eased by improvements in mining technology that would increase gold production. But gold supplies were merely a technical detail for Morimura. He believed gold was the trend of the moment and should be adopted regardless of practical issues. This a priori preference for gold led Morimura to bypass the guessing games of whether gold or silver was more likely to depreciate, which preoccupied other gold and silver proponents.

In fact, Morimura did believe that as gold became more popular demand would outstrip supply, which would cause gold to appreciate. A similar belief would have settled the argument in favor of silver for all silver proponents and the non-Matsukata majority of gold proponents who were focused on industry, commerce, and fears of silver's appreciation. But for Morimura a belief in limited gold supplies and thus in gold's impending appreciation simply meant that Japan needed to jump even more quickly on the bandwagon before supplies dried up.

For gold opponents, this sort of argument, where world standards morphed into a seasonal popularity contest, was worth "absolutely nothing" and gave currency choices the same weight as passing fads.[44] Merely because various people had gone "mad for gold" did not mean there were good reasons for their enthusiasm, just as there had been no good reason for people in seventeenth-century Holland to go mad for tulip bulbs. For those who dismissed the world-standards argument as equivalent to the notorious Dutch tulip bubble, Japan's giving up silver would damage agriculture and industry and throw away export advantages in pursuit of a system worth nothing. In this view the gold standard had already failed economically in Europe and the United States and was being sustained in a sort of international Ponzi scheme in which gullible countries adopted deflationary gold standards merely because other countries had made the same mistake.

The fad, or at least its technical form, was already showing signs of having hit its peak in the late 1890s. Despite the rush of countries to gold standards in the late 1890s, metallic currency itself was becoming increasingly a relic, replaced not only by convertible paper but also by an array of bills, checks, and accounting setoffs. This was a trend that would only increase—both in the world of practice and in the English economic theory that underlay the gold standard as it came to exist in the nineteenth century.[45] This trend also meant that, by the 1920s, attempts to reinstate the gold standard would come to be strangely disconnected from historical fact as countries nominally sought to restore a pre–World War I monetary order that itself had been evolving out of existence even before World War I brought it to a sudden end.

The result would be a striking mismatch between theory, history, policy, and practice in the 1920s as states imagined they were reinstating the substance of the turn-of-the-century gold standard when, in fact, they were obsessing about little more than its form. This incongruity between what the gold standard had been in practice and what its advocates in the 1920s imagined it had been would be left unresolved until countries abandoned the gold standard system entirely and turned economically inward in response to the Great Depression of the 1930s. That turn inward would mean not only an end to the gold standard itself but also to the flows of trade and finance that had coincided, for better or worse, with its heyday.

Sekai-teki to naru: The Meaning of Globalization

Whether one marks the end of the turn-of-the-century age of globalization with World War I or the Depression of the 1930s, it was the gold standard that rested at the center both of its emergence and its ultimate decline. And it was a very particular kind of globalization that carried with it a choice of one set of geographical influences over another. It was also riddled with the competing interplay of midcentury English political economy and late-century imperialism and protectionism. Nowhere was this more apparent than in Japan where the attempt to adapt to world standards could not do away with the fact that Japan's economy existed simultaneously within two separate world currency regimes—silver Asia and gold Europe. Nor could it avoid the fact that the adoption of mid-century English liberal forms was meant to serve the purposes of late nineteenth-century empire.

Switching from silver to gold also opened Japan to a new array of financial influences from Europe and the United States from which it had previously been isolated. After European and American military threats in the 1850s and 1860s, foreign influences on the Japanese economy took a less militaristic turn prior to the Sino-Japanese War, at which point militarism became much more of a two-way street.

In the late nineteenth century these economic changes made themselves directly felt in two ways: changes in overseas demand for Japanese silk and changes in the price of silver, which in turn directly affected silk demand. Demand for Japanese silk overseas in the 1890s had briefly declined due to improvements in Italian silk cultivation and appreciating silver. Then it increased dramatically due to the worldwide economic upturn and silver's depreciation. Silver's price, in turn, had fluctuated increasingly in the 1890s due to India's currency changes, decline in silver demand in India and other countries, and changes in silver production, which magnified increased demand for silk.

More general political and economic events overseas had trade effects as well. The 1892 and 1896 U.S presidential elections, with their impact on world silver and gold prices, political tensions in Europe, and the ups and downs of overseas financial markets all had worldwide effects. The effects on Japan, however, stopped at the level of trade. There was virtually no overflow in terms of finance. Throughout most of the preceding thirty years, Meiji Japan had essentially been on a silver standard no matter what the nominal system was at any time. During this period Japan had experienced significant industrial growth internally and export and commercial expansion externally. Only in terms of finance was Japan cut off from foreign countries. But capital was in high demand and interest rates had been high. Although outflows of capital overseas had ceased, there had not been large inflows. In short, Japan's economic relations with foreign countries had been limited to trade.

This isolation from the more volatile European and American financial markets had its advantages. When the U.S. financial panic of 1893 rippled to London and other European financial markets, Japan remained largely unaffected. The only effect on Japan of that financial crisis was in terms of trade: a decline in silk exports due to decreased demand. In 1896 interest rates rose dramatically in London and more generally throughout Europe and the United States, accompanied by specie outflows from London. Not only was Japan unaffected by these fluctuations, even merchants directly involved in foreign trade were, in general, unaware of these fluctuations due to the complete separation of Japanese and Euro-U.S. financial markets. Trade effects were felt; financial effects were not, unless or until they flowed over into trade.

This would all change with adoption of the gold standard. As a result Japan would be dealing more directly with Europe and the United States and economic ties would no longer stop at the level of tradable goods. The deeper financial ties would make economic links between Britain and Japan "as deep and broad as that between Britain and the U.S.," which in turn would cause Japan's financial system to become, in the words of one Meiji observer, "globalized" (*sekai-teki to naru*).[46]

For those who believed the supply and demand of capital determined the growth or stagnation of national economies, Matsukata's currency plan represented a great restoration (*ichidai ishin*) of the economy. In this view one great restoration had already arrived in the form of trade. Matsukata's plan would extend it to finance, fully incorporating Japan within the Euro-U.S. economic world. The question for Japan's politicians, economists, merchants, industrialists, bankers, and manufacturers was whether to proceed with this integration or not. Those who answered affirmatively saw this integration with Euro-U.S. financial markets as providing low-cost capital for domestic development. For those opposed, this sort of increased integration could only result in an "East-West commercial war" that Japan risked "losing."[47]

Being integrated into a larger world economy also meant Japan would need to pay attention to matters far outside its borders and beyond purely trade issues. What was the future of U.S. currency? What was the direction of U.S. trade with Europe? What was the position of English investors in U.S. industry? What would be the effect on English financial markets of moving Japanese specie reserves to London? What was the demand for gold in Germany, Italy, the Netherlands, and other gold standard countries with which Japan had until then only minor or nonexistent economic ties? What were the successes and failures among countries that had recently adopted gold standards, and what change in gold demand had this produced? What was the state of worldwide gold production? What of gold flows into and out of London? What were the movements in London interest rates? All these previously distant and largely irrelevant questions suddenly became crucial.

Japan was opening itself to what in the language of 1990s globalization were called hot money flows. Foreign funds would arrive suddenly and just as quickly depart in response not only to conditions in Japan but also to developments overseas. If foreign trade imports and exports were relatively predictable, foreign capital flows were not. Capital from England, France, Germany and the United States would flow into Japanese markets and be used to buy public debt or stocks. These funds, however, could withdraw not only in response to developments within Japan but also in response to circumstances having nothing to do with Japan, such as famine, war, or trade imbalances in other countries. This would subject Japan to the effects of foreign financial panics from which it had thus far been isolated. The goal then was to straddle the fine line separating the advantages and disadvantages of foreign capital.

The implications of foreign capital were not entirely economic. Adopting gold also meant paying attention to the military and diplomatic implications of finance as loans, trade balances, specie reserves, and the currency standard itself became tied in with territorial expansion, colonial rule, and military preparations. Most important for Japan in the aftermath of the Sino-Japanese War was Russia, with Russia's own adoption of the gold standard—and its rush to collect gold reserves—viewed, in Japan and elsewhere, as part of military preparations for hypothetical wars with the great powers of Europe and far less hypothetical wars with Japan over Korea and, perhaps, Manchuria as well. This interconnection between currency, finance, and military expansion was not, however, exclusive to Japan and Russia. It was all part of the great power priorities of the age.

9

Empire and the
Political Uses of Gold

Economic arguments about stability, industrial promotion, and world standards dominated discussions about the gold standard among merchants and industrialists. Among government officials and those concerned more with politics than economics another set of arguments emerged. These explicitly political arguments took precedence after Japan's victory in the Sino-Japanese War of 1894–95.

These political arguments consisted of psychological appeals to gold representing a particular level of civilization or great power development. This implied a particular level of international political and military power. These political arguments also emphasized more practical considerations concerning military development and imperial management. In particular these focused on the perceived need for foreign borrowing to develop war treasuries and military-use industry.

If merchants and silk manufacturers stressed depreciation to spur exports, political figures concerned with developing Japan's military and military-related heavy industry sought stable prices for machine imports from gold standard countries. Merchants and industrialists considered, if skeptically, the potential benefits of adopting the gold standard on foreign loans and domestic interests rates. But those concerned with future great power status and imperialist warfare took foreign loans far more seriously. They looked on gold as an essential means to fund those military endeavors.[1]

This did not mean that political advocates neglected the economic effects of adopting the gold standard. Proponents of the political uses of gold stressed the need to protect against the economic downsides of gold. In particular, they emphasized the importance of assuring that the gold standard did not cause deflation or alter the relative positions of debtors and creditors.[2] But these were defensive measures. They advocated gold for primarily noneconomic reasons.

By the late 1890s the argument within the government had become less one of whether to adopt the gold standard than one of technical procedures and timing. The Sino-Japanese War indemnity provided an infusion of reserves to establish a conversion fund—a fund that Argentina did not have. Japan could thus "align with the currency system of civilized nations" without immediately worrying about negative trade balances.[3] Experience from Europe and the United States led government officials to see the gold standard as deflationary. This centered government discussions on how to switch from a silver standard to the gold standard without producing price declines. This led to devaluing the official exchange rate in order to avoid price deflation and an economic downturn.[4]

This emphasis on assuring that adopting gold did not affect prices—combined with Matsukata's own considerable pressure to adopt gold—undercut what opposition there was from exporters who supported silver or bimetallism. Equally important, neither the existing silver standard nor a bimetallic standard seemed indisputably superior to gold in the context of the 1890s when currency systems were changing rapidly worldwide and future gold and silver prices remained uncertain. Even the staunchest export and industrial development advocates could not clearly say whether gold or silver would depreciate in the future, particularly in light of new gold discoveries. Given their inability to state definitively that silver or bimetallism would produce a depreciating yen, even Currency Commission members, such as Taguchi Ukichi, who had advocated silver or bimetallism in the early and mid-1890s, by 1897 had fallen in line with Matsukata's move to adopt the gold standard.[5]

This uncertainty among an opposition that was not even sure it was opposed left the way open for the government to adopt the gold standard primarily for political reasons. For the government, the gold standard formed part of a political vision of a militarized, imperial Japan: a Japan that was a great power like England, France, Germany, and the United States.

Great Power Priorities

This great power view of the world dominated Matsukata's thinking. It emphasized empire, military-use industry, and control of—rather than mutual benefit from—foreign trade.[6] In Matsukata's rendering, gold was "the world's great power" and represented a means to "leave Asia and enter Europe."[7] Others argued for gold as a means to tie Japan to Britain in a political alliance against Russia, France, and Germany.[8]

Support for the gold standard did not necessarily mean support for an alliance with Britain. Itō Hirobumi, who had argued for the gold standard in the 1870s, looked politically to Russia rather than Britain. Itō favored a political settlement with Russia, trading Japanese interests in Manchuria off against Russian interests in Korea, rather than an anti-Russian alliance with Britain.

But for most Japanese leaders Britain in the 1890s looked preferable to Russia. In 1894 Britain became the first country to revise the hated unequal treaties from the 1850s. In contrast, Russia intervened at the end of the Sino-Japanese War, with France and Germany. They forced Japan to return to China the strategically located Liaotung Peninsula, which Japan had received as war spoils along with Taiwan and other colonial possessions. Russia shortly thereafter took the Liaotung Peninsula as its own, setting up Russian territorial interests squarely in the way of Japanese interests. This Triple Intervention created a political furor and thrust Russia to the forefront as a potential military adversary of Japan.

Britain, which refused to take part in the Triple Intervention, emerged as a natural counterweight to Russian maneuvers in East Asia. For its part, the British government saw Japan as a counterweight in East Asia to French, German, and Russian maneuvers. All this would ultimately lead to the Anglo-Japanese Alliance in 1902.[9] Under the alliance, Japan and Britain pledged to militarily aid each other. In this political climate, popular sentiment in the late 1890s opted for Japan to reshape itself as "the England of the East."[10]

Although abandoning silver might curb growth and exports, gold proponents argued that the difference could be borrowed overseas. And borrowing through London would further strengthen Japan's political and economic ties to Britain.[11] Much as Russia used its political alliance with France to finance debt on the Paris capital markets, so too, it was argued, Japan could simultaneously use its English economic ties to promote a political alliance and its English political alliance to promote economic ties. The British government took a far less active role in the London financial markets than did the French in Paris. But the British government had on occasion either formally guaranteed bonds of key political allies or informally made its sentiments in favor of certain countries known within London's financial community.[12]

By 1897 a view prevailed around Matsukata that "gold is necessary in order to be a first-rate nation which will lead the world in all affairs."[13] This distinctly political and nationalist view combined Listian economics from the early nineteenth century with colonial and imperial ideas from the late nineteenth century. In this view Japan needed to adopt the gold standard for the greater power and glory of the Japanese Empire: to compete politically and militarily with first rank powers, develop heavy industry, control trade flows, and collect foreign loans. Loans were to provide the means to pay for military and industrial imports and to establish war treasuries analogous to those piling up in Europe.[14]

Matsukata's newfound enthusiasm for foreign loans in the aftermath of the Sino-Japanese War rested on the image of Japan as a great power in competition with other great powers. Most arguments circulating popularly among merchants, industrialists, and bankers were private and economic. In contrast, even Matsukata's ostensibly economic arguments were framed in terms of national power and effects on territorial expansion, warfare, and great power status.[15]

One other great power priority involved establishing one's own financial center, on the lines of London, Paris, or New York, that could produce industrial and imperial financing without having to assume the risks of foreign funding. Of the five East Asian treaty ports set up in the first wave of European colonial expansion in the mid-nineteenth century, the British colony of Hong Kong remained the East's financial center and operated as the Asian center for foreign financial institutions.[16] Japanese treaty ports, forcibly incorporated into this system in the 1850s, were also part of the trade side of this system.

As with China and with Japan's newly acquired colony of Taiwan, Hong Kong's currency system was based on silver. If Japan adopted the gold standard, Japanese treaty ports would be the only Asian ports operating under the gold standard. For gold supporters in Japan, this implied that foreign merchants would become more inclined to center both trade and financial activities in Japanese ports rather than in Hong Kong or other silver-based treaty ports. And this, in turn, implied that as foreign merchants increasingly centered their transactions in Japan—and demanded Japanese currency in the process—foreign finance would shift from Hong Kong to Japan.[17]

The possibility of Japan becoming the financial center of East Asia underscored not only shifts in the 1890s in trade and financial relations in East Asia but also a shift in the nature of European imperialism. The European and U.S. treaty port system emerged from the wave of European imperialism in the aftermath of the Opium War in the 1840s. But that system—and the particular balance of power it represented—was on its way out by the early 1890s. It dramatically changed as a result of Japan's victory in the Sino-Japanese War. Above all, this change came from Japan's emergence as an economic and military power within the existing European treaty system. Revision of the unequal treaties and Britain's victory in the Sino-Japanese War moved Japan from the category of potentially colonizable to colonizer.

Japan's adopting the gold standard played into this process not only in the access it gave to foreign financial markets for military and industrial funding but also in making East Asian foreign trade a two-currency affair where it had previously been only silver. The treaty port system established in the 1840s and 1850s had been centered on China trade and, accordingly, had been centered on silver as well, with silver the mandatory currency in all treaty ports. For those like Matsukata who viewed the gold standard within an explicitly great power political and military context, adopting the gold standard was meant to shift not only the trade and financial balance in East Asia toward Japan but also the political one as well.

This shift in power relations in East Asia—the "rise of Japan" in the rhetoric of the age—also reflected a worldwide change in the nature of imperialism. The commercial imperialism of the mid-nineteenth century exemplified in East Asia by the treaty port system gave way to territorial imperialism: Europeans seeking to carve up the "Chinese melon"; the U.S. occupation of Hawaii and the Philippines; and Japan's territorial expansion and eventual colonization of Taiwan, Korea, and later, Manchuria. If these imperial moves risked conflict between the great powers—not to mention conflict with those people being colonized—the moves themselves were not seen as negatives. Rather, in the thinking of the age, they were the very signs of civilization and progress.

CIVILIZATION AND GOLD

The idea of "civilization" and its constant companions, progress, science, and modernity, were staples of late nineteenth-century thought and rhetoric in Japan, as they were in Argentina, the United States, and throughout Europe. Gold standard proponents in Japan, as elsewhere, were prone to argue that currency metals were linked to material progress, which in turn was linked to cultural progress, all coexisting under the giant umbrella of civilization.[18] Different nations occupied different levels of civilization and development. Different currencies and economic policies were associated with each.

According to Matsukata the gold standard was a modern, scientific system signifying the highest level of civilizational development. Silver, in contrast, was the currency of "uncivilized countries" and unworthy of first-rank countries, and the Japanese people would be incorrectly classed with the uncivilized were they to use it for their currency standard.[19] In Japan, this civilizational argument for gold appeared most often with a heavy overlay of political and military concerns. In Europe, it was tied tightly to imperialism and imperialist views.

The standard civilizational view of gold argued that in ancient times currency consisted of bronze. It then became copper, then silver, then silver and gold, and finally, in the ultimate "modern" stage of currency's natural progression, gold as currency came to reflect the general level of advanced civilization.[20] Or as Soeda Juichi, part of Matsukata's faction in the Finance Ministry argued, "The standard must conform to the necessities of the country in which it is applied. For uncivilized nations, shells and hides may do; but as we advance, something better, such as silver becomes necessary. As the unit of prices rises by still higher advance toward civilization, silver becomes too heavy, and something that embodies more value in less volume is needed. This need is best satisfied by gold. Therefore, for the advanced nations, gold must be made the standard by the very necessities of daily life, while for backward countries silver will be more suitable."[21]

To some degree this argument simply reflected the view that currencies only had value in relation to the materials from which they were made.

But it went beyond that in arguing for a permanent hierarchy of metals in which their respective values remained unchanged and ignoring the use of paper, credits, checks, and other nonmetallic money. This sort of progressional view of currencies also implied an end, at least in terms of currency, to the ongoing march of progress that so preoccupied European thought in the nineteenth century. But even as countries worldwide were adopting the gold standard in the 1890s, English political economy itself was moving away from the view of gold as the ultimate currency, although the shift in economic thought was still in its early stages in England.[22]

The nineteenth-century English enthusiasm for gold as an expression of a society's level of development appeared popularly in arguments such as those made by the economist and Diet member, and *Tōyō keizai* cofounder, Amano Tameyuki, who advocated gold because it was the standard of the world's civilized nations.[23] If this superficially resembled the world-standards argument, it was in fact fundamentally different, as Amano was concerned not with practical issues of trade, stability, and convenience, but with issues of relative prestige irrespective of the practical implications. Amano had supported adopting the gold standard since the 1880s because all of those he considered "first-rank," "enlightened countries" had already adopted gold.[24] It made no difference to him that Japan had no gold reserves.

This was, on one level, a stance by association. Amano looked at those great powers he felt Japan should model itself on and urged adopting the same institutions. In this, Amano resembled Matsukata's Finance Ministry protégé Sakatani Yoshio, who approached the issue primarily as one of international prestige. As Sakatani put it, "Of those countries presently subscribing to a silver standard, in truth not only are they extremely few, namely Korea, China, Siam, and Mexico, but in addition to their being extremely few in numbers, their status is not high. For our country, which has transcended such position through our military victory [in the Sino-Japanese War], we clearly cannot be ranked with such countries."[25]

Sakatani saw skepticism in London about the economic wisdom of Japan adopting the gold standard as attempts to exclude Japan from a privileged Western gold club and leave it lumped with the losers of Asia: "Those who argue for silver and against gold are those in the gold standard countries. They uniformly say that the gold standard is not good and that one should stick to silver but they remain gold standard countries. The remaining silver countries are China, Korea, Malaya, and Japan. If silver is good, why do the European and American people desert the silver standard?"[26]

Although Sakatani started from reputational concerns, he then followed Matsukata's lead in seeking to ameliorate gold's practical defects through devaluing the exchange rate. Amano, on the other hand, preferred not to acknowledge any practical difficulties in adopting the gold standard; instead, he sought to make the economic arguments match his reputational preference. In doing so, Amano ended up producing a mix of standard economic arguments from the time with extraeconomic emphases on progress, civilization, and empire that, in part, contradicted those arguments. Amano repeated the uncontroversial fact that having the same currency base as gold standard countries would simplify bookkeeping in trade with those countries, as well as the less clear, but still common, argument that adopting gold would ease foreign capital imports and help develop Japan's financial markets.

But in the late 1890s Amano added these rationales to a pro-gold position he had advocated for more than a decade. They did not form the basis of his support nor did Amano apply them in consistent, or even logical, ways. Amano's enthusiasm for gold rested on the fact that since Germany had adopted the gold standard in 1873, "the world's first-rank, enlightened countries" had "fought forward and dumped silver." It was thus "essential for Japan and its people" to adopt gold as well, in order to join the first-rank, enlightened elite.[27]

If Amano made nods, albeit inconsistent, to trade arguments, the then-vice minister of agriculture and commerce, and from 1898 minister, Ōishi Masami concentrated squarely on gold's role in promoting "the political civilization of Imperial Japan" (*Nihon teikoku no seiji-bunmei*). In Ōishi's view, the purpose of adopting the gold standard was to ensure the "future of the Empire" in a world of "extraordinarily intense Great Power competition." In this world of great power rivalry Japan would need to defend itself from being "trampled underfoot . . . like India or Annam . . . [by] other first-rate peoples."[28]

Accordingly, Japan would need to prepare to "defend the nation" against military moves by European powers in China and, more broadly, East Asia. For Ōishi the overriding concern of the age was the "black clouds" stretching over East Asia from Russian moves in China and the seemingly inevitable great power conflict this would produce, in which case Japan must be prepared to defend its interests in China "at any moment." Most immediately this meant foreign funding. Domestic funds were insufficient for the sorts of military expenditures required and needed for private industry, which could not develop if funding were monopolized for military purposes. Military funding thus would need to come from gold standard countries. Ōishi believed it was "exceedingly necessary that our currency system be revised to be the same" as the gold standard countries from which military funds would need to flow. Japanese bonds issued in perpetually depreciating silver would merely inspire "pity" in foreign markets and would be insufficiently attractive to the foreign investors needed to fund Japan's military operations.[29]

But there was more to the issue than just foreign funding. In Ōishi's view, Japan would in all matters need to be "on the same level" as "the world's first-rate peoples." Japan would need to triumph in the pursuit of "civilizationalism" (*bunmeishugi*) and "civilizational progress" (*bunmei shinpo*), devoting itself to "civilizational activities" (*bunmei jigyō*) such as upgrading the army, railroads, telegraphs, and postal service so that Japan could be equal to "the world's superior countries." Although the idea of civilization and national progress played an equally large role in Argentina, there was no idea of countries that were superior to Argentina. There might have been individual people or specific groups in Argentine society that were seen as outside the world current of civilization, but the country itself was viewed as equivalent to the United States or Europe, and any criticism from abroad inevitably prompted a heated defense of the nation's honor.[30]

Although Ōishi acknowledged that scholars in Europe and the United States had expressed doubts about the gold standard, and workers had suffered "hardships" due to its operation, this made no difference. As long as the "world's superior countries" used gold, adopting the gold standard became in and of itself a prerequisite of "civilizationalism."[31]

TAIWAN AND THE EMPIRE OF JAPAN

There was another prerequisite of civilizationism and great power status: colonies. And Japan's adoption of the gold standard raised the immediate question of what to do about its newly acquired colony, Taiwan. The same issue would apply to silver-based Korea, but as Japan's control over Korea did not emerge until after the Russo-Japanese War in 1905, that was an issue for the future.[32] The choices were either to leave the current silver system as it was, adopt a special silver system limited to Taiwan and entirely separate from the currency system in Japan proper, or establish the gold standard to match the Japanese system.[33] Keeping a silver standard made sense for trade with silver-based China and would, arguably, encourage industrial development in Taiwan by aiding exports to gold standard countries and promoting the China trade. Leaving Taiwan silver-based would also allow Japan to hedge its bets while the fate of bimetallism worked itself out worldwide. Forcing an appreciating gold standard on Taiwan would undercut Taiwan's exports. Here the arguments were essentially the same as the trade arguments for and against the gold standard in Japan with the added fillip that Taiwan's trade was overwhelmingly with China.

The key point economically was Taiwan's location. For Taiwan's perceived value as a colony was not simply as a supplier of primary products—principally sugar—to Japan proper. More important was its physical proximity to China and the resulting trade and financial ties with that country.[34] In terms of geography it was natural that most of its trade was, and would continue to be, with silver-based East Asia given that as of 1897 Taiwan's trade was 70%–80% with China, about 20% with Hong Kong, and about 10% with Japan.[35] One major cause of the increase in Japanese exports to China had been changes in comparative gold and silver prices, which made Japanese exports to China less expensive than European exports. This advantage would end, however, with Japan's adoption of the gold standard. Part of the trade disadvantage in going to the gold standard, however, could be made up for with a special silver system in Taiwan aimed at Asia-related trade and the colony's industrial development.[36]

A special silver system in Taiwan would allow continued coinage of the preexisting Taiwanese one-yen silver coin system in a way that would not cause disruption to the gold standard system in Japan. That is, the Japanese government would have no obligation to convert Taiwanese silver into gold, just as Britain had no obligation to convert the silver Indian rupee.[37] Taiwan would have its own system of silver coins, which would exist separately from the currency system in Japan proper. In this way Taiwan would become a self-contained silver zone. And as long as Taiwanese silver was not convertible into gold, Taiwan could be used as a dumping ground for silver that had already been turned into the Bank of Japan for conversion into gold. Once the Japanese government had received silver in exchange for gold, it then had to make sure that that silver was not consumed again within Japan proper. Otherwise there would be a never-ending cycle where the same piece of silver was converted to gold repeatedly, each time causing silver's price to fall further and each time causing greater losses for the Japanese treasury.

A special silver system to replace the existing chop dollar system—under which Japanese silver that had flowed in over the years had been specially marked thus rendering it unusable in Japan—would allow Taiwan to continue competing against imports from the United States and Europe without having to worry about exchange rate changes between gold and silver.[38] And as Taiwan industrialized through export growth, Japan would benefit as well, with the profits from Taiwanese industry being exportable back to Japan and also providing a self-sustaining basis for the Taiwanese economy. In fact, the chop dollar silver currency was only one of a variety of currencies, including paper, that were used in Taiwan. By 1897, however, virtually all transactions were conducted using some form of silver.[39] The key point for supporters of silver in Taiwan was not trade between Taiwan and Japan and how changes in the exchange market might affect it, but the trading relations between Taiwan, China, and Southeast Asia and how their having the same currency system would increase the prosperity and closeness of Japan's trade with all of them—either directly or through Taiwan.[40]

In this argument the proper order was to first develop Taiwan's industry and trade with China and Southeast Asia. For this silver was preferred. Then, once that industry and trade had "matured," to adopt in Taiwan the same gold standard system as in Japan. The important point for advocates of silver and Taiwan's own industrial development as part of the larger Japanese Empire was first to expand trade with China, East Asia, and Southeast Asia so that Japanese infrastructure and development efforts in Taiwan—electrification, railroads, industry—were not wasted efforts.

Economically, then, the primary question was whether one emphasized bilateral trade between Taiwan and Japan proper—in which case gold would be preferable—or whether one emphasized Taiwan as a gateway toward expanding trade with China and the rest of Asia—in which case silver would be preferred. Gold advocates did not entirely dismiss Taiwan's role in broader Asian trade, arguing that fluctuations in gold and silver values would cause fluctuations in the Taiwanese exchange market, which would in turn damage trade with silver standard countries even if Taiwan itself remained on a silver standard.[41]

Gold advocates also envisioned expanding the China trade more broadly into Japan. They argued that trade with Taiwan—and through it the larger China trade—should be switched from its present concentration among specialized coastal ports to more internal regions of Japan. This, it was argued, was made more difficult by keeping Taiwan's exports denominated in silver.

Arguments in favor of establishing the gold standard in Taiwan ranged from the intrinsic value of gold, to trade, to the practical difficulties of Taiwan being on a different currency standard from the rest of Japan. For those who followed the civilization-and-progress view of gold and viewed gold as intrinsically superior to other forms of currency, the Taiwanese preference for silver resulted neither from custom nor from Taiwan's trade being oriented toward China but from the simple fact that they had "not yet known the value of gold."[42] This idea existed alongside another civilizational view that argued that Taiwan was so "noticeably behind" Japan in terms of its degree of civilizational development—since "progress has been virtually non-existent for the past hundred years"—that it was not yet at a stage of development appropriate for the gold standard.[43]

Gold supporters also argued that it made sense to adopt gold because Taiwan's primary export products, for example, tea, were marketed in gold standard countries.[44] Gold supporters also argued that Taiwan's ties with Japan would become tighter as the island colony was integrated into the Japanese Empire, making a gold standard in Taiwan more logical. Finally, gold supporters argued that Hong Kong and Shanghai would likely soon make gold their trade currencies thus adding another incentive to enact the gold standard in Taiwan to match that in Japan.

If Taiwan were moved onto the gold standard, exchange-rate fluctuations could be avoided in trade between Japan and its colony. The argument that the gold standard in Taiwan would remove any potential problems with conversion of Taiwanese currency in Japan was more tenuous. The conversion problem could be handled by making silver from Taiwan ineligible for conversion. It was also argued—entering the realm of the ideological and the abstract—that a "morality problem" would arise from shipping silver to Taiwan when Japan had officially abolished silver in favor of the gold standard.[45]

The disadvantages to using the gold standard in Taiwan were more concrete. First, without Taiwan as a dumping ground for silver the Japanese government would have to come up with some other means of managing its expected accumulation of silver reserves as people converted silver to gold. Second, given the fact that the residents of Taiwan were used to silver and had every intention of continuing to use silver, there would be no avoiding resistance in Taiwan to any newly proclaimed, legally circulating gold currency. This problem could be resolved by forcing people in Taiwan to use gold—by requiring land taxes to be paid in and contracts to be made in gold.

Japanese proponents of the gold standard in Taiwan were ultimately less concerned with trade matters and hedging bets against gold's effects within Japan proper than they were with more abstract principles of national sovereignty and the presumed natural relations between colonies and metropoles. For gold supporters, Taiwan was "just like Shikoku, Kyūshū or Hokkaidō in making up one part of the Empire [of Japan]."[46] And "to have two currency systems in the same country damages the honor of the nation." A colony, under this argument, would be Singapore, India, or Hong Kong under the British Empire because they were treated as colonies, geographically and institutionally separate from the homeland. Taiwan, however, for those concerned that it not some day vanish from Japanese control, had to be treated as an integral part of the empire. The fundamental worry for advocates of the gold standard in Taiwan was that a mere colony was simply a "country's possession." It was not a part of the country itself and thus "at any time can be abandoned" or "sold off." Accordingly, if Japan "mistook" Taiwan for a colony, it would leave open the possibility that Taiwan might some day be lost to Japanese control.[47]

These arguments rested on a proprietary interest in showing that Taiwan had no independent institutional existence or tradition separate from its relationship to Japan. The common analogy from those who saw no reason to establish the gold standard in Taiwan was that of the British Empire—that is, the British pound was tied to gold, but both silver and gold standard countries belonged to the British Empire. For gold proponents, however, Taiwan could not be compared to British colonies because Taiwan was "one part" of Japan proper and a separate currency system in Taiwan would be like "in the feudal age when each fief had its own currency."[48] Establishing a special silver system in Taiwan would cause exchange-rate fluctuations between Taiwan and Japan proper and would gradually cause Taiwan to grow more distant from Japan. It would, in short, "become a colony" rather than a permanent part of Japan.[49]

The indecision over what to do with Taiwan's currency continued through the start of the gold standard in Japan in October 1897 and into mid-January 1898, when the Matsukata cabinet was replaced by one headed by Itō Hirobumi. The Itō cabinet chose to finesse the issue by establishing gold as the nominal accounting currency for Taiwan while keeping silver as the currency that would actually circulate. The cabinet established a special silver system in Taiwan under which Japan would coin special silver yen that could be used only in Taiwan and that would serve as backing for convertible paper notes issued under authority of the Japanese-appointed governor general.

The idea was to make gold the bookkeeping currency for trade with Japan and otherwise leave the silver system intact. In other words, gold would be the "money of account," but silver would be the "money of use." Money of account would apply only to salaries of Japanese officials in Taiwan, transactions with Japan proper, and transactions among Japanese within Taiwan. This two-tiered system resembled the early use of silver in Japan's own trading ports in the 1850s in which transactions with and among Japanese nationals were conducted in gold and all other transactions were conducted in silver.

For those wishing to solidify Taiwan as an indisputable part of Japan, this arrangement was, at best, foolish and ill informed and, at worst, treasonous. In the most extreme version of this argument, even establishing a pure gold standard in Taiwan would be insufficient because geography and custom would still push trade overwhelmingly toward China. A de facto silver standard would come to dominate the official, de jure gold standard. There was, accordingly, no choice for the most intense advocates of the integrated empire approach but to withdraw Chinese trading rights with Taiwan. By not doing so, Japanese officials were "without knowing it failing to prevent Taiwan from becoming part of the silver area."[50] The fact that Taiwan was accustomed to using a silver system, that that system worked well, and that imposing the gold standard would—even as those most pushing for it acknowledged—cause practical difficulties, was beside the point.[51] Above all, it was this distancing from Japan—and the potential it held that Taiwan could slip from Japanese control—that was to be avoided.

Finance and Foreign Borrowing

If ideas of great power prerequisites and stages of civilization established a need for military and industrial spending as a military, political, and ideological priority, there was one other absolute necessity: the funds to pay for it all. Ultimately, if one could establish heavy industry, reduce the need for industrial imports, and make colonies not merely self-sufficient but profitable, there would be sufficient funds internally to maintain and expand these various endeavors.

One could also attempt to recoup military expenses—and, with luck, make a profit—through ex post facto war indemnities such as Germany received from France after the Franco-Prussian War and Japan got from China after the Sino-Japanese War. But there was no guarantee that, even in victory, a war indemnity would be forthcoming, as the Meiji leadership learned in the aftermath of the Russo-Japanese War. In any case, enormous sums were needed for military, industrial, and infrastructure projects. For that, the only possible source was borrowing on foreign financial markets.[52]

Despite much discussion of trade, price stability, and the attributes of civilization, the prime motive behind Matsukata's push for gold after the Sino-Japanese War was a desire to attract foreign capital.[53] This was, for Matsukata, primarily a matter of military and industrial development. For others it was more broadly an argument that adopting the gold standard in Japan would attract low-cost foreign capital into Japan, which in turn would lower domestic interest rates and help fill import surpluses and specie outflows.[54] These two arguments were somewhat contradictory in the belief of a limitless pool of foreign capital for both private and public borrowing. It was public borrowing that impelled Matsukata to push for the gold standard.

This was not without its problems. First, it was unclear that gold would in fact ease foreign borrowing as Matsukata contended. Second, even if it did ease borrowing Matsukata's plans implied a potentially enormous debt burden.[55] Given the sums necessary for expansive military and industrial spending, in combination with the decline in export revenue that would come from abandoning silver in favor of gold, Japan would become a major debtor country, inviting a cycle in which repaying foreign debt and preserving gold convertibility would become increasingly difficult. Preserving gold convertibility itself would require taking on more foreign debt, which, longer term, would make preserving gold convertibility even more difficult.

Foreign borrowing, moreover, carried considerable baggage in Meiji Japan. Even while advocating establishment of the gold standard in 1871,

Meiji leaders steadfastly avoided foreign borrowing. They saw foreign borrowing as a national security threat that might increase Western power over Japan. Looking at China, they saw the Opium War linked to Britain's protection of its commercial interests in the opium trade. The Meiji leadership sought to avoid protection of foreign investments as a pretext for further Western encroachments on Japanese territory and sovereignty. The unequal treaties of the 1850s, modeled on those previously forced on China, had mandated territorial concessions, extraterritoriality, and loss of tariff autonomy. The Meiji leadership sought to avoid any excuse for further Western incursions of the sort that had occurred in China.

Foreign borrowing, accordingly, carried political risk in addition to the standard economic risk. Advocating foreign borrowing easily led to accusations of endangering national security. Seeking to adopt the gold standard in 1880, Matsukata's rival, Finance Minister Ōkuma Shigenobu, proposed floating a 50 million yen bond offering in London. Under pressure, Ōkuma had switched from a policy of industrial expansion to a Matsukata-style austerity policy.[56] He hoped to provide specie backing for the flood of paper currency issued since the mid-1870s as quickly as possible in order to salvage the remnants of his activist fiscal policies.[57]

The government split over the issue, with Matsukata leading the opposition. Even in 1880, Matsukata ardently backed gold. But he even more ardently opposed foreign borrowing. He had been in a fierce rivalry with Ōkuma for control of Meiji financial policy since at least 1878. Matsukata's security concerns, accordingly, coexisted easily with his interest in undermining Ōkuma politically.[58] By 1897, however, times had changed. The Western treaty powers led by Britain had agreed to revisions of the unequal trade treaties. The Sino-Japanese War had given Japan Taiwan and put Japan in the early stages of empire-building competition with Russia. The advance of the Trans-Siberian Railroad, linking western Russia with the Pacific, heightened security concerns and underlined the need for infrastructure improvements in Japan. Public, political, and business opinion turned in favor of closer ties with England and its financial markets. The English government and investors, in turn, showed new interest in Japan as an emerging economic and political power to balance Russia's ambitions in Asia.

Matsukata had also changed. By 1897 he needed foreign borrowing to reconcile gold with fiscal expansion. As late as 1896 Matsukata still opposed foreign borrowing.[59] Even with the Chinese indemnity, however,

Matsukata worried that both the gold standard and his post-Sino-Japanese War economic policies would remain unworkable without Western credit lines.[60] In 1897 Matsukata shifted positions and argued that foreign borrowing would spur development and gold would spur foreign borrowing. Matsukata made no mention of his previous opposition to foreign borrowing during the Diet debates on gold.

The wisdom of adopting the gold standard was not shared in London. On March 20, 1897, the *Economist* noted with skepticism Japan's stockpiling gold: "Large quantities of gold . . . are now being imported into Japan, which are, no doubt, in connection with the [Sino-Japanese War] indemnity money. On the other hand, silver is being freely exported. It is difficult to see what object Japan (a silver currency country) can have in view in deliberately importing gold when the balance of trade is against her, and silver is leaving the country. One can hardly think she is seriously contemplating placing the currency of the country on a gold basis, for nothing would be more disastrous to her trade and industries, and yet if there be no such move as this, where is the advantage of importing gold?"[61]

The *Economist* noted that Japan seemed intent on ignoring economic reality and pursuing gold for status reasons: "There is . . . an idea that as Japan now considers that she has the right to be regarded as a first-class Power, she ought to adopt for her currency the same standard of value as other first-class Powers."[62] Foreigners in Japan also argued against gold on economic grounds:

> Foreigners, and even foreign political economists, in this country [Japan] are nearly all trying to dissuade Japan from making the change [from silver to gold], clearly pointing out the disadvantages to trade and industries that would accrue from the adoption of the gold standard, and citing the experiences of India during the past four years as an example of the injury that can be done by tampering with the currency of a country; the trade and industries of India during that period having practically stood still, whilst those of Japan have more than doubled. Japan, however, is apparently not to be deterred by any argument. The Government is determined to carry the [Currency] Bill through at all hazards."[63]

Opinion in London also rejected Matsukata's claimed connection between Japan's adopting gold and its being able to borrow more easily. Commenting on Japan's apparent interest in gold as an entrée to London's financial markets, the *Economist* noted, "Why Japan, without altering her currency, should not borrow abroad in gold, as China has done, it is difficult to understand. If foreign political economists and others are right in their contention that the adoption of the gold standard in this country will injure the trade and industries of Japan, it seems unlikely that the credit of the country will be improved by the measure."[64] The American economist Garrett Droppers similarly argued that adopting the gold standard would make little difference in the ease of obtaining or the cost of foreign loans since they could be denominated in gold whether or not Japan's currency standard was gold.[65]

Despite the far from tight connection between gold currency and borrowing in London, a second line of opinion emerged in financial journalism—associated in particular with the American Charles Conant—that emphasized, somewhat contradictorily, the reluctance of Western investors to invest in silver-based countries and (reflecting views on the nature of late nineteenth-century imperialism similar to Hobson and Lenin) the need for Western investors to invest in Asia, Africa, and Latin America due to increasing savings but declining investment opportunities at home.[66]

Matsukata's newfound enthusiasm for foreign debt ran up against the question of whether adopting gold would actually make any difference in Japan's ability to borrow and against the even more fundamental question of whether borrowing large sums of foreign capital was a wise course of action. If tens of millions to a hundred million or more yen of overseas public debt were contracted, Japan would immediately become one of the most indebted countries in the world. Critics painted a worst-case scenario in which the value of Japan's entire rice production would flow overseas, the continuing depreciation of silver would lead to a decline in Japanese exports to silver countries, and exports to gold countries would decline in the face of competition from silver countries.[67]

This scenario envisioned Japan following in the steps of the crisis India faced, where agricultural exports and industrial production had been severely damaged in the attempt to shift to the gold standard under the theory of more firmly integrating it into the British imperial trade and financial system. Even without a crisis of that proportion, the difference in the amount of exports with Japan on gold rather than silver was conceivably substantial, raising the possibility—and more likely the probability—of gold outflows putting the sustainability of the gold standard itself in question, absent taking out more loans that would only increase the likelihood of a debt crisis and put more pressure on the exchange rate in a vicious cycle of declining exports, industrial stagnation, gold outflows, and mounting foreign debt. It also raised the possibility that faced with gold outflows and declining exports from Japan, foreign investors would sell off Japanese stocks and bonds, making financing the trade deficit increasingly difficult, if not impossible, and potentially precipitating a financial panic. Looked at from a long-term perspective, massive foreign borrowing could, it was argued, destroy the very industrial development it sought to encourage—or sought to encourage along with military development, the industrial and military aims being in large part complementary, but not entirely so.

Gold enthusiasts outside the government emphasized that in ordinary circumstances Japan would need foreign capital for industry as it needed know-how and technology from the United States and Europe.[68] It would also need foreign capital in the event of import surpluses, specie outflows, and financial panics. For those most committed to the gold standard, foreign borrowing would be nearly impossible without adopting the gold standard. This argument for ordinary capital requirements, however, overlooked the trade disadvantages of gold that brought about the need for dealing with import surpluses and specie outflows.

Putting aside the question of whether adopting gold really did make foreign borrowing cheaper and easier, abandoning depreciating silver for gold would make Japanese products more expensive thereby decreasing exports, increasing imports, and contributing to the very sort of import surpluses and specie outflows that gold proponents sought to ameliorate with foreign borrowing. This was borne out in Japan's first foreign borrowings after adopting gold. The loans were taken out in order to maintain the gold standard in light of trade deficits—and resulting gold outflows—resulting from a drop in exports after abandoning silver.

Merchants were less receptive to the interest rate argument, with even those merchants who supported gold for stability or depreciation reasons wary of the interest rate claims. Although the Yokohama silk merchants had split into separate silver and gold camps, both camps believed the foreign capital claims were an illusion.[69] For them, it was not realistic to expect that British financiers would suddenly lower interest rates on Japanese debt simply because Japan had adopted the gold standard. Given the "Far East problem" so widely discussed in London, it was unlikely that Japan's adopting the gold standard would suddenly produce a drop in interest rates on Japanese foreign debt. English investors were immensely concerned with Japan's intentions in Korea and the likelihood of a Japanese-Russian war over Korea, as well as continued uncertainty and great power jostling in China.

This was even more true given the view in London that the gold standard was economically disadvantageous for Japan. Add the possibility of non-Asian imperial wars such as the Boer War in South Africa pushing up interest rates in London generally, and the connection between Japan adopting the gold standard and its borrowing in London came to seem even more tenuous—particularly compared to a country like Argentina that, due to its traditional ties with Britain and an overflow of British banks and merchants, could borrow regardless of its currency standard.

In short, the foreign borrowing argument rested on the assumption that adopting the gold standard would automatically allow Japan to borrow in the London financial markets at the same interest rates as other gold standard countries.[70] This was not, however, how the London markets worked. Interest rates and available credit depended on a range of factors related to the perceived risk of the borrower, the availability of funds in London, the general investment climate. and other global circumstances, from wars to droughts, that might have nothing to do with the country seeking to borrow.

There were moments when London funds could be obtained nearly indiscriminately, but this was historically more likely in regions such as North and South America with closer generational and economic ties than in Japan's case. At its most extreme, the belief that adopting the gold standard would open the gates to cheap foreign capital and, by extension, cause domestic interest rates to decline, held that all existing public debt could be erased by borrowing overseas—that is, taking out foreign loans to pay off domestic loans.[71]

In the months after the gold standard was adopted, foreign capital did not come flowing in as Matsukata had predicted.[72] Foreign borrowing did increase as the government so desperately wanted. But this was not a natural inflow of funds—nor was it primarily directed at private industry. It was the result of the government's stance of borrowing at virtually any cost. Japan's first industrial boom of 1886–90 had flowed naturally from depreciating silver and proceeded largely free of state influence. Industrial growth from 1896 to 1900 resulted from government spending—primarily for military expenses or to develop heavy industry and infrastructure that could be used for military purposes.

Increased government spending and the imports it entailed put immediate pressure on the gold parity. To supplement its gold reserves, the government issued bonds in London in 1897, in the amount of 43.89 million yen, and in 1899 for 100 million yen. Debt skyrocketed with the Russo-Japanese War. The government floated bonds in London, New York, Germany, and Paris nine times between 1902 and 1910. Japan's foreign indebtedness rose from less than 100 million yen in 1903 to 1.4 billion yen by 1907. By the end of 1914 it stood at 1.1 billion yen.[73] Interest payments on foreign debt for 1913 alone totaled 70 million yen.[74] By the end of the Russo-Japanese War in September 1905, Japan's outstanding borrowing totaled 1,870 million yen of which 970 million yen was held abroad.[75]

The Russo-Japanese War marked the one time Japan paid for its wars with foreign borrowing. Japan financed its other modern wars—the Sino-Japanese War, World War I, and World War II—from domestic taxation and borrowing. Except for bonds issued in 1923 to fund earthquake recovery and conversions of Russo-Japanese War bonds, the central government did not issue any other overseas bonds until after World War II. In an address to the Bank of Japan Club's banquet on January 24, 1905, Takahashi Korekiyo—then vice governor of the Bank of Japan and Japan's chief loan negotiator in London—argued that Japan could finance the Russo-Japanese War on its own. Maintaining the gold standard simultaneously, however, left "no alternative" but to borrow abroad.[76] "Concerning the war, Japan has sufficient ability to pay its military expenses internally. However, reliance on foreign markets for borrowing is for the sake of preserving the currency convertibility system. It is a custom of warring states that their purchases of foreign goods are great during wartime. If the Bank of Japan uses up its hard currency reserves to pay for these amounts the end point will be that it will destroy the basis of a convertible currency system. Accordingly, we wish to borrow the money from abroad to purchase foreign goods."[77]

The result was continual gold outflows and a constant battle to refill Bank of Japan specie reserves. Even with enormous amounts of foreign loans—the bulk to pay for the Russo-Japanese War, but those in 1897 and 1899 to replenish gold reserves—Bank of Japan reserves relative to the number of convertible notes declined by half between 1897 and 1914.[78] Still, no one seriously considered going off the gold standard prior to September 1917 when the United States prohibited gold exports, which changed the situation completely.

If gold made foreign borrowing obligatory, it did not in Japan's case necessarily make it any cheaper. Initially interest rates on bonds fell after 1897, but they had been trending downward before Japan adopted gold. Bond yields at issue fell from 9.2% (nominal interest of 9%) in 1870 to 7.6% (nominal interest, 7%) in 1873 at a time when investors knew little about Japan or its finances.[79] By 1897 yields at issue had fallen to 4.9% (nominal interest, 5%). The 1899 offering went off at a 4.4% yield and 4% nominal interest rate. Thereafter, yields at issue ranged from 6.6% to 4.2%. Interest rates reacted to a range of political and economic factors in addition to gold. Enactment of the Anglo-Japanese Alliance in 1902 decreased interest rates and eased access to borrowing in London.[80] The British government also at times made its preference for Japanese borrowing known to London financial houses. Increased investor interest in overseas lending, the expanding British economy of the late 1890s and early 1900s, and the vicissitudes of the Russo-Japanese War also played into interest rate calculations.[81]

Whatever the interest rate, by 1914 Japan faced a daunting debt burden. The outbreak of World War I produced an unexpected export boom that turned Japan from a net debtor to net creditor. In response to foreign demand, Japan's trade balance went from a deficit of 706.5 million yen in 1908–13 to a surplus of 1,197.5 million in 1914–19. Its balance in invisibles went from minus 435.9 million yen in 1908–13 to plus 1827.5 million in 1914–19.[82] By 1915 the current accounts surplus was more than 200 million yen. The current accounts surplus peaked at 1 billion yen in 1917 and totaled 3 billion yen from 1915 to 1919.[83] By the beginning of 1920 Japan had become a creditor nation of 2.77 billion yen.[84] Outstanding foreign debt (both public and private) as a percentage of GNP decreased from a peak of 41.8% in 1910 to 10.2% by 1920. During the same period, Japan's gold reserves increased from 472 million yen to 2,179 million.[85] The export boom had broader effects as well, pushing GNP growth rates to an average 3.3% per year following the gold-induced slump of the late 1890s and early 1900s.[86] From 1910 to 1920 real net domestic product increased 61.5%.[87] Between 1914 and 1918 alone Japan's gross national product increased by 40%, for an average annual growth rate of almost 9%.[88]

All of that, however, came after the gold standard had ceased to exist as even a partial world system, having been suspended in Europe and Argentina in 1914 and in the United States and Japan in 1917. If war treasuries and military expansion partly fueled the adoption of gold in the late nineteenth century by countries such as Germany, Russia, and Japan, it was those same great power priorities that ultimately led to the demise of the gold standard with the outbreak of World War I. The connection between nineteenth-century great power politics, empire building, and militarism and the gold standard was obscured after World War I in the rush to reinstate the form of the gold standard while ignoring its substance and the varied rationales and motivations that had supported it. Despite the rose-colored hues of nostalgia that flourished after the war, the gold standard did not exist in some magical land separate from the rest of the late nineteenth-century world. For better or worse, the gold standard was as much a part of the age of empire as it was of the age of industry.

Epilogue

The Rules of Globalization

Prominent in the market euphoria of the late twentieth and early twenty-first century was a line of thinking that found the years before World War I analogous to the present. In this view, the turn of the twentieth century marked an earlier age of market dominance and laissez-faire triumph. The 1990s and early 2000s meant a hundred-year delayed return to a past of laissez-faire, neoclassical economics, and English liberal ideals.

This is a story with immense appeal for those who prefer that governments not take an explicit role in the economy. In practice, this reluctance comes down to opposition to government undertaking the sort of explicit industrial promotion role common to the second nineteenth century of List, Pellegrini, and Matsukata. It also usually means opposition to social welfare expenditures associated in the United States and Britain with the years after World War II: pensions, health insurance, unemployment compensation, disability payments, and so on. Yet lost in the search for laissez-faire triumph is the fact that these sorts of expenditures and government roles have their roots in the second nineteenth century rather than emerging out of nowhere after World War II. That, however, is an issue for another book.

Far less criticized in the market triumphalist story have been late nineteenth-century-style military expenditures of the kind Matsukata so diligently pursued. Economic critiques of these expenditures rarely, if ever, appear in present-day financial debates. It would seem that, in much market-triumph thinking, military expenditures involve no government spending, raise no issues of government size and scope, require no economic choices, and carry no economic consequences. That, too, however, is an issue for another book.

The Anglo laissez-faire triumph story also has immense appeal for those members of English-language audiences who prefer to see an idealized view of English history at the center of the world's past and present. Whether by reason of habit or simple lack of curiosity, it remains a fact of life that many people raised in the UK or its former colonies have difficulty seeing the world without an English institutional and ideological heritage at its base.

But the years before World War I were hardly an age of unfettered liberal economics and one-world, one-market harmony even regarding something so central to English economic liberalism as the gold standard. Nor was British influence anywhere near as strong as a mere listing of countries that adopted ostensibly British institutions might imply. Britain was indeed a powerful country. But it was not the only one, and it held a monopoly on neither institutions nor ideas.

The years before World War I were a period of industrial promotion, protectionism, empire, and massive government expenditures rooted in a very different conception of the world than that dominant a century later. It was a worldview that looked not to Britain but to the European continent and North America for its ideological models even as it borrowed, and reworked, institutions from Britain.

For advocates of the gold standard, globalization enthusiasts, and fin de siècle nostalgists, the favorable and stable world economy was cut short by the outbreak of World War I. But this economic tale of an Anglo paradise lost has always existed uncomfortably with the politics of the late nineteenth-century world and the chronology of the years before World War I.

Adoption of the gold standard in the 1890s was facilitated by new gold discoveries and declining worldwide interest rates. After twenty years of deflation in the wake of Germany's and France's abandonment of silver and bimetallism, respectively, the 1890s ushered in a new period of worldwide economic growth. Economies boomed as countries expanded industrial and military endeavors. Military expenditures were sustainable for countries whose military efforts remained colonial conflicts or hypothetical great power strategizing. The financial burdens were heavier for states that engaged in evenly matched warfare. By World War I Japan was facing a potential debt crisis from its Russo-Japanese War debts. Russia's teetering government found itself financially strapped as well.

Despite the ex post facto image of the prewar World War I world economy as an Eden of liberal prosperity, by 1913 the twentieth century was already being described by observers as an era of large state wars and economic instability.[1] The development of not only great power arms races but also state welfare policies meant to deal with the defects of midcentury liberalism made even professed liberals such as David Lloyd George and Joseph Caillaux less advocates of eighteenth-century English economic liberalism than advocates of a different, and increasingly statist, turn in economic management.

European countries abandoned the gold standard with the outbreak of World War I as combatant countries sought to horde their gold reserves to pay the enormous costs of the war. The war was less disastrous for those countries positioned to profit from it. The United States was a special case due to its size, relatively unopposed territorial expansion, linguistic and colonial ties to English financial markets, and rapid industrialization. Both Japan and Argentina were far more dependent on world markets and international conditions beyond their direct control. Nonetheless, after the initial shock of the war on global finance and trade, they both adapted during the war.

In Argentina the abandonment of gold convertibility in 1914 resulted not from the peso's instability or a lack of gold reserves, but from the fact that Britain had blocked gold exports. After a panic because of the outbreak of war, the Argentine economy turned to supplying Allied forces with beef, wool, and grains. Reduced imports of British capital and capital goods put downward pressure on the economy. But, simultaneously, this decline in British imports translated into record trade surpluses and protected domestic industries from foreign competition. The surplus reached $200 to $300 million during these years, an amount not repeated until the 1940s.

In Japan the change was more dramatic. Although Argentina's economy remained centered on cattle and grain exports, in Japan textiles and raw silk were joined in the war years by a burst of heavy industry. Government finances reversed course dramatically due to the wartime export boom. In 1914 massive debt outstanding from the Russo-Japanese War had weighed on the economy. But by 1919 Japan had been transformed into a net creditor—and was willing to use its new financial strength as a political and diplomatic tool, particularly in China.

Unlike the devastated European economies, Japan and Argentina entered the 1920s with flush reserves. For both countries, though, the situation quickly changed. In Argentina the balance of payments began to deteriorate. But the worst came with the fall in the terms of trade in the years following the war. In 1923 the peso's value fell to 330 pesos per dollar versus the official, now suspended, convertibility rate of 227 established by Law 3871. Interest group battles increased with importers pressuring the government for a return to the gold standard at the old 227 rate. Simultaneously, the government saw the cost of servicing its external debts in pesos rise until it subjected its debt payments to a preferential exchange rate.

Beginning in 1924 recovery in the prices of agricultural and cattle products improved the terms of trade at the same time that it underscored the Argentine economy's continuing reliance on global primary product prices. With the increase in the value of the dollar, exporters could sell overseas in more favorable conditions, and domestic prices inevitably reflected these higher overseas prices as well. Here the depreciation of the peso was associated with higher food prices, which aroused the opposition of parties most interested in workers' living conditions, especially the Socialist Party.

In Japan the war boom that had so dramatically changed the structure of the Japanese economy grew into a bubble at war's end, finally bursting in 1920. The exchange rate fluctuated throughout the 1920s as governments intermittently sought to prop up the yen. Increased imports to rebuild after the 1923 earthquake and the effects of the 1927 financial panic pushed the yen in the opposite direction. Deflation, however, was not a serious, economy-wide problem until governments in the mid-1920s began to adopt deflation as official policy in order to force a return to the gold standard at the by then overvalued prewar rate.

The government of the Minseitō party and its financial leader Inoue Junnosuke made deflation a national priority upon taking office in mid-1929. They instigated anticonsumption campaigns, police suasion, and public denunciations of trading firms choosing to purchase dollars rather than yen.[2] This deflation compounded the distress in Japan's agricultural sector, floundering under the price declines from the worldwide overproduction that affected Argentina as well. It was this economic distress among farmers that supplied the bulk of the recruits to Japan's right wing associations and fueled the military coups, political instability, and popular fever for military expansion in Manchuria and China that overtook Japan in the 1930s.[3]

Gold Standard Orthodoxy

Reactivating the gold standard was treated as the preeminent global economic issue of the 1920s. But the nature of the return, and its effects, played out differently according to whether countries emphasized stabilizing exchange rates or deflating their economies in order to return to the prewar exchange rate. In the most extreme cases, such as Japan, returning to the gold standard became a means to achieve an independently valued policy of inducing recessions.

In Germany and France, most directly affected by the war, paying off wartime debts and digging out of the rubble of warfare and hyperinflation, took precedence. In Argentina, although returning to the gold standard was a priority for the Socialist Party and the banking industry, no government pushed the issue as long as the exchange rate remained below the prewar level.

For the United States, the issue was simple. It could have the gold standard, the prewar exchange rate, and an expanding economy with no particular hardship. Flush with revenue and assets from World War I, the United States found sustaining convertibility relatively easy. Quickly reactivating the U.S. gold standard at the prewar exchange rate provided a further impetus to the wartime shift of global financial activity from London to New York.

For Britain the calculations were more complicated.[4] Much was made of the government's new policy of allowing foreign exchange reserves to be counted along with gold as backing for the gold standard: a "gold exchange standard" rather than the presumably purer gold standard used prior to World War I. But outside of Britain using foreign exchange reserves to supplement gold reserves was nothing new. Countries as diverse as Belgium, Bulgaria, Finland, Italy, Russia, Austria, Denmark, Greece, Norway, Portugal, Romania, Spain, Sweden, and Japan had followed the practice prior to World War I.[5]

More significant for Britain was the issue of returning to the gold standard at the prewar exchange rate. As in Japan and other countries, this meant deflating the domestic economy back to the prewar price level, which meant industrial and commercial stagnation, unemployment, and labor unrest. English advocates believed returning to the gold standard at the prewar rate offered a way to reassert the supremacy of the City of London over Wall Street. But this practical desire to regain English financial preeminence coexisted with a general fixation on World War I, the future of the British Empire, and fears of the end of a supposedly uniquely English era.[6] Despite the countervailing pressure of an increasingly powerful labor movement and the critiques of John Maynard Keynes and others, the desire to return to the gold standard at the prewar exchange rate proved dominant.[7]

Taken to its extreme, this preference for deflating the economy meant inducing a depression. In both Japan and Britain it reflected a consensus or orthodox view, a "gold standard ideology"[8] or "gold standard mentality."[9] This gold standard ideology existed worldwide among financial, political, and media figures who took pride in being associated with what they took to be the most respectable and soundest views of Wall Street and the City of London.[10]

Among academic economists the trend away from beliefs in the value of the gold standard and its benefits was already noticeable in the 1890s.[11] In the interwar period economic theory was in flux, with various theories competing against each other and no dominant orthodoxy in control.[12] Economists such as Gustav Cassel, Irving Fisher, and John Maynard Keynes readily discussed the defects and limitations of the gold standard. Their critiques would be instrumental in the development of a new monetary orthodoxy after World War II. But others such as Joseph Schumpeter, Friedrich von Hayek, and Lionel Robbins remained advocates of the full orthodox trio of gold standard supremacy, prewar exchange rates, and deflation.

Although gold standard orthodoxy was sharply challenged in all countries, it remained the dominant guide to government action. It was also inevitably referred to by its supporters, and a sympathetic daily press, as sound opinion. Underlying this orthodoxy was a belief that governments in the prewar years had remained hands-off observers of the world economy. In this view, governments were believed to have let the gold standard work its automatic ways as described in eighteenth-century liberal theory.

Governments, it was argued, had refused to tamper with the market's natural rhythms by devaluing their exchange rates.

This orthodoxy came to be known most commonly as part of the consensus thinking among employees of the British Treasury and the Bank of England in the 1920s.[13] It had its official expression in Britain's Cunliffe Commission report of 1919 and that report's establishment of the idea that certain "rules of the game" rooted in eighteenth-century English theory had controlled the prewar workings of the gold standard. In this view, governments had refrained from intervening in financial markets to prevent the otherwise natural inflows and outflows of gold that would quickly and smoothly adjust prices to match the level of gold.

That was not what the prewar gold standard—or the prewar world economy—had been. The global gold standard emerged in the 1890s as states sought to lock in devalued exchange rates and intervened in trade flows through protective tariffs. Even in Britain, the lone island of global free trade, the gold standard was hardly left untouched. The Bank of England regularly adjusted interest rates to control flows of gold into and out of England.[14] In countries that adopted gold standards in the 1890s, the true believers in gold standard orthodoxy stood at the margins. The laissez-faire believers in "true and universal money" and the deductive certainties of English theory were sideshows except where they overlapped with the more concrete interests of importers, bankers, or merchants. The main stage belonged to the Pellegrinis and Matsukatas who were intent on using the gold standard for their own industrial and military purposes.

March of Folly

Looking back at the 1920s and the return to the gold standard, the obvious question is why did so many countries insist on inducing depressions in order to return to the gold standard at overvalued exchange rates? And why in the 1930s did the most steadfast gold supporters remain adamant in their support for the gold standard and prewar exchange rates, and why did they insist that continued deflation was unavoidable and would eventually cleanse economies of their unhealthy excesses?

The key issue remained devaluation or the lack thereof. Germany and France were so devastated by the war and ensuing inflation that the old exchange rate remained beyond the recommendation of even the most avid advocates of prewar exchange rates. But elsewhere governments consistently refused to reinstate the gold standard at a devalued exchange rate roughly reflecting the prevailing market rate and the underlying state of the economy. States had devalued as a matter of course at the turn of the century. They did not do so in the 1920s.

This refusal to consider what even opponents at the time regarded as the simplest, easiest, and most realistic solution extended beyond political and financial communities. The mass media and, through them, public opinion in general reflected this view as well. In effect, all these groups looked at the facts, acknowledged that devaluation would be the easiest way to stabilize the economy, that returning to the prewar exchange rate would at the very least cause a recession, very likely a financial panic, and perhaps a depression, and then freely and unabashedly chose the latter course of action.

It was this that made these gold enthusiasts seem such dreamers and fanatics to their critics.[15] For most of the 1920s, however, it was these dreamers and fanatics who were most widely regarded as embodying serious and sound opinion. Even in Argentina, where no government attempts were made to return to the gold standard until the exchange rate had recovered to its prewar level in 1927, devaluation was considered out of the question, as was any ultimate refusal to return to the gold standard.

There was nothing to prevent a government from reactivating the gold standard at an exchange rate different from that used prior to World War I. In Japan's case the exchange rate had been in effect for twenty years. In Argentina's case, the prewar exchange rate nominally lasted fifteen years, although actual gold conversion lasted barely more than a decade. These were standard periods of time for fixed exchange rate regimes. They were slightly less than the quarter century of the Bretton Woods system after World War II, slightly more than the scant decade-long currency board in Argentina in the 1990s and the European Monetary System of the 1980s. There was no particular sense or logic in assuming that an exchange rate that roughly reflected the relative state of an economy in 1914 should be the same a decade later, even without the changes brought about by World War I.

If advocates for reinstating prewar exchange rates were in essence the hard money supporters of the 1890s who benefited from appreciating currencies and deflation, several new elements had been added to the mix in the 1920s. First were claims that saving, suffering, and retrenchment reflected and promoted national and individual character. Second was the idea that the exchange rate served as a proxy for national worth and value, with currency devaluation being tantamount to devaluing national honor and status. Finally, there was the idea of competitive trade benefits to be obtained by deflating economies through liquidation and rationalization. These were by no means the only views at the time, nor did they always prevail. But they existed in all countries. They prevailed in Japan and England, and at least rhetorically in the United States. In Argentina, they ultimately gave way to more practical considerations.

STATUS AND MORAL CHARACTER

Although status arguments had existed in the 1890s, they were far more influential in the 1920s. Gold standard supporters had linked currency metals to stages of civilization in the 1890s, but currency decisions rested on more concrete concerns of export promotion, industrial development, and foreign loans. But in the 1920s currency became much more an indicator of moral value. In particular, an idea took hold that a more appreciated or stronger currency was a symbol of national worth.

As in the 1890s there was concern in Japan about being lumped with the world's losers rather than its winners. Even the otherwise skeptical vice governor of the Bank of Japan Fukai Eigo argued that it would be useful to adopt the prewar exchange rate in order to avoid the damage to Japanese self-esteem in being associated with the devaluing countries of Germany, France, and Italy.[16] And status arguments became far more widely circulated in the 1920s than they had been in the 1890s. The main Tokyo and Osaka newspapers, in particular, stressed the loss of national honor that would result from failure to return to the gold standard at the prewar exchange rate.

In Argentina, a similar emphasis on national honor marked a shift from the 1890s when even the gold standard's most fervent supporters argued from what they considered to be universal economic truths, not questions of status, image, and honor.[17] Opponents of Pellegrini's conversion plans in the 1890s had argued that devaluing the peso's exchange rate with gold amounted to robbery. They argued that only a 1:1 paper to gold exchange rate was truly money. But they made no link between currency and national honor. Foreign opinion mattered to the extent that it affected borrowing rates in London. Any other opinions foreigners might hold were considered irrelevant.

Status concerns went much further in Japan than they did in Argentina. In Japan they morphed into questions of moral character and willpower. They became part of a more general critique of a society viewed as suffering from corrosive and "ever more shallow" "modern social conditions." Hard work and character were seen as having been subverted by the boom years of World War I, the free-spending ways of a new class of wealthy businessmen, and the corrupting influences of mass urban consumption. This social corruption was contrasted with the supposedly simpler, agrarian virtues of rural Japan. Repeatedly, Japan's main newspapers, Diet members, and government officials argued that failing to make the effort necessary to return to the prewar exchange rate was synonymous with weak national character. It meant an inability to endure hardship that risked subverting all of Japanese society. In this view, devaluation would result in "people running away, avoiding all difficulty and easily giving up," and would undermine "the habit of enduring difficulty."[18]

LIQUIDATION

The most forthright argument in favor of the prewar exchange rate accepted that reinstating the gold standard at the old exchange rate would cause deflation. This, it was argued, was a good thing because it would promote the economy's "liquidation" and thereby establish its future health.[19] The most fervent proponents of the prewar exchange rate argued that a depression ought to be welcomed. This stemmed in part from a general consensus that inflation was fundamentally unhealthy and deflation a cleansing process. This latter view predominated among bankers, urban journalists, newspaper owners, and others who gained under deflation and suffered losses under inflation.

As expressed in mass circulation magazines and newspapers in the 1920s, this was essentially a matter of common sense. It was discussed less in terms of evidence and economic practicalities than it was in terms of moral arguments and analogies. Economists such as Keynes in Britain and Ishibashi Tanzan and other devaluation advocates in Japan ridiculed liquidationism. But liquidationism remained the dominant economic theory of governments in the 1920s. It was supported in particular by the U.S. treasury secretary Andrew Mellon, the Bank of England's Montague Norman, and economists such as Joseph Schumpeter, Friedrich von Hayek, and Lionel Robbins. Like Inoue Junnosuke in Japan, Robbins would argue at the height of the Great Depression that the greatest economic danger the world faced was inflation and that the only way out of the Depression was more deflation, not less, the "sharp purge" rather than the "lingering disease."[20]

Although liquidation was a distinct concept from gold standard orthodoxy, liquidation and gold standard supporters almost inevitably overlapped. The two concepts ultimately blurred into one idea that reached its height in Japan where liquidation and returning to the gold standard came to serve as rationales for each other.

"Rationalization" (*gōrika*) provided an industrial spin to liquidationism by adding an element of industrial promotion. Through the general economic purge of deflation and their own belt-tightening, individual industries and companies would become newly "rationalized." Industrial promotion in the 1890s had centered on increasing exports and economic growth through inflating the economy and depreciating the currency. Liquidation and rationalization took the opposite tack. They emphasized reducing export prices through domestic deflation, mass campaigns to restrict consumption, and forcing "uncompetitive" industries and firms out of business.

Typical of liquidationist and rationalization arguments, prohibiting gold exports or reinstating the gold standard at a devalued exchange rate was seen as allowing uncompetitive industries—artificial industries in 1890s parlance—to survive. They should be left to die what was viewed as a natural and inevitable death. In this view, the World War I boom for countries like Japan and Argentina had been a curse rather than a benefit. For liquidationists, that boom and the devalued exchange rates it brought acted "like a greenhouse in which industries have been protected and are unprepared for the cold winds of international competition."[21]

According to liquidationists, "In order to forge the strength to compete internationally," it was necessary to reinstate the gold standard at a rate that would produce economic contraction, business failures, and unemployment. In this view, the purpose of reinstating the gold standard at the prewar exchange rate was not to stabilize the exchange rate, aid industry, promote commerce, clean up bad loans, or any other independent goal. At its most extreme, as it was practiced in Japan, the purpose of reinstating the gold standard was to provide an independent excuse for deflating the economy back to its prewar level.[22]

The liquidationist argument, however, could only exist by assuming that the prewar price level, and the prewar exchange rate, reflected a natural, true state of the economy around which all other aspects of society were to adjust. This was something that neither Matsukata, Pellegrini, nor anyone else involved in setting the 1890s exchange rates ever claimed.

Devaluation supporters saw lifting the gold embargo as simply a matter of stabilizing the exchange rate. But liquidationists viewed stabilizing the exchange rate as, at best, a secondary concern. In accepting that the prewar exchange rate was natural, they viewed any economic growth under another exchange rate as artificial and representing "a false balance sheet."[23] The economy's true state could only be seen at the prewar exchange rate, and the success or failure of individual businesses and industries could only be judged at that rate.

Liquidationists accepted that devaluing the exchange rate would be relatively easy and painless. For liquidationists this was precisely the problem. Accepting the existing market price level and exchange rate would merely perpetuate the "false balance sheet" and allow companies that would otherwise fail at the "natural" prewar exchange rate to remain inefficiently in business. Liquidationist arguments ostensibly emphasized the need to reduce production costs. But they most often boiled down to ideological, almost mystical arguments of moral fortitude. Enduring the suffering that would result from reinstating the gold standard at the prewar exchange rate would "produce the strength to unblock the economy and the birth of a constructive will." This overarching need to reawaken a vanished moral will could not, for the most extreme liquidationists, be forgone "simply in order to obtain exchange market stability."[24]

Gold and the Rules of Globalization

The liquidationist creed vanished from prominence by the mid-1930s as its de facto centerpiece, the gold standard, was abandoned worldwide.[25] The Argentine government went off the gold standard almost immediately after the 1929 Wall Street crash as gold outflows from Argentina increased. This reflected the continuing marginal political influence that hard money and deflation advocates held in Argentina. The Great Depression proved as devastating for Argentina as it did for most other countries as the economy remained—despite the efforts of Carlos Pellegrini and other industrial developmentalists in the 1890s—overwhelmingly dependent on exports.

If Argentina was exceptionally early in abandoning the gold standard, others eventually followed suit. As production and trade declined, unemployment increased, banks failed, and traders rushed to sell off currency from countries they believed unable to support their gold standard exchange rates; governments reacted by cutting back expenditures in order to prop up their exchange rates. This deepened the Depression and made financial systems even more fragile. Faced with further deflating their economies or abandoning the gold standard entirely, those countries that abandoned gold either de facto or de jure in 1931 or 1932, such as Britain and Germany, gained the freedom to reflate their economies without having to worry about supporting an overvalued exchange rate.

Slower to recover were countries such as the United States and France, which sought to use their massive gold reserves to sustain the gold standard even as it meant pursuing fiscal and monetary policies that worsened the Depression. Even these countries, however, could not withstand the perpetual downward spiral of deflation that supporting the gold standard without devaluation entailed. The United States finally abandoned the system in 1933; France, the last holdout, followed in 1936.

In Japan, meanwhile, the Great Depression was both homegrown and a reflection of worldwide disaster. The silk industry was devastated by a decline in demand from the United States and the Minseitō government insisted on even greater deflation to support the gold standard it had insisted on reinstating in January 1930 despite the U.S. stock market crash three months earlier.[26] The finance minister Inoue Junnosuke continued to support the liquidationist line—even when Britain was forced off the gold standard in September 1931 and nearly simultaneously Japanese troops revolted in Manchuria, giving vent to the economic devastation at home.

Only with the fall of the Minseitō government in December 1931 was the gold standard finally abandoned. The expansionary Seiyūkai regime of Takahashi Korekiyo, which shifted to inflationary measures, expanded domestic spending, and pursued a policy of letting the exchange rate fall freely, produced a rapid expansion of exports.[27] It was only then that the economy recovered.

Until Inoue's assassination in February 1932, he remained a fierce critic of Japan's departure from the gold standard as the country spiraled into militarism at home and abroad. But if Inoue was particularly stubborn in his views, he was hardly unique in his obsession with liquidation and the self-image he had constructed for himself as the courageous bearer of scientific truth. In accepting the gold standard orthodoxy and liquidation ideas wholeheartedly, Inoue had moved beyond merely pursuing his own personal interests or those of the banking community he had been nurtured by and trained to represent. He had become hostage to an abstract idea that had become wrapped in layers of historical confusion.

In this Inoue was as much a product of his time as Matsukata and Pellegrini had been of theirs. The difference was that both the gold standard orthodoxy idea and Inoue explicitly looked back to the years before World War I for support, with the Cunliffe Commission seeing apolitical automaticity where none had existed and Inoue repeatedly likening himself and his policies to Matsukata Masayoshi.[28]

This tendency to publicly, albeit unconsciously, rewrite the past so that its presumed highlights became a tale of continuity to the present occurred again at the turn of the twenty-first century. From Milton and Rose Friedman's 1980 TV and literary reimagining of Meiji Japan as a free-market, laissez-faire land of Reaganomics to post-1989 Washington consensus triumphalism, Anglo-American opinion came to embrace the turn of the twentieth century as an easily identifiable reflection of its own market triumphalism, ideas of globalization, and repudiation of the post-Depression, midcentury Keynesian years.

But despite global trade, international finance, and people traversing the globe, the beginning of the twentieth century was not the same as the start of the twenty-first. It was, in the parlance of the time, a globalized era but with characteristics, principles, and ideas different from the globalized laissez-faire triumphalism that defined the early twenty-first century. Neither era had a monopoly on the definition of globalization. Nor, for that matter, did the midcentury Keynesian years of Bretton Woods, GATT, multinationals, and an endless series of UN and other public and private international organizations lack global content. They were simply different kinds of global activity, based on different views of the world.

In essence, the neoliberal tale of global market triumphalism was the same tale told by the liquidationists of the 1920s and 1930s and the pre–World War I believers in a Platonic "true and universal money" based on gold. Believers in true and universal money and their descendants rarely found themselves at home outside the deductive certainties of theory, preferring a tidier view of the world that turned economics—and social relations in general—into a morality play of black and white, good and evil, and the triumph of human willpower.[29]

It is not at all coincidental that probably the most revered advocate of late twentieth- and early twenty-first-century market triumphalism—the U.S. Federal Reserve chairman Alan Greenspan—was raised on the super-hero fantasies of the über-laissez-faire theorist and novelist Ayn Rand. Like Rand, Greenspan advocated the gold standard as "the protector of property rights" and argued that "gold and economic freedom are inseparable."[30] Like civilizationists and true and universal money advocates, Greenspan argued that only commodities could be true money and that gold was best suited for "more civilized societies." [31] Nor is it coincidental that both the treasury and liquidationist views bubbled back to the surface along with the market triumphalism of the late-twentieth century.[32]

It was not, of course, all ideology. Hard money and deflation advocates overwhelmingly came from groups and institutions that benefited from hard money and deflation or individuals who wished to be included in such groups. But there is a difference between believing in ideologies that not so coincidentally favor one's own interests and conscious cynicism. For better or worse, it is a common feature of history for individuals to adopt—and, indeed, believe—ideas that put their own interests and ex-istences in the most favorable light. There is nothing inconsistent about being both an ideologue and self-interested.

There is, however, a practical danger in becoming prisoners to the ideo-logical certainties and historical unawareness of a given age. If an obses-sion with narrowly defined rules of global conduct in the 1920s led to economic disaster and, with it, a turn toward economic autarchy and yet more war in the 1930s and 1940s, this was in part the work of the most fervent advocates of 1920s internationalism and the sound, sensible, and scientific views they believed they were following. That these presumed rules of global conduct were not without their own internal logic only increased the divide between those most fervently intent on recapturing an imaginary prewar past and an interwar present stubbornly refusing to accept the belle époque of their collective imagination.

Notes

Introduction: Pasts Imperfect

1. The idea of a market triumphalist past—and its reemergence—was a staple of late twentieth- and early twentieth-first-century Anglo-American society. The trend was kicked off in the late 1970s reaction to oil shocks and inflation combined with ongoing opposition from various sectors of society to New Deal–Great Society programs in the United States and the British welfare state. Its most successful early mass popularization came in M. Friedman and Friedman (1980) and the accompanying TV series that, for their historical examples, selected Meiji era Japan as an exemplar of free market, laissez-faire virtues. For an updated version of the Friedman series attuned to globalization ideas of the 1990s, see Yergin and Stanislaw (1998) and the accompanying 2002 TV series. For other works placing liberal market economics at the center of the late nineteenth-century world, see Frieden (2006), Ferguson (2001, 2003, 2005, 2006, 2009), Lindsey (2001), James (2001), O'Rourke and Williamson (1999), Bordo, Taylor, and Williamson (2003), and Findlay and O'Rourke (2008). For blunter and more popular accounts, see in particular the *Washington Post* and *Wall Street Journal* editorial and op-ed pages, *Time, Newsweek, U.S. News & World Report, Forbes, Business Week,* and much of late twentieth- and early twenty-first-

century cable news programming in the United States. For public policy and political arguments, see Zoellick (2002).

2. The popular version of the brave new world theme can be found in journalistic accounts such as T. Friedman (1999, 2005) and in a steady stream of op-ed pieces, particularly at publications such as the *Washington Post* and various weekly business and general interest magazines. For scholarly studies, see Lawrence, Bressand, and Ito (1996), Zevin (1992), Sachs and Warner (1995), and Baldwin and Martin (1999). Bordo, Eichengreen, and Irwin (1999) provide an early summary of the two views while choosing to fall on the brave new world side.

3. For works drawing on the Pax Britannica and British hegemony tradition, the classic account is Kindleberger (1973). For later works developing the theme, see Gilpin (1987), P. Kennedy (1987), Landes (1998), Ferguson (2001, 2003, 2005, 2006, 2009), and Arrighi (2009). See also Soros (1998) who argues that turn-of-the-century globalization was based on Britain providing open markets, a stable monetary system (the gold standard), and an ideological consensus based on English liberalism. Eichengreen (1987b) and others have undercut the idea that Britain held a hegemonic position in international finance, although they have tended to keep the focus on Britain and English-language sources.

4. The classic theory of economic "late developers" being more state-centric is Gerschenkron (1962). Gerschenkron argued that countries such as Germany and Russia that industrialized after Britain had to rely more on centralized action and institutions (large banks or governments) than laissez-faire policies in order to industrialize.

5. There was, of course, one more nineteenth-century model: communism, as initially discussed by Karl Marx and Friedrich Engels. But until the twentieth century communism was an intellectual doctrine, not a governing one. Not until the Russian revolution of 1917 did a government attempt to establish communism in practice.

6. By the late nineteenth century, immigration was changing as well, with an increase in immigration restrictions worldwide that would continue after the turn of the century. See, for example, Goldin (1994) and McKeown (2008).

7. Historical scholarship has been an entirely different story; much work has extensively reevaluated the idea of British hegemony, financially and otherwise. For a summary of these trends related to the gold standard and British historiography, see Balachandran (2008).

8. Schumpeter 1994: 382.

9. Over the past thirty years a consensus view has emerged among economists and economic historians linking the gold standard and the Great Depression. The most developed synthesis of this view is Eichengreen (1992). For similar views, see Eichengreen and Temin (1997), Temin (1989), Bernanke and James (1991), Choudhri and Kochin (1980), Eichengreen (1984), Eichengreen and Sachs (1985), James (2001), and J. Hamilton (1987, 1988). The gold standard argument has

complemented work emphasizing Keynesian, demand-side views (Temin, 1976), debt deflation aspects of the Depression (Fisher, 1933; Bernanke, 1983; Bernanke and Gertler, 1990; Mishkin 1978), asymmetric information (Mishkin 1997), and those emphasizing the Depression as a monetary phenomenon (M. Friedman and Schwartz, 1963). For a representative synthesis view, see Romer (1992). For a comparison of gold standard arguments with other theories of the Depression, see Bernanke (1995). Related to the gold standard theory of the Depression is the idea of a monetary "trilemma" as developed by Robert Mundell (see principally 1960, 1961a, 1961b, 1961c, 1962, 1963, 1968) and J. M. Fleming (1962) in which governments can choose only two out of three objectives among fixed exchange rates, capital mobility, and independent monetary policy. For additional accounts of the worldwide return to the gold standard in the interwar period, see Simmons (1994) and Mouré (1991, 2002).

   10. On this point, see Bloomfield (1959, 1963), de Cecco (1974, 1996, 1997), Michie (1986), Triffin (1997), and Eichengreen (1987a, 1992). In particular, Eichengreen and Michie emphasize various ways in which the Bank of England managed the system so as to limit its need for actually using gold in its transactions. See also Lindert (1969), who emphasizes not only the British pound sterling but also the French franc and German mark as key currencies around which the pre–World War I gold standard functioned. The idea that governments and central banks refrained from interfering with financial flows came to be referred to in the 1920s as their following certain gold standard "rules of the game." The concept seems to have first gained prominence in 1919 in the British Cunliffe Commission report; it was summarized by Keynes (1925) using the term "rules of the game" and then adopted by Nurkse (1944) in an influential work arguing that the interwar gold standard had failed, in contrast to the turn-of-the-century gold standard, in part due to the failure of governments in the 1920s to follow these presumed rules of the game. Bloomfield (1959) and later works gradually chipped away at the rules of the game idea, while other works continued to appear based on Nurkse's attempt to determine whether governments in the 1920s had followed the rules of the game. For a rules-of-the-game argument on the gold standard in Japan, see Teranishi and Uchino (1986). In the twenty-first century (see, for example, Flandreau, Holtfrerich, and James 2003) the idea of rules of the game has been treated as a historical artifact rather than as a valuable line of economic inquiry. Sterilization means the actions of central banks or some similar institution preventing gold or other money flows from continuing on into the domestic economy. For example, to prevent inflation, central banks could "sterilize" the effect of gold inflows on the amount of money in circulation by selling securities in the domestic market thereby pulling money out of circulation. To prevent deflation, central banks could sterilize gold outflows by purchasing securities, thereby increasing the amount of money in circulation. In other words, by sterilizing

gold flows, governments sought to block, in whole or in part, Hume's specie flow mechanism and the presumed rules of the game.

11. That there was a late nineteenth-century backlash has been a common staple of political histories of the period. See, for example, Hobsbawm (1987) and Girault (1997). It has also featured prominently in European economic histories such as Asselain (1984). It has been less integrated into economic history studies in the United States, which have been less concerned with political factors than calculating economic losses from protectionism. One notable exception is James (2001).

12. Trying to resolve the presumed puzzle this presents of high growth coupled with factors currently associated with low growth has led to numerous studies. Bairoch (1972, 1989, 1997), Clemens and Williamson (2001), and O'Rourke (2000) support a correlation between high growth and protective tariffs, which is counterintuitive for neoclassical theory. Bértola and Williamson (2003) and Irwin (1997, 1998, 2002) argue that, although growth accompanied protective tariffs, there was no causation between protective tariffs and growth or, alternatively, that growth would have been higher without protective tariffs.

13. The primary references to the pre–World War I gold standard in Japan are the contemporary accounts published by the Japanese government under the name of Matsukata Masayoshi (Matsukata 1899 and, more briefly, Matsukata 1900), Patrick (1965), Bytheway (2001), Tamaki (1988, 1994), and the first part of Metzler (2006b). Ramseyer and Rosenbluth (1995) discuss Meiji finance and also provide a sketch of the interwar gold standard. In Japanese studies, the pre–World War I gold standard has received less attention than the return to the gold standard in the 1920s and the subsequent Depression. For discussions of the prewar gold standard, see Kojima (1981), Yūzō Yamamoto (1994), and Takemori (2006). Traditionally, Ford (1962) has been the standard reference for Argentina. Using English-language secondary sources, Ford (1962) looked at financial and goods flows between Britain and Argentina. He was not concerned with the reasons Argentines adopted the gold standard or with domestic Argentine politics or society. The key issue for Ford was how Argentina fit within the British system, not with the views and concerns of contemporary Argentine society. Ford did argue that the gold standard functioned differently in Argentina than it did in Britain. He also found, consistent with most rules-of-the-game studies, that the presumed rules did not seem to apply in Argentina. J. Williams (1920) and Díaz Alejandro (1970) are the other two main English-language works on monetary policy in Argentina, if not the gold standard per se. Della Paolera and Taylor (2001) have also discussed Argentine monetary institutions as established in the 1890s. The main sources on the gold standard's adoption in Argentina are Gallo (1996) and Llach 2007: 218–31. Post-Ford descriptions of the gold standard's functioning can be found in Della Paolera (1988) and Della Paolera and Taylor (2001). For the gold standard in Argentina in the interwar period, see Díaz Fuentes (1994, 1998).

1. The Late Nineteenth-Century World

1. There is an extensive body of literature on late nineteenth-century British decline. See, in particular, Levine (1967), Aldcroft and Richardson (1969), Landes (1969), W. Lewis (1978), Pollard (1982), Elbaum and Lazonick (1985), Crafts, Leybourne, and Mills (1989), Chandler (1990), Kirby (1992), Rubinstein (1993), Floud and McCloskey (1994), and Crafts (1997, 1998). There is little dispute about relative British decline. More in dispute has been the cause, with labor practices, capital markets and overseas investment, and cultural and class factors such as educational institutions and entrepreneurship being assigned varying degrees of blame. For labor, see Clegg, Fox, and Thompson (1964), Harley (1974), Cottrell (1980), Clegg, Fox, and Thompson (1985), A. Fox (1985), Price (1986), Lewchuck (1987), and Lazonick (1994). For capital markets and overseas investment see, Cairncross (1953), Imlah (1958), Ford (1965), Barratt Brown (1971), Fieldhouse (1973), Cottrell (1975), W. Kennedy (1976, 1987), More (1980), Edelstein (1982, 1994a, 1994b), Pollard (1985), Davis and Huttenback (1987), Michie (1987, 1988), Van Helten and Cassis (1990), Rowthorn and Solomou (1991), Offer (1993), M. Collins (1995, 1998), Watson (1996), and Cain and Hopkins (2001). For cultural factors, see McCloskey and Sandberg (1971), Sanderson (1972), Coleman (1973), Lazonick (1981), K. Williams, Williams, and Thomas (1983), Elbaum and Lazonick (1984), Coleman and Macleod (1986), Dintenfass (1988), Payne (1988), B. Collins and Robbins (1990), Foreman-Peck (1991), Pollard (1994), Broadberry (1997), Nicholas (1999), and Weiner (2004).

2. Ferguson 2001: 278–79.

3. Girault 1997: 48–49.

4. Frieden 2006: 59–60.

5. Takemori 2006: 26.

6. Frieden 2006: 59–60.

7. Bairoch 1997: 68–69.

8. In the 1890s it was the Eastern banker wing of the Democratic Party, exemplified by Grover Cleveland, that pushed hard money monetary policies and the gold standard. The economic lynchpin of the Republican Party was protective tariffs, with the Republican Rutherford Hayes' administration supporting the 1890 Sherman Silver Purchase Act in exchange for passage the same year of the protective McKinley Tariff. On the 1890 trade-off, see Eichengreen (1996: 22). For a discussion of the effects of the McKinley Tariff on promoting industrial development, see Irwin (1997).

9. Uematsu Kōshō, "Sekai sankin no taisei," Part 4, *Tōyō keizai shinpō*, September 5, 1907, 10.

10. In contrast to those such as Flandreau (1996b, 2000b, 2004) and Milward (1996) who have looked at the reasons for changes in supply and demand, another current of studies has taken supplies of silver and gold as given and then looked theoretically at

what this should mean for general price levels in a given economy. See, for example, Barro (1979).

11. Uematsu Kōshō, "Sekai sankin no taisei," Part 4, *Tōyō keizai shinpō*, September 5, 1907, 10.

12. Paul Leroy-Beaulieu, "Una nueva edad del oro, El aumente presente y próximo de la producción de ese metal y sus consecuencias," Part 1, *El Economista Argentino*, February 2, 1895, 4–5, reprint from *L'Economiste français*.

13. Ferguson 2001: 330, citing Cooper 1982: 9.

14. Takemori 2006: 57.

15. Much discussion has also focused on technological advances reducing costs. For the debate over the Great Depression, see Saul (1986) and Landes (1969). For the relation between the gold standard and prices, see Nocken (1998). For contemporary treatment of price declines, see A. De Foville, "El oro y la plata," *El Economista Argentino*, March 23, 1895, 5–6; and Paul Leroy-Beaulieu, "La agitación en favor del bimetalismo," *El Economista Argentino*, May 25, 1895, 6–7, reprint from *L'Economiste français*.

16. On bimetallism in general, see Flandreau (1996b, 1997a) and Redish (1990, 2000). On the decline of French bimetallism and the Latin Monetary Union, see Flandreau (1996b, 2000a, 2004), Einaudi (2000, 2001), and Gallarotti (1993). For debates on the nature of bimetallism in Britain, see Howe (1990) and Green (1988, 1990).

17. For the British shift to free trade, see Howe (1998), Marrison (1998), and Cain and Hopkins (2001).

18. On List and Listian national economics, see List (1841), Johnson (1967), Szporluk (1988), Senghaas (1991), Semmel (1993), Levi-Faur (1997a, 1997b), Todd (1998), Winch (1998), Harlan (1999), Helleiner (2002), and Metzler (2006a). For nationalist and protectionist trends in Europe and the United States, see Poinsard (1893), Gerschenkron (1943), Golob (1944), M. Smith (1980), Lebovics (1988), Lake (1988), and Verdier (1994).

19. For a summary of tariff rates worldwide from the mid-nineteenth century, see Williamson (2003). For critiques of protectionism that mix history and theory, see Bhagwati (1988) and Irwin (1996).

20. See Clemens and Williamson (2002) for a comparison of high tariff rates in Latin America and low tariff rates in Asia. Although they acknowledge that Asian countries were subject to colonial or semicolonial restrictions, they argue that low tariff rates in Asia reflected other factors as well.

21. The move to higher tariffs in Asia commenced with Burma, India, the Philippines, Siam, and Turkey from the late 1880s (Williamson 2003). Although the first of Japan's unequal treaties was revised in 1894, Japan did not regain full tariff autonomy until 1911.

22. Herbert A. L. Fisher, "The Protectionist Reaction in France," *Economic Journal* 6, no. 23 (Sept. 1896): 341.

23. Ullrich 1997: 92–93. See also Winkler (1997), Wehler 1995: 620–61, and Nipperdey 1992: 382–408. For an analysis of the working of the gold standard under German protectionism, see Fechter (1974).

24. Frieden 2006: 41. For a fuller survey of tariff rates, see Bairoch (1989).

25. Frieden 2006: 41.

26. Gourevitch 1986: 104. For the "apostle" reference, see Georges Michel, "Discusiones de la Sociedad de Economía Política de Paris, Es la moneda una mercancia?" *El Economista Argentino*, September 21, 1895, 3–4.

27. The figures for Mexico, Colombia, and Brazil come from Findlay and O'Rourke 2003: 51. All other figures come from Bairoch 1997: 294. For a fuller discussion of the prevalence of protective tariffs through the start of World War I, see Bairoch (1989).

28. On this point, see Kinghorn and Nye (1996).

29. American writers concerned with economic competition from Japan, China, and other countries have made virtually identical arguments since the 1980s. These have included the same invocation of "fair trade" rather than "free trade." For "fair trade" usage, see Girault 1997: 161. For a sampling of the vast Japan–China–foreign competitor fear and neo-List literature, see Tolchin (1988), Choate (1990, 2005), Thurow (1992), Prestowitz (1993), Fallows (1994), and Fingleton (1995, 2008). Most of these writers have argued, implicitly or explicitly, for the United States to adopt Listian policies. For a general List as policy guide argument, see Lind (1998).

30. Aristarco, "Retrospecto," *El Economista Argentino*, December 29, 1900, 1.

31. Listian ideas of national economics and infant-industry protection were reflected, under different names, in Latin America after World War II in dependency theory writings and in industrialized countries from the late 1970s under the rubric of "fair trade," and then strategic trade theory. For dependency theory parallels, see Gourevitch 1986: 46.

32. Oddly, Hamilton in the 1990s became something of a poster boy for proponents of free trade, free market economics. This generally rested on Hamilton's support for the banking industry and reducing government debt. Lost in this interpretation was Hamilton's equally fervent support for industrial promotion and protective tariffs. For the 1990s view of Hamilton see Brookhiser (1999), Bordo and Végh (2002), and Chernow (2004).

33. Quoted in Irwin 1996: 127.

34. On Henry Carey see Gordon 1991: 241–43, Conkin (1980), and Dawson (2000).

35. Nor has the infant-industry argument been discarded in the present day even by the most enthusiastic free traders. See, for example, Irwin (1996) and Bhagwati (1988).

36. Irwin 1996: 127, 135. This did not prevent other critics from attacking the protectionist movements of the age. The Russian sociologist Jacques Novicow called the "protectionist lunacy" of the age a "moral epidemic" that had "risen up" and "infected" "all countries" ("Teorizantes y practicones," *El Correo Español*, October 27, 1899, 1).

37. For a contemporary account of French protectionism, see Herbert A. L. Fisher, "The Protectionist Reaction in France," *Economic Journal* 6, no. 23 (Sept. 1896), 341–55. On Leroy-Beaulieu and French imperial ideology, see Leroy-Beaulieu (1874), Said (1978) and Murphy 1948: 89, 110, 136.

38. For Schmoller and the German historical school, see Bruhns (2004) and Grimmer-Solem (2003).

39. "Jiyū bōeki ka, hogo bōeki ka," Part 1, *Tōyō keizai shinpō*, January 25, 1909, 2. For the influence of List in Japan, see also Morris-Suzuki (1989) and Metzler (2006a).

40. Taussig 1905: 65 quoted in Irwin 1996: 3.

41. Irwin 1996: 225–26.

42. See, for example, Bértola and Williamson (2003), Clemens and Williamson (2001, 2002), and Irwin (1997, 1998).

43. For the link between gold production, interest rates, and adoption of the gold standard, see Flandreau, Le Cacheux, and Zumer (1998). For a contemporary description of the same phenomenon, see Ōkuma Shigenobu, "Sekaiteki kōkeiki ni tsuite," *Tōyō keizai shinpō*, February 5, 1907, 11–13.

44. Joaquin M. Ruiz, "La baja del interés del dinero," *El Economista Argentino*, January 12, 1895, 2.

45. Frieden 2006: 19.

46. "Yushutsu bōeki no shinsei," *Tōyō keizai shinpō*, April 25, 1907, 7.

47. On the expansion of cash substitutes, see Laidler (1991).

48. Ferguson 2001: 332.

49. "Yushutsu bōeki no shinsei," *Tōyō keizai shinpō*, April 25, 1907, 7.

50. "Notas," *El Economista Argentino*, October 28, 1899, 1.

51. Paul Leroy-Beaulieu, "La muerte del Mikado, El Japon y el mundo," *El Economista Argentino*, September 7, 1912, 5, reprint from *L'Economiste français*.

52. Paul Leroy-Beaulieu, "De la producción y el empleo del oro en el mundo," Part 2, *El Economista Argentino*, June 10, 1899, 6, reprint from *L'Economiste français*.

53. Hobsbawm 1987: 350.

54. Warship tonnage figures come from P. Kennedy 1987: 203.

55. Production figures come from Paul Leroy-Beaulieu, "La producción de metales preciosos en el mundo en 1911, El oro," *El Economista Argentino*, March 30, 1912, 5, reprint from *L'Economiste français*. As of 1912, 1 pound sterling equaled 25.22 francs; 1 U.S. dollar, 5.181 francs; 1 yen, 2.58 francs; and 1 German mark, 1.235 francs (Girault 1997: 41).

56. There are two basic scholarly trends about increased state presence in the late nineteenth-century world economy. One emphasizes the state as an active promoter of industrialization. Gerschenkron (1962) is the classic account. see also Chang (2002) and, for later periods, Amsden (1989, 2001). The second emphasizes the state as a reactive or complementary agent responding to the development of large-scale business enterprises. For examples of this second trend, see Sklar (1988), Chandler (1977, 1990),

and Lamoreaux (1985). Both trends emphasize the importance of size and economies of scale and scope resulting from the second Industrial Revolution of the late nineteenth century (steel, chemicals, and other heavy industry). This is contrasted with the British-centered Industrial Revolution of the late eighteenth and early nineteenth century (textiles and other light industry).

57. "Kisho: Kin to tetsu," *Tōyō keizai shinpō*, March 5, 1897, 32.

2. National and International Money

1. For interpretations of worldwide silver flows, see Pomeranz (2000), Bin Wong (1997), Flynn and Giráldez (1995), and Findlay and O'Rourke (2003).

2. For the nationalization of currency in the nineteenth century, see Helleiner (2003).

3. On the establishment of nineteenth-century national traditions and institutions more generally, see Hobsbawm and Ranger (1983) and Anderson (1983).

4. On the relationship between central banks, the gold standard, economic nationalism, and activist state policy, see de Cecco (1974) and Helleiner (2002, 2003).

5. Some studies have seen a single gold standard operating continuously from its adoption in Britain in 1821. See, for example, A. Schwartz (1984). The literature on the gold standard is enormous, with most of it at least implicitly seeking to draw contrasts between the gold standard at the turn-of-the-century and the gold standard in the interwar period. In addition to Eichengreen (1984, 1987a, 1987b, 1996), Eichengreen and Flandreau (1996), Eichengreen and Sachs (1985), Eichengreen and Temin (1997), Flandreau (1996a, 1996b, 1997b), Milward (1996), and Gallarotti (1995), see also Polanyi (1944), Mouré (1991, 2002), Frieden (1996), and Simmons (1994) for a political economy focus. Since Kydland and Prescott's (1977) and Barro and Gordon's (1983) theoretical work on time inconsistency, a strand of macroeconomic literature has studied the role of commitment rules in economic policy. This has influenced interpretations of the turn-of-the-century gold standard as being, at least in part, based on credible commitment to certain gold standard rules reminiscent of, but distinct from, the Cunliffe Commission and Keynes idea of rules of the game. See, in particular, Bordo and Rockoff (1996), Bordo and MacDonald (1997), and, for the interwar period, Bordo, Edelstein, and Rockoff (1999). Eichengreen (1987a, 1987b, 1992) and Bayoumi and Eichengreen (1996) argue that the success of the pre–World War I gold standard rested on both credible commitment and central bank cooperation. Kindleberger (1973) has also discussed central bank cooperation, but Eichengreen's conception is less institutionalized and more ad hoc. Flandreau (1997b) emphasizes the piecemeal, nonreciprocal, noninstitutionalized character of central bank cooperation and questions its role.

6. Flandreau 1996b: 862.

7. P. C., "La Crísis de la Plata," *El Economista Argentino*, March 17, 1894, 6.

8. On the French "Crime of '73" and the decline of French bimetallism and the Latin Monetary Union, see Flandreau (1996b, 2000b, 2004), Einaudi (2000, 2001), and Gallarotti (1993). On the political context of Germany's abandonment of silver, see Milward (1996). On bimetallism more generally, see Flandreau (1996b, 1997a) and Redish (1990, 2000). In contrast to the more political focus of Flandreau, Einaudi, and Milward, Redish focuses on subsidiary token coinage and argues that bimetallic standards functioned prior to establishment of the classic gold standard because they provided a superior medium of exchange.

9. Paul Leroy-Beaulieu, "Una nueva edad del oro, El aumente presente y próximo de la producción de ese metal y sus consecuencias," Part 3, *El Economista Argentino*, February 23, 1895, 3–4, reprint from *L'Economiste français*.

10. The primary article is Bordo and Rockoff (1996).

11. Ferguson 2001: 278. See also Bagehot (2006): 104. For a fuller argument, see Enaudi (2001).

12. Joaquin M. Ruiz, "Oro y plata," *El Economista Argentino*, March 9, 1895, 5.

13. There is an enormous literature on push (factors at home) versus pull (factors abroad) in describing British overseas capital flows. See, for example, Edelstein (1982).

14. Ferguson 2001: 278, citing Edelstein 1982: 24, 48, 313.

15. Bordo and Rockoff (1996) argue that adopting the gold standard did lower borrowing costs. Flandreau and Zumer (2004) dispute this, arguing that adherence to the gold standard did not lower the cost of capital for sovereign borrowers. Mauro, Sussman, and Yafeh (2006b) contend that institutional reforms had relatively little effect on bond rates, particularly compared with major news events such as wars or other political disturbances. For further discussion of bond rates, see Mauro, Sussman, and Yafeh (2006a).

16. To get some sense of the enormity of the borrowing, by 1913 foreign investors owned one-half of the Argentine economy (Frieden 2006: 20). Despite the enormous number, loans to Argentina were not necessarily cheap compared to other nations borrowing in London. Llach 2007: 111 finds bond yields consistently higher for Argentine debt from 1885 to 1990 than for similar debt from Brazil, Chile, and New South Wales.

17. See, for example, "La conversión en Chile," Part 1, *El Economista Argentino*, March 2, 1895, 5–6; "El problema económico en Chile," *La Tribuna*, December 11, 1899, 1.

18. On this point, see McKinnon (2005), McKinnon and Ohno (1997, 2001), Cargill, Hutchison, and Ito (1997), and Amyx (2004). For additional views on Japan's economy in the 1990s, see Grimes (2001), Wright (2002), Bailey, Coffey, and Tomlinson (2007), and Hutchison and Westermann (2006). For an argument on exchange rates and nineteenth-century economic development, see Nugent (1973).

19. "Gloom Grows as Japanese Exports Suffer Record Fall," *Financial Times*, December 23 2008; "Toyota Expects First Loss in 70 Years Amid 'Unprecedented Emergency,'" *Financial Times*, December 23, 2008.

20. On this post-2002 Argentine policy, see, for example, "Top Official on Economy Steps Down in Argentina," *New York Times*, April 26, 2008.

21. U.S. criticism of Chinese currency policy has been steady for years. See, for example, Jackie Calmes, "Geithner Hints at Harder Line on China Trade," *New York Times*, January 22, 2009. For an analysis of revaluing the yen in Japan under Bretton Woods, see Itō (2009).

22. It was only in the 1880s that the deflation of the 1870s consistently came to be associated with adoption of the gold standard. See, for example, Barsky and DeLong (1991). On usage of the term "money question" in the United States, see Frieden 2006: 14. In Argentina the phrase was "cuestión monetaria"; in Japan, "kahei mondai."

23. For a contemporary account of these conferences, see Russell (1898).

24. Domingo Lamas, "La cuestión monetaria, El ejemplo de los Estados-Unidos, Parentesis de actualidad," *Revista Económica (del Río de la Plata)*, May 10, 1899, 61. The quotations are from, in order: Francis Amasa Walker (U.S.; first president of the American Economic Association, director of the 1870 and 1880 U.S. censuses, professor of economics at Yale, and president of MIT from 1881 to his death in 1897), and Luigi Luzatti (Italy; treasury minister in the 1890s and later interior minister and prime minister [1910-1911]). Walker's views reflected those of the founders of the American Economic Association, which was established in 1885 by institutionalists critical of English liberal theory. Its founder, Richard T. Ely, planned an association of "economists who repudiate laissez-faire as a scientific doctrine," which he regarded as "unsafe in politics and unsound in morals" (Gordon, 1991: 247). All of the other founding members were trained in Germany under Gustav von Schmoller and other members of the German historical school.

25. Domingo Lamas, "La cuestión monetaria, El ejemplo de los Estados-Unidos, Parentesis de actualidad," *Revista Económica (del Río de la Plata)*, May 10, 1899, 61.

26. Ibid. Quotations come from, in order: the archbishop of Dublin, Arthur Balfour, and George Goschen.

27. Marshall 1925: 192, quoted in Eichengreen 1996: 19. Various proposals for bimetallic, quasi-bimetallic, indexed, or currency basket-style systems emerged during the late nineteenth century. W. Stanley Jevons (1875) favored an indexed system under which currency values would be adjusted for changes in the price level. Marshall favored a similar indexed standard for long-term contracts. Both Marshall and Edgeworth supported a variation on bimetallism that Edgeworth called "symmetallism," which functioned as a basket of gold and silver currency (Marshall 1926: 12–15, 26–31; Edgeworth 1895: 442). Léon Walras (1874) favored a managed gold standard with a "silver regulator" to keep prices stable. Irving Fisher (1911) favored a "compensated dollar" system under which the gold equivalent of the dollar would be varied to keep a broad-based price index constant. For a fuller discussion of these monetary proposals, see M. Friedman (1990a).

28. Frieden 2006: 114 citing Jones 1964: 14.

29. For contemporary support for the silverite view, see M. Friedman (1990b). On *The Wizard of Oz* as a gold standard analogy, see Rockoff (1990). For a general interpretation of Bryan and the silver movement, see Kazin (2006).

30. Domingo Lamas, "La cuestión monetaria, El ejemplo de los Estados-Unidos, Parentesis de actualidad," *Revista Económica (del Río de la Plata)*, May 10, 1899, 61.

31. Ferguson 2001: 333 citing Bordo and Rockoff (1996).

32. Domingo Lamas, "La cuestión monetaria, El ejemplo de los Estados-Unidos, Parentesis de actualidad," *Revista Económica (del Río de la Plata)*, May 10, 1899, 61.

33. Ibid., 6.

34. For contemporary reflections on nationalism as the basis for currency choices, see A. De Foville, "Las variaciones del poder monetario," *El Economista Argentino*, July 27, 1895, 6, and "Saikin ginka bōraku no genin ikan," *Tōyō keizai shinpō*, May 15, 1897, 28.

35. Melchor G. Rom, "La crísis en Estados-Unidos y la crísis en la Argentina, Iguales causas producen siempre los mismos efectos," *El Economista Argentino*, March 9, 1895, 1.

3. Nations and Gold

1. Histories of the gold standard in English have tended to be histories of the gold standard in Britain or how Britain interacted, and ostensibly led, the rest of the world. For works taking a particular interest in the gold standard within Britain prior to World War I, see Sayers (1953, 1957, 1976) and Eichengreen (1987a).

2. Michie (1986) discusses the effectiveness of changes in the London bank rate on short-term capital flows.

3. For the emergence of the gold standard in Germany and France, see Flandreau (1996b, 2000b, 2004), Einaudi (2000, 2001), Gallarotti (1993), and Milward (1996).

4. For the gold standard in Russia, see Gregory (1979), Drummond (1976), Gregory and Sailors (1976), Von Laue (1963), Crisp (1953, 1976), Witte (1960, 1990), and Harcave (2004).

5. Witte (1899).

6. For the gold standard in the United States, see M. Friedman (1990b), M. Friedman and Schwartz (1963), Bensel (2000, 2008), Ritter (1997), Goodwyn (1976), and Rockoff (1990).

7. Nationalist claims cut both for and against the gold standard. Gold opponents argued that adopting the gold standard would serve British rather than American national interests. The 1896 Democratic Party platform called the gold standard "a British policy," the adoption of which had "brought other nations into financial servitude to London," and a policy that was "not only un-American but anti-American." See also "Has the Gold Standard Hurt Us and Benefited Great Britain?" *Commercial and*

Financial Chronicle, August 15, 1896. For the full text of the platform, see Schlesinger (2002). For the full proceedings of the convention, see *Official Proceedings of the Democratic National Convention* (1896). For a biography of the platform's primary author, see Graham (1990).

8. See Bensel (2000) for the correlation between support for the gold standard and support for protective tariffs.

9. On Bryan and the 1896 election, see Bensel (2000, 2008), Bryan and Cherny (1996), Bryan and Bryan (1925), Burnham (1965, 1970), Phillips (2003), Cherny (1994), Kazin (2006), Graham (1990), Ritter (1997), Sanders (1999), Rockoff (1990), and Schlesinger (2002).

10. See Bensel (2000) for how monetary benefits from protective tariffs were used to hold together a Republican majority in support of the gold standard and northern industrialization. Benson argues that a "tariff policy complex" provided protection for industry and revenue to pay Union Army pensions that helped solidify a Republican political majority. For late nineteenth-century U.S. tariff debates, see Bensel (2000) and Reitano (1994).

11. Phillips 2003: 81–82. In 1891, while campaigning for governor of Ohio, McKinley criticized Grover Cleveland for "dishonoring" and "discrediting" silver (Bensel 2000: 369–70).

12. In 1900 Bryan campaigned as an anti-imperialist against the McKinley administration's enthusiasm for imperial expansion and overseas colonies. In 1896 Bryan received 46.7% of the vote and 176 electoral votes; in 1900, 45.5% and 156 electoral votes.

13. On Indian currency and British financial policy in India, see Keynes (1913), Chaudhuri (1968), Ambirajan (1978, 1984), Kaminski (1980), Banerjee (1982), Tomlinson (1993), Rothermund (1993), Cain and Hopkins (2001), and Balachandran (2008).

14. "La conversión en Chile," Part 1, *El Economista Argentino,* March 2, 1895, 5–6.

15. See Bordo and Rockoff (1996) for yield rates on Chilean bonds. Underlying a problem with using bond rates as the only evidence of gold standard motivations, the authors admit to being unable to explain why the bond rate data for Chile do not match up with their expectation that adopting the gold standard would cause bond rates to fall.

4. Gold and Industrial Developmentalism

1. The literature on the ideas of the "generation of '80" is voluminous. See in particular Halperín Donghi (1987a), Gallo (1993), Botana (1977), and Botana and Gallo (1997). For state promotion of economic and institutional development, see Dorfman (1942), Gallo (1988), Rocchi (2006), Duncan (1981, 1983), Villanueva (1972), and Cortés Conde (1979). Rocchi (2006) is particularly notable in describing early

industrialization in Argentina from the 1870s and state efforts to support industry through tariffs.

2. On the dissolution of the Spanish Empire and gradual emergence of ideas and institutions of an Argentine nation, see Adelman (1999, 2006), Botana (1984), Halperín Donghi (1995b), Chiaramonte (1997), and Botana (1984). For the classic work on the economic aspects of the pre-1853 Argentine federation, see Burgin (1946).

3. See Botana (1977) and Halperín Donghi (1995a) for the idea of 1880 as the start of a new phase of Argentine history. See Gerchunoff, Rocchi, and Rossi (2008) and Llach (2007) for a detailed discussion of the continued economic competition between Buenos Aires and Argentina's interior provinces after 1880, the consolidation of national economic power in the 1890s, and the relative decline of interior influence politically and economically after the turn of the century.

4. On English-Argentine relations, see Ferns (1960) and Platt (1972, 1977).

5. On Argentine industry, see Rocchi (2006), Dorfman (1942), and Guy (1976, 1980, 1982, 1984). On agriculture and agricultural capitalism, see Adelman (1994), Hora (2001), Scobie (1964), and Amaral (1998). For debates over these two models in the 1860s and 1870s, see Chiaramonte (1971).

6. On foreign capital in Argentina, see Regalsky (1994, 1997, 2001, 2002). On foreign capital and debt crises, see Marichal (1989), Cortés Conde (1989), and Della Paolera and Taylor (2001). For foreign direct investment, see C. Lewis (1983).

7. On immigration, see Gallo (1983) and Halperín Donghi (1987b).

8. Melchor G. Rom, "Decadencia de las Naciones Latinas de Europa, Enseñanzas que es necessario aprovechar, Deberes de los gobiernos y de los pueblos," *El Economista Argentino*, January 6, 1894, 1–2.

9. These ideas remained common after World War I. See, for example, "Colonización en vasta escala, al alcance de todos, Divisa financiera-económica-mundial, Sin seguridad económica la democracia es confusion y desorden (Conclusion)," *La Argentina Económica*, August 15, 1925, 7–11.

10. "La futura Presidencia de la República, El Dr. Hipolito Irigoyen," *La Argentina Económica*, April 15, 1928, 3.

11. On the key role that currency appreciation and a desire for a depreciated exchange rate played in Argentina's 1899 gold standard law, see Gallo (1996) and Llach 2007: 159–60. Llach, in particular, points out the overlapping interests of coastal exporters and nascent inland industry in favor of using the 1899 gold standard law to assure a depreciated exchange rate.

12. On Pellegrini, see Gallo (1997) and Guy (1979). On protectionism in Latin America, see Coatsworth and Williamson (2004). Bértola and Williamson (2003) describe high Latin American tariff rates and their trade protection effects but argue that governments enacted high tariffs primarily for revenue needs related to midcentury warfare rather than industrial promotion. Williamson (2003) deals more directly

with the influence of List from the 1890s but is most concerned with results showing that protectionism retarded growth in Latin America rather than promoting it. Irwin (2002) notes that protective tariffs accompanied high growth in the late nineteenth century but argues that protective tariffs were not responsible for that growth.

13. On protectionism worldwide, see Williamson (2003), Bairoch (1989, 1997), and Chang (2002) as well as the discussion in chapter 1. For late nineteenth-century protectionism in Argentina, see Hora (2000), Rocchi (2006), and Llach (2007). For earlier Argentine protectionism debates, see Chiaramonte (1971).

14. Domingo Lamas, "Supremacia del criterio nacional en la aplicación de los principios económicos," *Revista Económica (del Río de la Plata)*, April 10, 1899, 4.

15. Ives Guyot, "El espíritu proteccionista, Sus riesgos sus cargas," Part 1, *El Economista Argentino*, July 13, 1912: 6.

16. On PAN, see Botana (1977) and Alonso (2000).

17. *DSCD*, September 19, 1913, 397, quoted in Rocchi 2006: 219.

18. "La cuestión monetaria, El discurso del Doctor O'Farrell," *El Tiempo*, October 19, 1899, 1. Llach 2007: 177 calculates that ad valorem protection increased from 20% to 90% during the 1880s, and then held steady through the 1890s. Lach 2007: 160–206 discusses the increased protectionism of the 1880s and the failure of free traders to challenge it successfully in the 1890s.

19. "Nuestras finanzas en el extranjero," *La Tribuna*, September 5, 1899, 2.

20. Pellegrini emphasized this point during the 1899 tariff debates immediately after pushing through adoption of the gold standard. See *DSCD*, December 12, 1899.

21. "Con el Palo del Rucio," *Don Quijote*, November 19, 1899, 4.

22. On the historical division of protectionism and free trade along regional and industry lines, see Llach (2007), particularly 154–59. Llach traces how national protectionist and free trade policies tracked the relative power of interior provinces versus Buenos Aires in national politics. As the relative popular and political power of Buenos Aires increased, the protectionist dominance of the 1880s shifted to free trade by the 1910s. See also Gerchunoff, Rocchi, and Rossi (2008) for similar ideas framed in terms of the economic crises of the 1880s and 1890s.

23. There were exceptions. Sheep and cattle industries in the Pampas that relied on exports favored low tariffs as did export-import merchants based in Buenos Aires. The wheat industry in the Pampas, however, traditionally favored more protection because of its intensive labor requirements. See Llach 2007: 155, as well as Rocchi (2006) and Chiaramonte (1971).

24. Pedro S. Lamas, "La orientación económica del mensaje, La industria nacional, Un gran plan de gobierno," *Revista Económica (del Río de la Plata)*, May 10, 1899, 53–58.

25. "Los proyectos financieros, Opiniones autorizadas," *El Tiempo*, September 1, 1899, 1.

26. On pre-1880s currency, see Irigoin (2000) and Della Paolera (1994).

27. Conversion ceased de facto in December 1884 when note-issuing banks stopped exchanging paper for gold. Conversion was officially suspended (ostensibly, temporarily) by the government in March 1885. It was suspended indefinitely in December 1886 (Della Paolera and Taylor 2001: 47–48). In contemporary accounts the rate was generally expressed multiplied by 100 so that a rate of 1.00 was referred to as a rate of 100.

28. Della Paolera and Taylor 2001: 89. On the financial crisis, referred to as the Barings Crisis in Britain due to the losses suffered by the Barings Bank, see Cortés Conde (1989).

29. Domingo Lamas, "La cuestión monetaria, El ejemplo de los Estados-Unidos, Parentesis de actualidad," *Revista Económica (del Río de la Plata)*, May 10, 1899, 60–63. Llach 2007: 179 finds that depreciating currency from 1889 to 1895 combined with protective tariffs to increase fourfold the real price that Argentine sugar producers received relative to the international price. He finds similar results for wine (Llach 2007: 181). For a contemporary English account of depreciating currency aiding Argentine agriculture, see William Bear, "The Agricultural Progress of the Argentine Republic," *Economic Journal* 5, no. 20 (December 1895): 516–26, cited in Llach 2007: 183.

30. "La moneda legal," *El Correo Español*, September 8,1899, 1; Rocchi 2006: 44.

31. Della Paolera and Taylor 2001: 114.

32. "Crisis imaginarias," *La Tribuna*, July 6, 1899, 1; "Avidez insaciable," *El Correo Español*, July 1, 1899, 1.

33. "El comercio y la moneda, Adhiriendo a los proyectos, La petición al Congreso," *Revista Económica (del Río de la Plata)*, September 20, 1899, 281; "Las dos encuestas de 'La Argentina Económica' has despertado gran interes," *La Argentina Económica*, July 30, 1926, 9. See also Gesell (1898) for an analysis of the dangers of appreciation.

34. Domingo Lamas, "La cuestión monetaria," *Revista Económica (del Río de la Plata)*, May 20, 1899, 73–76.

35. "La cuestión monetaria," *El Tiempo*, August 25, 1899, 1.

36. Roca and Pellegrini were cofounders of PAN, but by the late 1890s policy and personal disagreements had made their alliance tenuous. Pellegrini's appointment was widely viewed as an attempt by Roca to preempt Pellegrini from joining the opposition or forming his own party, which he did in 1901 after breaking definitively with Roca. The intra-PAN Pellegrini-Roca rivalry was exacerbated by the fact that Roca's second term as president (1898–1904), unlike his first (1880–86), was nominally backed by the Buenos Aires political faction led by the Mitre family and former president Bartolomé Mitre. The Mitre family and its newspaper, *La Nación*, fiercely opposed Pellegrini's gold standard plans. This opposition led to Mitre's faction leaving the governing alliance (or *Acuerdo*, as it was called). For detailed descriptions of political parties and party alliances in the 1890s, see Alonso (2000, 2003) and Etchepareborda (1980). For contemporary accounts of the role Pellegrini's gold standard plans played in destroy-

ing the *Acuerdo* between PAN and Mitre's Unión Cívica Nacional, see "Vacilaciones, dudas y dulce de naranja (tres cosas buenas)," *Don Quijote*, September 10, 1899, 4; Mayol, "Los primers efectos," *Caras y Caretas*, November 11, 1899; "Ecos, Consecuencias políticas," *La Tribuna*, October 21, 1899, 1.

37. "Situación financiera, La industria y la moneda," *La Tribuna*, August 22, 1899, 1. For arguments about tariff retaliation, see Hora (2000).

38. "Situación financiera, La industria y la moneda," *La Tribuna*, August 22, 1899, 1.

39. "Notas," *El Correo Español*, September 11, 12, 1899, 1.

40. "El principio del fin," *El Correo Español*, September 17, 1899, 1. In Argentina as elsewhere at the turn of the century, the image of the evil speculator was prominent and served as an all-purpose foil. After the 1890 financial panic, a series of popular novels appeared in which the lives of innocent youth were ruined through the sinister maneuvering of financial speculators. Pellegrini framed the debate over his currency proposals in terms of "speculators without conscience" versus "the sacred interests of the country." "Crónica parlamentaria, Senado, Los proyectos financieros, El discurso integro de Pellegrini, Réplica del Senador Uriburu," *El Correo Español*, September 20, 1899, 1. For a discussion of the "evil speculator" in Europe and the United States, see James 2001: 22.

41. Pedro S. Lamas, "La orientación económica del mensaje, La industria nacional, Un gran plan de gobierno," *Revista Económica (del Río de la Plata)*, May 10, 1899, 56

42. "Crónica Parlamentaria, Senado," *El Correo Español*, December 13, 1899, 2.

43. For the same breakdown of creditors and hard-money advocates versus inflationists in Chile, see "El problema económico en Chile," *La Tribuna*, December 11, 1899, 1.

44. Opponents countered that appreciated currency was not healthy currency but destructive currency. see Domingo Lamas, "La cuestión monetaria, El ejemplo de los Estados-Unidos, Parentesis de actualidad," *Revista Económica (del Río de la Plata)*, May 10, 1899, 60–63.

45. Pedro S. Lamas, "La orientación económica del mensaje, La industria nacional, Un gran plan de gobierno," *Revista Económica (del Río de la Plata)*, May 10, 1899, 56.

46. Ibid., 56.

47. "Los proyectos financieros, Adhesion del comercio," *El Tiempo*, September 7, 1899, 1. See also "Adhesion a los proyectos, Los ultimos telegramas," *El Tiempo*, September 13, 1899, 1, and "Los proyectos financieros, Siguen las adhesions," *El Tiempo*, September 22, 1899, 1. On political action by industrialists and merchants more generally, see Hora (2003b).

48. "En favor de los proyectos monetarios, La reunión de hoy," *El Tiempo*, September 8, 1899, 1.

49. "El Comercio y la cuestión monetaria," *El Correo Español*, September 10, 1899, 1; "¿Es eso lo que se busca?" *El Correo Español*, August 30, 1899, 1.

50. "¿Es eso lo que se busca?" *El Correo Español*, August 30, 1899, 1.

51. "Manifiesto de adhesion a los proyectos financieros," *El Tiempo*, September 12, 1899, 1. See also "Tribuna libre, La inmigración y los proyectos," *La Tribuna*, September 18, 1899, 1; "La cuestión del día," *El Correo Español*, August 26, 1899, 1.

52. "Tribuna libre, Cuestiónes conexas con los proyectos monetarios," *La Tribuna*, October 7, 1899, 1.

53. "Tribuna libre, Sesión memorable, Los Sres. Anadón, Pellegrini y Uriburu," *La Tribuna*, September 23, 1899, 1.

54. "La cuestión monetaria, De sofisma en sofisma," *El Tiempo*, September 4, 1899, 1.

55. "El principio del fin," *El Correo Español*, September 17, 1899, 1. See also "Indiferentismo," *El Correo Español*, October 21, 1899, 1; "Notas," *El Correo Español*, October 22, 1899, 1.

56. "Atrancar la puerta," *El Correo Español*, October 7, 1899, 1.

57. As summarized by J. Williams (1920), "The measure provoked a storm of controversy, such as perhaps has never been called forth by any other proposal or event in Argentine history. The speeches delivered on the subject in Congress fill six volumes. The plan was opposed by the press (led by the distinguished newspaper *La Nación*). Five former finance ministers attacked it. . . . Petitions of merchants and industrials with four thousand signatures appealed to Congress to defeat the bill. Similar petitions were formulated by the Chamber of Commerce of the Stock Exchange, and by the Italian and French Chambers" (J. Williams 1920: 157). The petitions of "merchants and industrials" in opposition reflected the views of importers (who opposed the proposals) versus exporters (who favored them) (ibid., 159).

58. "Notas," *El Economista Argentino*, May 6, 1899, 2; Junius, "La cuestión monetaria, Significado de las declaraciones del mensage, Reorganización del Banco de la Nación," *El Economista Argentino*, May 6, 1899, 1–2.

59. "Apoteosis," *Don Quijote*, October 1, 1899, 1. Regarding the currency proposals as part of general wasteful spending, government budget deficits, PAN electoral fraud, and government nepotism, see "Villancicos," *Don Quijote*, December 24, 1899, 1.

60. "Lanzadas," *Don Quijote*, October 1, 1899, 1. A bubonic plague outbreak struck Argentina in 1899, making plague references common.

61. Pandora's box: "Ultima hora," *Don Quijote*, September 3, 1899, 4; Columbus egg: *Don Quijote*, "Huevos," September 3, 1899, 4. Argentina's political cartoonists regularly portrayed political figures as animals. The notably tall Pellegrini inevitably became a giraffe.

5. Strange Bedfellows

1. Tornquist and his supporters favored a 250 rate rather than Pellegrini's 227.

2. "Los proyectos financieros, Opiniones autorizadas," *El Tiempo*, September 1, 1899, 1.

3. "La Conversión Chilena, La Nuestra," *La Tribuna*, October 10, 1899, 1.

4. "Los hallazgos de los grandes organos, Los de hoy," *La Tribuna*, October 11, 1899, 1.

5. "La cuestión del día, El ejemplo de la Rusia," *El Tiempo*, September 5, 1899, 1. See also "Crónica Parlamentaria, Cámara de diputados," *El Correo Español*, October 23, 24,1899, 1.

6. "La solución monetaria, La oficina de cambio, Mensaje y proyectos del Poder Ejecutivo," *El Economista Argentino*, September 2, 1899, 1–3. The complete Senate debates can be found in *DSCS* organized by date.

7. "El mensaje y los proyectos financieros," *El Correo Español*, September 1, 1899, 1.

8. "Los proyectos financieros," *La Tribuna*, September 8, 1899, 1.

9. "Ecos, El Dr. Pellegrini, Su discurso," *La Tribuna*, September 18, 1899, 1. See also "El debate financiero," *El Tiempo*, September 18, 1899, 1.

10. All Pellegrini statements in this paragraph are from "Crónica parlamentaria, Senado, Los proyectos financieros, El discurso integro de Pellegrini, Réplica del Senador Uriburu," *El Correo Español*, September 20, 1899, 1.

11. "Los debates de ayer, La intervención y los proyectos," *El Tiempo*, September 22, 1899, 1.

12. "Ecos, Los proyectos financieros," *La Tribuna*, September 11, 1899, 1. See also "Congreso, Comisión de Hacienda del Senado, El pedido de la intervención," *El Tiempo*, September 5, 1899, 1; "El nuevo régimen monetario, Antecedentes," *El Tiempo*, November 2, 1899, 1.

13. "Crónica parlamentaria, Senado, Los proyectos financieros, El discurso integro de Pellegrini, Réplica del Senador Uriburu," *El Correo Español*, September 20, 1899, 1.

14. Ibid., 1.

15. "Los proyectos, Discurso del Senador Uriburu," *Revista Económica (del Río de la Plata)*, September 30, 1899, 292–93.

16. Ibid., 293.

17. Ibid., 293.

18. Ibid., 293, 295.

19. Ibid., 295.

20. Ibid., 296.

21. "Crónica parlamentaria, Cámara de diputados," *El Correo Español*, October 19, 1899, 2.

22. "La cuestión monetaria, El discurso del Doctor O'Farrell," *El Tiempo*, October 19, 1899, 1.

23. "Crónica parlamentaria, Cámara de diputados," *El Correo Español*, October 19, 1899, 1.

24. Ibid., 2.

25. Ibid., 1.

26. "Tribuna libre, La oposición y los proyectos, El dictamen en disidencia," *La Tribuna*, October 11, 1899, 1.

27. "Ecos del día, Los proyectos financieros," *El Correo Español*, October 9, 10, 1899, 1–2.

28. "Crónica parlamentaria, Cámara de diputados," *El Correo Español*, October 19, 1899, 1.

29. "Boers y Ingleses," *Don Quijote*, October 22, 1899, 4.

6. Law 3871 and the Gold Standard

1. The *Times* of London criticized the Argentine government for not obtaining "the services of European financial experts" and blamed the country's economic difficulties on "the political pressure brought to bear by the clique of persons interested in sustaining the spoon-fed industries, which are only kept alive by excessive protection to the detriment of the real source of the wealth of this country, consisting of pastoral and agricultural enterprise" (*Times*, September 25, 1899, 6). In reporting that "the Senate has passed the Conversion Bills, which are meant to counteract appreciation," the *Times* lamented that "the prestige of President Roca is nullified by Dr. Pellegrini's ascending influence" and warned that "the economic situation is bad owing to the Conversion Bills" (ibid., 4).

2. "Tribuna libre, Cuestiónes conexas con los proyectos monetarios," *La Tribuna*, October 4, 1899, 1.

3. "¡Estamos Frescos!" *Don Quijote*, August 13, 1899, 1.

4. "¿Es eso lo que se busca?" *El Correo Español*, August 30, 1899, 1.

5. "Semana que promete, Regreso del Presidente, Novedades financieras y políti-cas," *El Tiempo*, August 21, 1899, 1. See also "Los proyectos financieros, Para esta se-mana, El doble despacho," *El Tiempo*, September 11, 1899, 1.

6. "La cuestión financiera en la Comisión de Hacienda, Los despachos, Discusión para el viernes," *El Tiempo*, October 6, 1899, 1; "El presupuesto y los proyectos mon-etarios," *El Tiempo*, October 6, 1899, 1. An additional 5% import duty was added in the Cámara de Diputados.

7. "Economizando . . . ," *El Tiempo*, September 13, 1899, 1.

8. "Lanzadas," *Don Quijote*, March 25, 1900, 1, and "Lanzadas," *Don Quijote*, April 1, 1900, 1, for funding from Banco de La Nación; "Varapalos," *Don Quijote*, March 25, 1900, 4, and "Lanzadas," *Don Quijote*, May 20, 1900, 1, regarding gold inflows and outflows from Caja.

9. "La ley monetaria, Garantía y conversión, El plan del gobierno," *La Tribuna*, November 7, 1899, 1.

10. Limiting conversion was not unique to Argentina. France, Belgium, Switzer-land, and the Netherlands also made conversion discretionary. On the various excep-tions to gold convertibility worldwide prior to World War I, see Bloomfield (1959).

11. "El corte de cuentas," Part 1," *El Correo Español*, August 21, 22 1899, 1.

12. *DSCS*, October 18, 1899. For Rosa's later comments on Law 3871, see Rosa (1909).

13. "Crónica parlamentaria, Camára de Diputados," *El Correo Español*, October 19, 1899, 1.

14. "Nuestras finanzas en el extranjero," *La Tribuna*, September 5, 1899, 2.

15. "Tribuna libre, Cuestiones conexas con los proyectos monetarios," Part 3, *La Tribuna*, October 6, 1899, 1.

16. The literature on the "Argentine climacteric" or "Argentine puzzle" as it has been called is enormous and has served as the primary analytical frame in Argentine economic history since at least the 1970s. The most frequent framing question has compared per capita GDP figures showing Argentina ranked in the top half dozen of countries surveyed at the turn of the century with contemporary figures that show a lower rank, and asks why this change occurred. In the 1950s and 1960s the dominant dependency and structural school approach exemplified by Raul Prebisch and Aldo Ferrer (Ferrer 1963), argued that the structure of the international trading system—in particular, disadvantageous terms of trade—was the problem. Borrowing a stages-of-development framework taken from Rostow (1960) and Gerschenkron (1962) (and also appearing in Ferrer), Di Tella and Zymelman (1967) argued from the perspective of set stages of economic development. From the mid-1970s the dominant approach shifted to finding fault with domestic Argentine institutions, either post–World War II (Díaz Alejandro 1970) or pre–World War II (although generally accepting Díaz Alejandro's critique of postwar state policies). For a pre–World War II view that draws on the "new institutionalism" movement popular from the early 1990s and associated, in particular, with Douglass North, see Taylor (1992a, 1992b), Della Paolera and Taylor (2001), and Della Paolera and Taylor (2003). For a synthesis of views, see Cortés Conde (1996), and Gerchunoff and Llach (2003, 2004). For a broader framing of issues in Latin American economic history, see Coatsworth (1998) and Coatsworth and Taylor (1998). For the most recent expression of the puzzle/climacteric idea, see Beattie (2009) emphasizing the Great Depression and then Peron. For works that look farther back into the nineteenth century for the sources of Argentina's future economic growth path, see Crafts and Venables (2003) and Coatsworth (1998) who emphasize the divergence of per capita GDP figures for Argentina (as well as all of Latin America) and the United States over the course of the nineteenth century. A variation on the Argentine puzzle literature has sought to compare Argentina with Australia, Canada, New Zealand, the United States, or all four in asking why Argentina apparently diverged economically from these seemingly similar English settler colonies—much land, little population, natural resources favorable to agriculture and exports. The comparative Argentina, former English colonies literature is extensive, but see in particular Smithies (1965), Diéguez (1969), Moran (1970), Dyster (1979), Gallo (1979), Fogarty (1979), Platt and Di Tella (1985), Duncan and Fogarty (1984),

H. Schwartz (1989), Schedvin (1990), Korol (1992), Adelman (1994), Asensio (1995), Bértola and Porcile (2002), Sanz Villarroya (2003), Prados and Sanz Villarroya (2004), and Gerchunoff and Fajgelbaum (2006).

17. "El proyecto monetario, Viajando . . . sobre congeturas," *El Tiempo*, August 30, 1899, 1.

18. "Los proyectos financieros, Su discusión en el Senado," *La Tribuna*, September 20, 1899, 1.

19. "Tribuna libre, El oro para la conversión, De hecho, en pleno régimen metálico," *La Tribuna*, September 16, 1899, 1.

20. "Notas," *El Correo Español*, September 27, 1899, 1.

21. For criticism of Pellegrini as an inflationist (or "emisionista"), see Gallo 1997: 37.

22. "Ecos, Los proyectos financieros, Reunión de la comisión," *La Tribuna*, September 2, 1899, 1. "Ecos, Los proyectos financieros," *La Tribuna*, September 5, 1899, 1.

23. "Emisión ilimitada," *El Correo Español*, October 6, 1899, 1.

24. "La ley . . . del embudo," *El Correo Español*, November 5, 1899, 1.

25. "Emisión ilimitada," *El Correo Español*, October 6, 1899, 1.

26. Junius, "El oro y la marcha del tesoro, hay que derogar o reformar fundamentalmente la ley monetaria," *El Economista Argentino*, July 28, 1900, 1–2.

27. "Tribuna Libre, Batiendose en retirada, Inmigración, producción, trabajo," *La Tribuna*, September 19, 1899, 1.

28. "Lanzadas," *Don Quijote*, May 20, 1900, 1

29. Ibid., June 10, 1900, 1. "Caja" can mean an office or bureau as in "Conversion Office" "Conversion Bureau," or a supply of wealth or goods (or, in everyday life, simply a "basket"). Thus the "Caja de Conversión" (Conversion Office) became an "office" with neither a gold "supply" nor "conversion."

30. Junius, "El oro y la marcha del tesoro, hay que derogar o reformar fundamentalmente la ley monetaria," *El Economista Argentino*, July 28, 1900, 1.

31. On Pellegrini usurping Rosa's role, see "Los debates de ayer, La intervención y los proyectos," *El Tiempo*, September 22, 1899, 1; "Notas," *El Correo Español*, October 22, 1899, 1, and "Notas," *El Correo Español*, October 28, 1899, 1.

32. "La ley monetaria y sus efectos," *El Tiempo*, November 6, 1899, 1.

33. "Situación financiera, Leyes económicas," *La Tribuna*, August 24, 1899, 1.

34. "Los cívicos alborotados, Asustando al Presidente," *El Tiempo*, September 4, 1899, 1.

35. "La cuestión monetaria, A proposito del libro del señor Vedia," *El Tiempo*, September 13, 1899, 1. See also "En el Senado, Los dos asuntos," *El Tiempo*, September 13, 1899, 1; "Notas," *El Correo Español*, September 1, 1899, 1.

36. "El corte de cuentas," Part 2, *El Correo Español*, August 26, 1899, 1.

37. "Ecos, El debate finaciero, La sesión de ayer, Nuevas oradores," *La Tribuna*, October 26, 1899, 1.

38. "La cuestión monetaria, El diputado Mitre Proteccionista," *El Tiempo*, October 26, 1899, 1.

39. "Notas," *El Correo Español*, October 23, 24 1899, 1.

40. On the political effects of the currency proposals, see "Vacilaciones, dudas y dulce de naranja (tres cosas buenas)," *Don Quijote*, September 10, 1899, 4; Mayol, "Los primers efectos," *Caras y Caretas*, November 11, 1899, 2; "Ecos, Consecuencias políticas," *La Tribuna*, October 21, 1899, 1; "Ecos, La política del acuerdo y el discurso del senado," *La Tribuna*, November 3, 1899, 1.

41. "Crónica parlamentaria, Camára de diputados," *El Correo Español*, October 26, 1899, 1.

42. "La cuestión monetaria, El diputado Mitre Proteccionista," *El Tiempo*, October 26, 1899, 1.

43. "Crónica parlamentaria, Camára de diputados," *El Correo Español*, October 26, 1899, 1.

44. "Crónica Parlamentaria, Camára de diputados," *El Correo Español*, October 23, 24, 1899, 1.

45. Ibid., 1.

46. Ibid., October 26, 1899, 1.

47. Ibid., October 23, 24, 1899, 1.

48. Ibid., October 26, 1899, 1.

49. Rocchi 2006: 215.

50. "Notas," *El Economista Argentino*, October 28, 1899, 1.

51. "Tribuna libre, Sesión memorable, Los Sres. Anadón, Pellegrini y Uriburu," *La Tribuna*, September 23, 1899, 1.

52. Ibid., 1.

53. "Crónica Parlamentaria, Senado," *El Correo Español*, September 23, 1899, 1.

54. Ibid., 1.

55. "Los proyectos financieros, Sanción en general," *La Tribuna*, September 23, 1899, 1.

56. "Crónica Parlamentaria, Senado," *El Correo Español*, September 23, 1899, 1.

57. "Atrancar la puerta," *El Correo Español*, October 7, 1899, 1.

58. "Crónica Parlamentaria, Senado," *El Correo Español*, September 23, 1899, 1.

59. "Notas," *El Correo Español*, December 14, 1899, 1.

60. "Los proyectos monetarios y el crédito argentino," *El Tiempo*, November 2, 1899, 1.

61. Rocchi 2006: 221, 233.

62. "Tribuna libre, Los proyectos monetarios, Refutación necesaria," *La Tribuna*, September 28, 1899, 1. For a review of contemporary views on the nature of money, see J. O. Machado, "Las Emisiones," *El Economista Argentino*, January 16, 1892, 3.

63. "La cuestión del día," *El Correo Español*, August 26, 1899, 1.

64. "Tribuna libre, Los proyectos monetarios, Refutación necesaria," *La Tribuna*, September 28, 1899, 1.

65. Ibid., Part 5, *La Tribuna*, October 3, 1899, 1.

66. Ibid., Part 2, *La Tribuna*, September 29, 1899, 1.

67. "¿Hablaba usted de mi pleito?" *El Correo Español*, September 3, 1899, 1; "Notas," *El Correo Español*, September 6, 1899, 1.

68. "Mas opiniones extrañas, Su escaso valor, Otros proyectos," *El Tiempo*, August 18, 1899, 1.

69. Ibid., 1.

70. "Los proyectos monetarios," *La Tribuna*, November 22, 1899, 1.

71. "La suba del Oro, o la desvalorización de nuestro peso papel moneda producirán a la inversa, de un día para otro, una lógica y agradable sorpresa," *La Argentina Económica*, June 30, 1930, 3.

72. "¿Los Defensores del Dr. Schacht, quienes son?" *La Argentina Económica*, June 30, 1927, 3, 5; See also "Jamás 'La Argentina Económica' estuvo de acuerdo con la ley de conversion del viejo marco aleman, inspirada por el Dr. Schacht," *La Argentina Económica*, April 15, 1929, 3.

7. The Meiji Gold Standards

1. On late Meiji ideology and civilization as a state enterprise, see Gluck (1985).

2. For a detailed discussion of the treaties and early Meiji attempts to renegotiate them, see Auslin (2004).

3. See, for example, the arguments in "Kinka seido jisshi no hōhō ni tsukite," *Tōyō keizai shinpō*, March 5, 1897, 1.

4. Bordo and Rockoff (1996) argue that the adoption of gold brought about a decline in interest rates. Flandreau, Le Caucheux, and Zumer (1998) argue that this emphasis on interest rates confuses cause with effect. Rather than widespread adoption of the gold standard triggering interest rate convergence as Bordo and Rockoff argue, Flandreau et al. contend that interest rate convergence encouraged states to adopt gold. In this argument, increasing gold supplies, price levels, and economic activity in the 1890s led to declining debt and interest rates, which allowed states the financial leeway to adopt the gold standard.

5. The description here comes from Metzler 2006b: 15–18 and Takemori 2006: 38. See also Yūzō Yamamoto (1994). See Frost (1970) for an earlier view of this late Tokugawa (*bakumatsu*) currency crisis.

6. For a contemporary account, see Ōkuma Shigenobu, "Ishin zengo no zaisei jōtai to waga kuni no shōrai," Part 3, *Tōyō keizai shinpō*, July 25, 1909, 28. See also Yūzō Yamamoto (1989).

7. Matsukata 1899: 5. The industrialist Shibusawa Eiichi later claimed that the Ministry of Finance had prepared Itō's proposal in advance and that Shibusawa (who then worked at the ministry as head of the office responsible for proposing reforms, *Minbushō kaisei kakari*) had arbitrarily selected gold (Takemori 2006: 54–55).

8. On the use of Mexican silver in Asia, see Wolters (2005) and Andrew (1904).

9. On Latin American silver in Asia, see Wolters (2005).

10. For the breakdown of Spanish silver as a global currency and the rise of rival, national currency areas, see Chalmers (1893).

11. Wolters 2005: 184. On the Japanese silver yen, see Hamashita (1983).

12. On Meiji industrialization policies, see T. Smith (1955) and, more briefly, Samuels (1994). The policies were known as *shokusan kōgyō*, which literally means "industrial promotion."

13. Ishibashi Tanzan, "Waga kuni kin hon'isei no kenkyū," *Tōyō keizai shinpō*, January 11, 1930, 13.

14. On the 1881 shift in power, see Ōishi (1989) and Lebra (1959, 1973).

15. In setting up the Bank of Japan, Matsukata followed the advice of the French finance minister Leon Say, who recommended modeling the Japanese bank on the Belgian central bank. Yoshino (1975) vol. 1; Takemori 2006: 97.

16. On the Matsukata deflation and comparisons with Ōkuma's financial policies, see Muroyama (2004, 2005), Nakamura and Umemura (1983), and Ōishi (1989).

17. In Japanese this period is referred to as *kigyō bōkō*, which means "a burst of industrial activity." This period also corresponds with the economic boom of the 1880s in Argentina that also came to an end in 1890. In Argentina's case the boom collapsed with the 1890 financial crisis. In Japan, the height of the boom ended with silver's appreciation in response to passage of the Sherman Silver Purchase Act in the United States. Once silver began declining again after the early 1890s, industrial activity rebounded.

18. Takemori 2006: 107–8. The figures in the rest of the paragraph are from the same source.

19. "Kisho: Gin wa teiraku subeki ka kōki subeki ka," *Tōyō keizai shinpō*, February 25, 1897, 31–32.

20. The commission was to address five specific questions: (1) What were the causes of the recent fluctuations in value between gold and silver? (2) What was the general result of these fluctuations? (3) What effects have these fluctuations had on our economy? (4) In light of these fluctuations, is there any need to change our currency system? (5) If so, what system should be adopted and how? The full commission report is in *NKS-M*, vol. 16.

21. Ishibashi Tanzan, "Waga kuni kin hon'isei no kenkyū," *Tōyō keizai shinpō*, January 11, 1930, 15.

22. Takemori 2006: 145–46.

23. "Sho daika heisei iken," *Tōyō keizai shinpō*, March 5, 1897, 28–29, reprint from *Jiji shinpō*.

24. Ishibashi Tanzan, "Waga kuni kin hon'isei no kenkyū," *Tōyō keizai shinpō*, January 11, 1930, 18.

25. The Franco-Prussian War indemnity is discussed in Flandreau (1996b) and Einaudi (2000). For a pre–World War I discussion of the indemnity, see Angell (1913).

26. Tokutomi 1935: 125.

27. See, for example, "Kinka ronsha ni shu ari," *Tōyō keizai shinpō*, February 25, 1897, 3.

28. "Kinka hon'i to gaikoku bōeki; 3/16 Nihon bōeki kyōkai reikai ni oite," Part 1, *Tōyō keizai shinpō*, April 5, 1897, 19.

29. "Kinka mondai," *Tōyō keizai shinpō*, February 25, 1897, 2.

30. Twenty-first-century scholarly studies looking at the effects of imperial ties (including use of a common currency) on the amount of trade support this contemporary understanding of the advantages of a common currency for trade. See, for example, Mitchener and Weidenmier (2008). Mitchener and Weidenmier find positive effects on trade associated with going onto the gold standard. They find greater effects associated with being part of an empire.

31. "Heisei kaikaku ihō," *Tōyō keizai shinpō*, March 5, 1897, 36, reprint from *Chūgai shōgyō shinpō*.

32. "Kinka hon'i to gaikoku bōeki; 3/16 Nihon bōeki kyōkai reikai ni oite," Part 2, *Tōyō keizai shinpō*, April 15, 1897, 16.

33. "Sho daika heisei iken," *Tōyō keizai shinpō*, February 25, 1897, 18.

34. "Kisho: Kinka hon'isei to kyoryūchi bōeki," *Tōyō keizai shinpō*, March 5, 1897, 32.

35. Nakamura 1990 : 36; Metzler 2006b: 30.

36. "Kinka hon'i to gaikoku bōeki; 3/16 Nihon bōeki kyōkai reikai ni oite," Part 2, *Tōyō keizai shinpō*, April 15, 1897, 16.

37. Matsukata 1899: 190.

38. Ibid., 190–91.

39. "Kinginka hendō no hyōjun," *Tōyō keizai shinpō*, March 5, 1897, 3.

40. Ibid.

41. For Droppers' views, see Droppers (1895, 1898).

42. "Sho daika heisei iken," Part 2, *Tōyō keizai shinpō*, March 5, 1897, 27, reprint from *Jiji shinpō*.

43. Nakamura 1985: 50–51.

44. Nakamura 1983: 39.

45. Muroyama 1984: 217.

46. Nakamura 1983: 39.

47. Ohkawa and Shinohara 1979: 10.

48. "Heisei kaikaku ihō," *Tōyō keizai shinpō*, February 25, 1897, 34.

49. "Hojo kahei shūsei iken, " *Tōyō keizai shinpō*, March 15, 1897, 5.

50. Ishibashi Tanzan, "Waga kuni kin hon'isei no kenkyū," *Tōyō keizai shinpō*, January 11, 1930, 15. For more on the Currency Commission see "Meiji 29nen keizai shoshi," Part 5, *Tōyō keizai shinpō*, March 5, 1897, 5–9.

51. Saikin ginka geraku no genyu," *Tōyō keizai shinpō*, March 25, 1897, 28.

52. "Ginka geraku no heisei kaikaku ni oyobosu eikyō ikan," *Tōyō keizai shinpō*, August 15, 1897, 3.

53. Saikin ginka geraku no genyu," *Tōyō keizai shinpō*, March 25, 1897, 29.

54. "Hojo kahei shūsei iken," *Tōyō keizai shinpō*, March 15, 1897, 4.

55. Ishibashi Tanzan, "Waga kuni kin hon'isei no kenkyū," *Tōyō keizai shinpō*, January 11, 1930, 15.

56. For favorable European opinion of Matsukata's move, see Georges Michel, "Las discusiones de la Sociedad de Economía Política de Paris, Reunión del 6 de Septiembre de 1897, Presidencia de M. Ives Guyot," *El Economista Argentino*, October 23, 1897, 2.

57. "Ginka geraku no heisei kaikaku no oyobosu eikyō ikan," *Tōyō keizai shinpō*, August 15, 1897, 4.

58. "Kinka seido to Taiwan Ginkō to no kankei ikan," *Tōyō keizai shinpō*, April 5, 1897, 4.

59. For arguments favoring Japan as a gold financial center, see "Kisho: Kinka hon'isei to kyoryūchi bōeki," *Tōyō keizai shinpō*, March 5, 1897, 32. In the 1920s both main political parties favored variations on yen blocs and Tokyo as the center of East Asian finance. Their emphases, however, were different, with the Minseitō seeing returning to the gold standard as the key and the Seiyūkai seeing loans to, and investment in, China and Manchuria as the key.

8. Industry and the Economic Uses of Gold

1. "Kinka ronsha ni shu ari," *Tōyō keizai shinpō*, February 25, 1897, 3.

2. For more on the tendency of countries in the 1890s to adopt the currency systems of their main trading partners, see Eichengreen and Flandreau (1996) and Meissner (2005).

3. The U.S. Congress passed the Sherman Silver Purchase Act in 1890 mandating U.S. government silver purchases.

4. "Kinka ronsha ni shu ari," *Tōyō keizai shinpō*, February 25, 1897, 3.

5. Currency Commission members argued that depreciating silver had increased exports and "promote[d] the continued prosperity of industry, agriculture and commerce" (*NKS-M*, 1:34).

6. Nakamura 1990: 11.

7. Droppers 1898: 165.

8. Nakamura 1990: 11.

9. The figures in this paragraph come from Hashimoto and Ōsugi 2000: 34.

10. Hashimoto and Ōsugi 2000: 34.

11. In 1910 Britain exported US$453.2 million in cotton goods, Japan exported US$26.2 million, Italy US$23.9 million, France US$23.4 million, and the United States US$8.5 million (U.S. House of Representatives 1912, appendix A).

12. "Sho daika heisei iken," *Tōyō keizai shinpō*, March 15, 1897, 14, reprint from *Jiji shinpō*.

13. "Heisei kaikaku ihō," *Tōyō keizai shinpō*, February 25, 1897, 33, reprint from *Jiji shinpō*.

14. Ibid., 34.

15. "Heisei kaikaku ihō," *Tōyō keizai shinpō*, March 5, 1897, 36.

16. "Sho daika heisei iken," Part 2, *Tōyō keizai shinpō*, March 5, 1897, 25 reprint from *Jiji shinpō*.

17. "Heisei kaikaku ihō," *Tōyō keizai shinpō*, March 5, 1897, 35.

18. "Sho daika heisei iken," *Tōyō keizai shinpō*, February 25, 1897, 16, reprint from *Jiji shinpō*; "Sho daika heisei iken," *Tōyō keizai shinpō*, February 25, 1897, 19, reprint from *Kokumin shinbun*.

19. "Sho daika heisei iken," *Tōyō keizai shinpō* (*Kokumin shinbun* reprint), February 25, 1897, 19, reprint from *Kokumin shinbun*. For more on the McKinley proposals and their reception in Japan, see "Bankoku kahei kaigi masa ni hirakaren to su (ginka no shōrai)," *Tōyō keizai shinpō*, March 25, 1897, 27–28; "Fukuhon'i-ron no sūsei ikan," *Tōyō keizai shinpō*, March 25, 1897, 13–15; "Dai yonkai bankoku kahei kaigi no unmei ikan," *Tōyō keizai shinpō*, January 25, 1897, 2–3; "Beikoku no heisei—genkō seido to Gaychi-shi no kaikakuan," *Tōyō keizai shinpō*, March 15, 1898, 11–14. For similar McKinley coverage in Argentina from the perspective of bimetallism, see Domingo Lamas, "La cuestión monetaria, El ejemplo de los Estados-Unidos, Parentesis de actualidad," *Revista Económica (del Río de la Plata)*, May 10, 1899, 63.

20. "Sho daika heisei iken," Part 3, *Tōyō keizai shinpō*, March 15, 1897, 16. reprint from *Jiji shinpō*.

21. "Kisho: Fukuhon'i-ronsha ni koku," *Tōyō keizai shinpō*, February 25, 1897, 30.

22. "Sho daika heisei iken," *Tōyō keizai shinpō*, March 5, 1897, 22–24.

23. "Sho daika heisei iken," *Tōyō keizai shinpō*, March 15, 1897, 14, reprint from *Jiji shinpō*.

24. Matsukata 1899: 54.

25. Ibid., 55.

26. Kotegawa 1897: 5.

27. Ohkawa and Shinohara 1979: 334.

28. The attempt to adapt to world standards by adopting the gold standard in the 1890s—a path-dependency argument—has been discussed by Eichengreen and Flandreau (1996) and Meissner (2005). Kemp and Wilson (1999) and Wilson (2000) also make path-dependency arguments.

29. "Kisho: Heisei mondai no Sekigahara," *Tōyō keizai shinpō*, February 25, 1897, 32.

30. Ibid., 32.

31. "Sho daika heisei iken," *Tōyō keizai shinpō*, March 5, 1897, 28, reprint from *Jiji shinpō*.

32. "Sho daika heisei iken," *Tōyō keizai shinpō*, February 25, 1897, 15, reprint from *Nihon shinbun*.

33. Ibid.

34. "Sho daika heisei iken," *Tōyō keizai shinpō*, March 5, 1897, 24, reprint from *Jiji shinpō*.

35. "Sho daika heisei iken," *Tōyō keizai shinpō*, February 25, 1897, 16, reprint from *Jiji shinpō*.

36. "Kisho: Fukuhon'i-ronsha ni koku," *Tōyō keizai shinpō*, February 25, 1897, 30.

37. *Tōyō keizai*'s founder, the politician Machida Chūji, finished his career as head of the Minseitō in the early 1930s after the Minseitō's disastrous attempt at reinstating the gold standard—an attempt opposed by the editors of *Tōyō keizai*.

38. "Kinka mondai," *Tōyō keizai shinpō*, February 25, 1897, 1.

39. Ibid.

40. Ibid.

41. Ibid.

42. Ibid., 2.

43. "Sho daika heisei iken," Part 2, *Tōyō keizai shinpō*, March 5, 1897, 27, reprint from *Jiji shinpō*.

44. Ibid., 28.

45. On this point, see Laidler (1991).

46. Kaneko Hatsutarō, "Kinkasei shikkō ni kanshi sejin no chūi o unagasu," *Tōyō keizai shinpō*, March 15, 1897, 9.

47. Ibid.`

9. Empire and the Political Uses of Gold

1. On post-Sino-Japanese War spending priorities, see Nakamura (1985), Teranishi (1990), Takamura (2006), Sakairi (1988), and Nishikawa and Abe (1990). On foreign borrowing, see Suzuki (1994) and Tamaki (1994).

2. "Kinka hon'i etsu ni tsukite," *Tōyō keizai shinpō*, February 15, 1897, 23.

3. Ibid.

4. "Nōmin ijime no kinka hon'i etsu," *Tōyō keizai shinpō*, February 15, 1897, 23.

5. Ibid., 23.

6. See for example, Ōishi Masami, "Kinka hon'i wa kokuze no hōshin ni dezu," *Tōyō keizai shinbun*, March 5, 1897, 11–15. Ōishi served as minister of agriculture and commerce in the first Ōkuma cabinet (1898).

7. Nakamura 1990: 18; Nakamura 1985: 84.

8. Kotegawa 1897: 5–7.

9. On the Anglo-Japanese alliance, see Nish (1966, 1972).

10. Droppers 1898: 168.

11. Kotegawa 1897: 6–7.

12. Suzuki 1994: 86–87.

13. Nakamura 1985: 84.

14. Ōishi Masami, "Kinka hon'i wa kokuze no hōshin ni dezu," *Tōyō keizai shinbun*, March 5, 1897, 11–15.

15. "Kinka hon'i no waga keizaishakai no oyobosu eikyō ikan," Part 1, *Tōyō keizai shinpō*, March 25, 1897, 3–6.

16. "Kisho: Kinka hon'isei to kyoryūchi bōeki," *Tōyō keizai shinpō*, March 5, 1897, 32.

17. Ibid., 32.

18. "Sho daika heisei iken," *Tōyō keizai shinpō*, March 15, 1897, 15, reprint from *Chūgai shōgyō shinpō*. A number of scholars have mentioned prestige motivations for countries adopting the gold standard. See, for example, Yeager (1984), Schumpeter (1994), Gallarotti (1995), Milward (1996), and Helleiner (2002). Similar to the conflicts between papelista and metalistas in Argentina, other Japanese saw currency as a simple means of exchange that could be fulfilled by any entity accepted by people as money—including unbacked paper. The Meiji luminary Fukuzawa Yukichi (founder of Keio University and the *Jiji Shinpō* newspaper) shared this latter view (Fukuzawa Yukichi, "Tsūkaron," [1882], reprinted in Fukuzawa [1958–64]).

19. Matsukata 1899: 145, 184.

20. The civilizational view was also common among economists. Even while arguing for an indexed, "tabular" currency system rather than a pure, laissez-faire gold standard, the English economist W. Stanley Jevons also subscribed to the civilizational view, with Britain and the gold standard occupying the highest level of civilizational progress (Jevons 1875). Jevons saw civilization developing from "hunting states," through "pastoral states," "agricultural states," to commercial, industrial and the most "civilized countries." As Jevons put it, "The gold standard has . . . made great progress, and it will probably continue to progress" among those countries Jevons viewed as appropriately civilized or civilizing. "An extensive monetary change is hardly to be expected in Russia, although it is very remarkable that in the province of Finland, a part of the empire highly distinguished for intelligence and good education . . . [a]

great step towards a future international coinage is thus effected. Like changes are impossible among the poor, ignorant, conservative nations of India, China, and the tropics generally. Hence, we arrive, as it seems to me, at a broad, deep distinction. The highly civilized and advancing nations of Western Europe and North America, including also the rising states of Australasia, and some of the better second-rate states, such as Egypt, Brazil, and Japan, will all have the gold standard. The silver standard, on the other hand, will probably long be maintained throughout the Russian Empire, and most parts of the vast continent of Asia; also in some parts of Africa, and possibly in Mexico. Excluding, however, these minor and doubtful cases, Asia and Russia seem likely to uphold silver against the rest of the world adopting gold." Jevons 1875:148–49 (chapter 12).

21. Soyeda (Soeda) 1896: 537. Soeda would finish out his career as head of the Bank of Taiwan.

22. On this point, see Laidler (1991).

23. "Sho daika heisei iken," *Tōyō keizai shinpō*, March 5, 1897, 24–25, reprint from *Chūgai shōgyō shinpō*. Along with Taguchi Ukichi and Fukuzawa Yukichi, Amano was considered as one of Japan's three main Meiji-era economists.

24. Amano Tameyuki, "Heisei kaikaku ron," *Tōyō keizai shinpō*, March 15, 1897, 1–4.

25. "Ki jukusu to Sakatani Yoshio ga ensetsu," *Kokumin shinbun*, February 24, 1897, reprinted in *Meiji nyūsu jiten* 1983–86, 5:133–34. Sakatani, a consummate careerist, would go on to become minister of finance, mayor of Tokyo, and a member of the Upper House of the Diet. He would also become Shibusawa Eiichi's son-in-law.

26. *Sakatani Yoshio den* 1951: 188–89.

27. Amano Tameyuki, "Heisei kaikaku ron," *Tōyō keizai shinpō*, March 15, 1897, 2.

28. Ōishi Masami, "Kinka hon'i wa kokuze no hōshin ni dezu," *Tōyō keizai shinbun*, March 5, 1897, 11–12.

29. Ibid., 12.

30. Ibid.

31. Ibid., 13.

32. "Chōsen no kinka hon'i mondai," *Tōyō keizai shinpō*, August 25, 1898, 21.

33. Kobayashi Shō, "Amano bungakushi no Taiwan kahei mondai ni tsuki," *Tōyō keizai shinpō*, September 25, 1897, 17–18. See also Amano Tameyuki, "Taiwan heisei mondai," *Tōyō keizai shinpō*, July 25, 1897, 2.

34. "Heisei kaikaku ihō," *Tōyō keizai shinpō*, March 5, 1897, 37.

35. "Tōkyokusha wa shirasu shikirasu no aida ni Taiwan ni ginkaseido wo shikkō shitsutsuari," *Tōyō keizai shinpō*, February 25, 1898, 3.

36. Kobayashi Shō, "Amano bungakushi no Taiwan kahei mondai ni tsuki," *Tōyō keizai shinpō*, September 25, 1897, 17.

37. Amano Tameyuki, "Taiwan heisei mondai," *Tōyō keizai shinpō*, July 25, 1897, 2.

38. Kobayashi Shō, "Amano bungakushi no Taiwan kahei mondai ni tsuki," *Tōyō keizai shinpō*, September 25, 1897, 17.

39. "Sumiyaka ni Taiwan no heisei wo kakutei seyo," *Tōyō keizai shinpō*, January 15, 1898, 3.

40. Kobayashi Shō, "Amano bungakushi no Taiwan kahei mondai ni tsuki," *Tōyō keizai shinpō*, September 25, 1897, 17.

41. "Kinka seido to Taiwan Ginkō to no kankei ikan," *Tōyō keizai shinpō*, April 5, 1897, 4.

42. "Kinka hon'i jisshi go ni okeru keizaikai (shodaika no iken)," *Tōyō keizai shinpō*, October 5, 1897, 34.

43. Kobayashi Shō, "Amano bungakushi no Taiwan kahei mondai ni tsuki," *Tōyō keizai shinpō*, September 25, 1897, 16.

44. "Kinka hon'i jisshi go ni okeru keizaikai (shodaika no iken)," *Tōyō keizai shinpō*, October 5, 1897, 34.

45. Amano Tameyuki, "Taiwan heisei mondai," *Tōyō keizai shinpō*, July 25, 1897, 3.

46. "Kinka seido to Taiwan Ginkō to no kankei ikan," *Tōyō keizai shinpō*, April 5, 1897, 4.

47. "Tōkyokusha wa shirasu shikirasu no aida ni Taiwan ni ginkaseido wo shikkō shitsutsuari," *Tōyō keizai shinpō*, February 25, 1898, 2.

48. "Kisho: Kaheihō ha sumiyakani Taiwan ni shikkō saseru hekarasu," *Tōyō keizai shinpō*, July 25, 1897, 16.

49. "Taiwan wa danjite ginkachi to nasu bekarasu," *Tōyō keizai shinpō*, April 5, 1898, 4.

50. "Tōkyokusha wa shirasu shikirasu no aida ni Taiwan ni ginkaseido wo shikkō shitsutsuari," *Tōyō keizai shinpō*, February 25, 1898, 3.

51. "Taiwan no heisei ni tsuite," *Tōyō keizai shinpō*, April 25, 1898, 13.

52. For English-language sources on Japanese borrowing overseas, see Suzuki (1994) and Hunter (1993, 2004).

53. "Gaishi yunyū ron," Part 1, *Tōyō keizai shinpō*, February 15, 1898, 12; "Heisei kaikaku ihō," *Tōyō keizai shinpō*, February 25, 1897, 33.

54. "Kinka hon'i to gaikoku bōeki; 3/16 Nihon bōeki kyoukai reikai ni oite," Part 2, *Tōyō keizai shinpō*, April 15, 1897, 17. See also "Sho daika heisei iken," *Tōyō keizai shinpō*, March 5, 1897, 22–24 for the same opinion.

55. Whether adopting the gold standard really did lower the cost of foreign borrowing is still an open question. Bordo and Rockoff (1996) argue that it did. Flandreau and Zumer (2004) argue that it did not.

56. Ōishi 1989: 215–20; Minami 1986: 11.

57. Muroyama 1984: 21.

58. *NKS-M*, 4:979.

59. Tokutomi 1935: 536.

60. Fujimura 1982, 4:296.

61. *Economist*, March 20, 1897, 413.

62. Ibid., April 24, 1897, 603.

63. Ibid., March 20, 1897, 413.

64. Ibid., April 24, 1897, 603.

65. "Sho daika heisei iken," *Tōyō keizai shinpō*, March 5, 1897, 27, reprint from *Jiji Shinpō*.

66. See, for example, Conant (1900, 1905).

67. Aoyama Shō, "Kisho: Fusaishukoku to narite no ue no kakugo wo yōsu," *Tōyō keizai shinpō*, February 25, 1897, 27.

68. Amano Tameyuki, "Heisei kaikaku ron," *Tōyō keizai shinpō*, March 15, 1897, 1.

69. "Heisei kaikaku ihō," *Tōyō keizai shinpō*, March 5, 1897, 36.

70. "Kisho: Kinka hon'i to kinkagyō," *Tōyō keizai shinpō*, February 25, 1897, 30.

71. Ibid., 30.

72. "Gaishi yunyū ron," Part 1, *Tōyō keizai shinpō*, February 15, 1898, 13.

73. Crawcour 1988: 436; Yamamura 1974: 302.

74. Crawcour 1988: 437.

75. Nakamura 1990: 27.

76. Takahashi 1936: 655.

77. *NKS-M*, 6:1061.

78. Ishibashi Tanzan, "Waga kuni kin hon'isei no kenkyū," *Tōyō keizai shinpō*, January 11, 1930, 16.

79. Bond figures from Suzuki 1994: 198.

80. Nish 1966: 253–56; Suzuki 1994: 75; Sussman and Yafeh 2000: 459.

81. Sussman and Yafeh 2000: 455.

82. Yamamura 1974: 303.

83. Crawcour 1988: 437.

84. Yamamura 1974: 302.

85. Teranishi 1990: 73.

86. Ohkawa and Shinohara 1979: 10.

87. Yamamura 1974: 301.

88. Crawcour 1988: 436.

Epilogue: The Rules of Globalization

1. Paul Leroy-Beaulieu, "Las reservas de oro en el mundo, La tasa de descuento y la circulación de los billetes," *El Economista Argentino*, November 15, 1913, 3.

2. The day before the gold standard went back into effect on January 11, 1930, the Finance and Interior Ministries had the main Tokyo stock and currency traders called

into police headquarters for a lecture on their duties to support Japanese financial markets ("Zaikai yōpō," *Tōyō keizai shinpō*, January 18, 1930; "Kinkaikin jisshi no seimei o yomite," *Tōyō keizai shinpō*, January 25, 1930, 7). Inoue also joined nationalist groups in their public denunciations of Japanese currency traders buying dollars as being unpatriotic. On frugality campaigns, see Metzler (2004, 2006b) and Garon (1997, 1998).

3. On agrarianism and militarism, see Young (1998).

4. On the return to the gold standard in Britain, see Eichengreen (1992, 1996), Moggridge (1969, 1972), Boyce (1987), and Cain and Hopkins 2001: 453–60.

5. For countries supplementing gold with foreign exchange prior to World War I other than India and Japan, see Eichengreen 1996: 61. For India, see Cain and Hopkins 2001: 299. For Japan, see Kojima (1981) and Itō (1989).

6. On World War I and its cultural effects in England, see Fussell (1975).

7. For Keynes' arguments, see Keynes (1925).

8. Temin (1989).

9. Fukai Eigo 1938: 2. For a discussion of Fukai's views, see Chō 2001: 79–82.

10. Inoue Junnosuke's correspondence with J. P. Morgan & Co. in New York is full of Inoue's references to his belief in "sound" (in Inoue's usage, deflationary) policies even as Morgan & Co. was urging him to devalue. For more on gold standard ideology, see Yeager (1984). For gold standard ideology as followed by central bankers in the interwar period, see Ahamad (2009).

11. Laidler (1991) provides a detailed description of changes in thinking among English economists in the 1890s and how this served as a foundation for later Keynesian ideas. See also Marshall 1925: 188–211 for a discussion of prices and wages that anticipates Keynes.

12. Laidler (1999). In a follow-up to his 1991 work, Laidler traces the development of interwar English economic thinking and shows how various trends coalesced into Keynesian economics.

13. Gold standard orthodoxy is sometimes included with something more specifically known as the "Treasury view" in describing interwar Treasury consensus views. See, for example, Sayers (1976). The phrase "Treasury view" is more specifically used to describe the idea held at the Treasury about the powerlessness of government fiscal intervention in the economy—that is, the idea that any government spending automatically crowds out an equal amount of private spending. On the Treasury view, see DeLong (2009), Meltzer (1989), Peden (1988, 2005), Sayers (1976), and Middleton (2005).

14. See Bloomfield (1959, 1963), de Cecco (1974, 1996, 1997), Triffin (1997), and Eichengreen (1987a)

15. "Las dos encuestas de 'La Argentina Economica' han despertado gran interés," *La Argentina Economica*, July 30, 1926, 15.

16. "Moto heika kaikin no fuesaku o ronji, Enka kirisage no kyūmu o shuchōsu," *Tōyō keizai shinpō*, March 16, 1929, 47.

17. "Los Defensores del Dr. Schacht, quienes son?" *La Argentina Economica*, June 30, 1927, 3, 5; See also "Jamás 'La Argentina Economica' estuvo de acuerdo con la ley de conversión del viejo marco aleman, inspirada por el Dr. Schacht." *La Argentina Economica*, April 15, 1929, 3.

18. "Sumiyaka ni kinkaikin o okonau ni wa, heika kirisage no hoka nashi," *Tōyō keizai shinpō*, March 16, 1929, 63.

19. For a Japanese liquidation argument, see "Shin heika kinkaikin ron ni taisuru, hantai ron o bakusu motoheika kinkaikin ni wa hatashite dō, ikan naru rieki ga aru ka?" *Tōyō keizai shinpō*, May 4, 1929, 9.

20. Robbins quotations from DeLong 1990: 8. For Hayek's views, see Hayek (1931, 1935). For liquidation arguments in Japan, see "Kin yushutsu kai," *Jiji shinpō*, February 25,1926; "Kawasedaka to seika gensō chūshi," *Jiji shinpō*, February 25, 1926; "Kinyushutsu kaijo no ben," *Yorozu chōhō*, February 25, 1926; "Kaikin jisshi," *Jiji shinpō*, January 11, 1930; "Hikaikin seimei no hangeki," *Tōkyō Asahi Shinbun*, September 17, 1922; and "Shasetsu: Honnen no zaikai kaiko, Buji na nen matsu," *Ōsaka mainichi shinbun*, December 30, 1930.

21. Morita Hisa, "Kinkaikin to sangyō gōrika no tettei," *Tōyō keizai shinpō*, March 16, 1929, 67.

22. Ibid., 67. See also Chō 2001: 67–68, quoting Fukai (1941).

23. Morita Hisa, "Kinkaikin to sangyō gōrika no tettei," *Tōyō keizai shinpō*, March 16, 1929, 69. See also "Kyū heika kaikin ni ha dō, ikan naru rieki ga aru ka, *Tōyō keizai shinpō*, April 27, 1929, 9–11; "Shin heika kinkaikin ron ni taisuru, hantai ron o bakusu motoheika kinkaikin ni wa hatashite dō, ikan naru rieki ga aru ka?" *Tōyō keizai shinpō*, May 4, 1929, 9.

24. Morita Hisa, "Kinkaikin to sangyō gōrika no tettei," *Tōyō keizai shinpō*, March 16, 1929, 69.

25. Fervent liquidationists—and fervent gold standard supporters—still, however, remained if at the margins. The Austrian economist Ludwig von Mises (1953: 416–23) summarized the continuing faith of those most concerned with true and universal money in arguing that "the gold standard appears as an indispensible element of the body of constitutional guarantees that make the system of representative government function" and "the gold standard did not collapse. Governments abolished it in order to pave the way for inflation." As Mises explained, "The whole grim apparatus of oppression and coercion—policemen, customs guards, penal courts, prisons, in some countries even executioners—had to put into action in order to destroy the gold standard. . . . The position of gold as the world's standard is impregnable. . . . Sound money still means today what it meant in the nineteenth century: the gold standard." Support for reinstatement of the gold standard has also been a staple of various factions and personalities of the contemporary U.S. Republican Party including supporters of supply side economics such as Jude Wanniski and Steve Forbes, and

Ron Paul. See also Gillian Tett, "Insight: Gold Standard debate roars on," *Financial Times*, April 8, 2009.

26. The most extensive English-language secondary source for the Interwar gold standard in Japan is Metzler (2006b). Drawing on an extensive array of Japanese primary sources and secondary sources, Metzler provides a detailed account of the competing Japanese financial policies of the 1920s and early 1930s including the competition between expansionist economic policies and policies promoting liquidation and induced depressions. Other noted points of reference in English are Patrick (1971) and Nakamura (1987). There are shorter discussions in Ramseyer and Rosenbluth (1995) and Kindleberger (1973). Compared with the scarcity of Japanese language work on the pre–World War I gold standard, there is an enormous literature on the interwar gold standard and Depression in Japanese. Frequently cited accounts are Nakamura (1994), Chō (2001), Yoshihiko Yamamoto (1989), and Tanaka (1969). More recent works include Iwata (2004), Miwa (2003), Adachi (2006), and Takemori (2006).

27. On Korekiyo, see Metzler (2006b) and Smethurst (2007).

28. Inoue accepted the Cunliffe Commission's views in contrast to the later (1930) views of the follow-up MacMillan Commission, which emphasized currency stability, devaluation, and flexibility rather than the emphasis on prewar exchange rates and deflation in the Cunliffe report. For Inoue's views, see Inoue (1926, 1929, 1931).

29. For the dominance of deduction over induction in economics at the end of the twentieth century and beginning of the twenty-first, see Barry Eichengreen, "The Last Temptation of Risk," *National Interest*, April 30, 2009.

30. On Rand, see Burns (2009) and Heller (2009). Rand is best known for the novels *The Fountainhead* (1943) and *Atlas Shrugged* (1957) in which heroes of self-interested capitalism triumph over the collectivist mediocrities around them. Greenspan was a follower of Rand from the early 1950s until her death in 1982 and contributed regularly to Rand's newsletter *The Objectivist*.

31. Greenspan (1986).

32. For updated liquidationist and Treasury view arguments, see John Lippert, "Friedman Would Be Roiled as Chicago Disciples Rue Repudiation," *Bloomberg*, December 23, 2008; John Taylor, "Why Permanent Tax Cuts Are the Best Stimulus: Short-term Fiscal Policies Fail to Promote Long-term growth," *Wall Street Journal*, November 25, 2008; John Cochrane, "Fiscal Stimulus, Fiscal Inflation, or Fiscal Fallacies?" (University of Chicago), January 27, 2009, http://faculty.chicagogsb.edu/john.cochrane/research/Papers/fiscal2.htm; Eugene Fama, "Bailouts and Stimulus Plans," (University of Chicago), www.dimensional.com/famafrench/2009/01/bailouts-and-stimulus-plans.html; Kevin Hassett, "Trillion-Dollar Spree Is Road to Ruin, Not Rally," *Bloomberg*, January 12, 2009. Revived liquidationist and Treasury view arguments are closely related to a strain of economic thought developed since the 1960s called the efficient market hypothesis (EMH). For a recent survey of EMH thinking and its origins, see J. Fox (2009).

References

Books and Articles

Adachi, Seiji. 2006. *Datsu defure no rekishi bunseki—"seisaku rejimu" tenkan de tadoru kindai Nihon*. Tokyo: Fujiwara Shoten.

Adelman, Jeremy. 1994. *Frontier Development: Land, Labor, and Capital on the Wheatlands of Argentina and Canada, 1890–1914*. Oxford: Clarendon Press.

———. 1999. *Republic of Capital: Buenos Aires and the Legal Transformation of the Atlantic World*. Stanford: Stanford University Press.

———. 2006. *Sovereignty and Revolution in the Iberian Atlantic*. Princeton: Princeton University Press.

Ahamad, Liaquat. 2009. *Lords of Finance: The Bankers Who Broke the World*. New York: Penguin.

Aldcroft, Derek H. and Harry W. Richardson. 1969. *The British Economy, 1870–1939*. London: Macmillan.

Alonso, Paula. 2000. *Between Revolution and the Ballot Box: The Origins of the Argentine Radical Party*. Cambridge: Cambridge Latin American Studies.

———. 2003. "La política y sus laberintos: El Partido Autonomista Nacional entre 1880 y 1886." In *La vida política en la Argentina del siglo XIX. Armas, votos y voces,* ed. Hilda Sábato and Alberto Lettieri, 277–92. Buenos Aires: Fondo de Cultura Económica.

Alvarez, Juan. 1929. *Temas de historia económica Argentina*. Buenos Aires: El Ateneo.

Amaral, Samuel. 1998. *The Rise of Capitalism on the Pampas: The Estancias of Buenos Aires, 1785–1870*. Cambridge: Cambridge University Press.

Ambirajan, Sanjay. 1978. *Classical Political Economy and British Policy in India*. Cambridge: Cambridge University Press.

———. 1984. *Political Economy and Monetary Management: India, 1766–1914*. Madras: Affiliated East-West Press.

Amsden, Alice H. 1989. *Asia's Next Giant: South Korea and Late Industrialization*. Oxford: Oxford University Press.

———. 2001. *The Rise of "the Rest": Challenges to the West from Late-Industrializing Economies*. New York: Oxford University Press.

Amyx, Jennifer. 2004. *Japan's Financial Crisis: Institutional Rigidity and Reluctant Change*. Princeton: Princeton University Press.

Anderson, Benedict. 1983. *Imagined Communities: Reflections on the Origin and Spread of Nationalism*. New York: Verso.

Andrew, A. Piatt. 1904. "The End of the Mexican Dollar." *Quarterly Journal of Economics* 18: 321–50.

Angell, Norman. 1913. *The Great Illusion: A Study of the Relation of Military Power to National Advantage*. New York: Putnam.

Arrighi, Giovanni. 2009. *The Long Twentieth Century: Money, Power, and the Origins of Our Times*. 2nd ed. New York: Verso.

Asensio, Miguel. 1995. *Argentina y los otros: Historia económica del fracaso y del éxito*. Buenos Aires: Ediciones Corregidor.

Asselain, Jean-Charles. 1984. *Histoire économique de la France du XVIIIe siècle à nos jours, tome 1: De l'Ancien Régime à la Première Guerre mondiale*. Paris: Seuil.

Auslin, Michael R. 2004. *Negotiating with Imperialism: The Unequal Treaties and the Culture of Japanese Diplomacy*. Cambridge, MA: Harvard University Press.

Bagehot, Walter. 1873. *Lombard Street: A Description of the Money Market*. London: Henry S. King.

Bailey, David, Dan Coffey, and Phil Tomlinson, eds. 2007. *Crisis or Recovery in Japan: State and Industrial Economy*. Northampton, MA: Edward Elgar.

Bairoch, Paul. 1972. "Free Trade and European Economic Development in the Nineteenth Century." *European Economic Review* 3: 211–45.

———. 1989. "European Trade Policy, 1815–1914." In *Cambridge Economic History of Europe*, ed. Peter Mathias and Sydney Pollard, 1–160. Vol. 8. Cambridge: Cambridge University Press.

———. 1993. *Economics and World History: Myths and Paradoxes*. Chicago: University of Chicago Press.

———. 1997. *Victoires et déboires: Histoire économique et sociale du mond du XVIe siècle à nos jours.* Paris: Gallimard.

Balachandran, Gopalan. 2008. "Power and Markets in Global Finance: The Gold Standard, 1890–1926." *Journal of Global History* 3: 313–35.

Baldwin, Richard E. and Philippe P. Martin. 1999. "Two Waves of Globalization: Superficial Similarities, Fundamental Differences." NBER Working Paper No. 6904.

Banerji, Arun. 1982. *Aspects of Indo-British Economic Relations, 1858–1898.* Oxford: Oxford University Press.

Barratt Brown, Michael. 1971. *Economics of Imperialism.* Harmondsworth: Penguin.

Barro, Robert. 1979. "Money and the Price Level Under the Gold Standard." *Economic Journal* 89: 13–33.

Barro, Robert and David Gordon. 1983. "Rules, Discretion, and Reputation in a Model of Monetary Policy." *Journal of Monetary Economics* 12: 101–22.

Barsky, Robert and J. Bradford DeLong. 1991. "Forecasting Pre–World War I Inflation: The Fisher Effect and the Gold Standard." *Quarterly Journal of Economics* 106, no. 3: 815–36.

Bayoumi, Tamim and Barry Eichengreen. 1996. "The Stability of the Gold Standard and the Evolution of the International Monetary System." In *Modern Perspectives on the Classical Gold Standard*, T. Bayoumi, B. Eichengreen, and M. Taylor, 165–88. Cambridge: Cambridge University Press.

Beattie, Alan. 2009. *False Economy: A Surprising Economic History of the World.* New York: Viking.

Bensel, Richard Franklin. 2000. *The Political Economy of American Industrialization, 1877–1900.* Cambridge: Cambridge University Press.

———. 2008. *Passion and Preferences: William Jennings Bryan and the 1896 Democratic Convention.* Cambridge: Cambridge University Press.

Bernanke, Ben. 1983. "Nonmonetary Effects of the Financial Crisis in the Propagation of the Great Depression." *American Economic Review* 73 (June): 257–76.

———. 1995. "The Macroeconomics of the Great Depression: A Comparative Approach." *Journal of Money, Credit, and Banking* 27: 1–28.

Bernanke, Ben and Mark Gertler. 1990. "Financial Fragility and Economic Performance." *Quarterly Journal of Economics* 105: 87–114.

Bernanke, Ben and Harold James. 1991. "The Gold Standard, Deflation, and Financial Crisis in the Great Depression: An International Comparison." In *Financial Markets and Financial Crises*, ed. Glenn Hubbard, 33–68. Chicago: University of Chicago Press.

Bértola, Luis and Gabriel Porcile. 2002. "Rich and Impoverished Cousins: Economic Performance and Income Distribution in Southern Settler Societies." Paper presented at 13th International Economic History Congress, Buenos Aires.

Bértola, Luis and Jeffrey G. Williamson. 2003. "Globalization in Latin America Before 1940." NBER Working Paper No. 9687.

Bhagwati, Jagdish. 1988. *Protectionism*. Cambridge, MA: MIT Press.

Bin Wong, R. 1997. *China Transformed: Historical Change and the Limits of European Experience*. Cornell: Cornell University Press.

Bloomfield, Arthur. 1959. *Monetary Policy Under the International Gold Standard, 1880–1914*. New York: Federal Reserve Bank of New York.

——. 1963. *Short-Term Capital Movements Under the Pre-1914 Gold Standard*. Princeton: Princeton Studies in International Finance.

Bordo, Michael D., Michael Edelstein, and Hugh Rockoff. 1999. "Was Adherence to the Gold Standard a 'Good Housekeeping Seal of Approval' During the Interwar Period?" NBER Working Paper No. 7186.

Bordo, Michael D., Barry Eichengreen, and Douglas A. Irwin. 1999. "Is Globalization Today Really Different from Globalization a Hundred Years Ago?" *Brookings Trade Forum* 1–50.

Bordo, Michael D. and Finn E. Kydland. 1995. "The Gold Standard as a Rule: An Essay in Exploration." *Explorations in Economic History* 32: 423–65.

Bordo, Michael D. and Ronald MacDonald. 1997. "Violations of the 'Rules of the Game' and the Credibility of the Classical Gold Standard, 1880–1914." NBER Working Paper No. 6115.

Bordo, Michael D. and Hugh Rockoff. 1996. "The Gold Standard as a 'Good Housekeeping Seal of Approval.'" *Journal of Economic History* 56: 389–406.

Bordo, Michael D., Alan M. Taylor, and Jeffrey G. Williamson, eds. 2003. *Globalization in Historical Perspective*. Chicago: University of Chicago Press.

Bordo, Michael D. and Carlos A. Végh. 2002. "What If Alexander Hamilton Had Been Argentinean? A Comparison of the Early Monetary Experiences of Argentina and the United States." *Journal of Monetary Economics* 49, no. 3: 459–94.

Botana, Natalio. 1977. *El orden conservador: La política argentina entre 1880 y 1916*. Buenos Aires: Sudamericana.

——. 1984. *La tradición republicana: Alberdi, Sarmiento y las ideas políticas de su tiempo*. Buenos Aires: Sudamericana.

Botana, Natalio and Ezequiel Gallo. 1997. *De la república posible a la república verdadera, 1880–1910*. Buenos Aires: Ariel.

Boyce, Robert W. D. 1987. *British Capitalism at the Crossroads, 1919–1932*. Cambridge: Cambridge University Press.

Broadberry, S. N. 1997. *The Productivity Race: British Manufacturing in International Perspective, 1850–1990*. Cambridge: Cambridge University Press.

Brookhiser, Richard. 1999. *Alexander Hamilton, American*. New York: Free Press.

Bruhns, Hinnerk, ed. 2004. *Histoire et économie politique en Allemagne de Gustav Schmoller à Max Weber: Nouvelles perspectives sur l'école historique de l'économie*. Paris: Éditions de la Maison des sciences de l'homme.

Bryan, William Jennings and Mary Baird Bryan. 1925. *The Memoirs of William Jennings Bryan by Himself and His Wife, Mary Baird Bryan*. Philadelphia: John C. Winston.

Bryan, William Jennings and Robert W. Cherny. 1996. *The Cross of Gold : Speech Delivered Before the National Democratic Convention at Chicago, July 9, 1896*. Lincoln: University of Nebraska Press.

Burgin, Miron. 1946. *The Economic Aspects of Argentine Federalism, 1820–1852*. Cambridge, MA: Harvard University Press.

Burns, Jennifer. 2009. *Goddess of the Market: Ayn Rand and the American Right*. New York: Oxford University Press.

Burnham, Walter Dean. 1965. "The Changing Shape of the American Political Universe." *American Political Science Review* 59: 7–28.

——. 1970. *Critical Elections and the Mainsprings of American Politics*. New York: Norton.

Bytheway, Simon James. 2001. "Japan's Adoption of the Gold Standard: Financial and Monetary Reform in the Meiji Period." In *Evolution of the World Economy, Precious Metals, and India*, ed. J. McGuire, P. Bertola, and P. Reeves, 79–95. New Delhi: Oxford University Press.

Cain, P. J. and A. G. Hopkins. 2001. *British Imperialism, 1688–2000*. 2nd ed. Harlow: Longman.

Cairncross, A. K. 1953. *Home and Foreign Investment, 1870–1913: Studies in Capital Accumulation*. Cambridge: Cambridge University Press.

Cargill, Thomas, Michael M. Hutchison, and Takatoshi Ito. 1997. *The Political Economy of Japanese Monetary Policy*. Cambridge, MA: MIT Press.

Cauwes, Paul. 1878. *Cours d'économie politique*. Paris.

Chalmers, Robert. 1893. *History of Currency in the British Colonies*. London: Eyre and Spottiswoode.

Chandler, Alfred D., Jr. 1977. *The Visible Hand: The Managerial Revolution in American Business*. Cambridge, MA: Belknap Press, Harvard University Press.

Chandler, Alfred D., Jr. 1990. *Scale and Scope: The Dynamics of Industrial Capitalism*. Cambridge, MA: Belknap Press, Harvard University Press.

Chang, Ha-Joon. 2002. *Kicking Away the Ladder: Development Strategy in Historical Perspective*. London: Anthem Press.

Chaudhuri, K. N. 1968. "India's International Economy in the Nineteenth Century: An Historical Survey." *Modern Asian Studies* 2, no. 1: 31–50.

Chernow, Ron. 2004. *Alexander Hamilton*. New York: Penguin.

Cherny, Robert W. 1994. *A Righteous Cause: The Life of William Jennings Bryan*. Norman: University of Oklahoma Press.

Chiaramonte, José Carlos. 1971. *Nacionalismo y liberalismo económicos en la Argentina, 1860–1880*. Buenos Aires: Solar-Hachette.

——. 1997. *Ciudades, Provincias, Estados: Orígenes de la Nación Argentina (1800–1846)*. Buenos Aires: Ariel.

Chō, Yukio. 2001. *Shōwa kyōkō, Nihon fashizumu zenya*. Tokyo: Iwanami Shoten.

Choudhri, Ehsan U., and Levis A. Kochin. 1980. "The Exchange Rate and the International Transmission of Business Cycle Disturbances: Some Evidence from the Great Depression." *Journal of Money, Credit, and Banking* 12: 565–74.

Clegg, H. A., Alan Fox, and A. F. Thompson. 1964. *1889–1910*. Vol. 1 of *A History of British Trade Unions Since 1889*. Oxford: Oxford University Press.

——. 1985. *1911–1933*. Vol. 2 of *A History of British Trade Unions Since 1889*. Oxford: Oxford University Press.

Clemens, Michael A. and Jeffrey G. Williamson. 2001. "A Tariff-Growth Paradox? Protection's Impact the World Around, 1875–1997." NBER Working Paper No. 8459.

——. 2002. "Closed Jaguar, Open Dragon: Comparing Tariffs in Latin America and Asia Before World War II." NBER Working Paper No. 9401.

Coatsworth, John H. 1998. "Economic and Institutional Trajectories in Nineteenth-Century Latin America." In *Latin America and the World Economy Since 1800*, ed. John H. Coatsworth and Alan M. Taylor, 23–54. Cambridge, MA: David Rockefeller Center for Latin American Studies, Harvard University.

Coatsworth, John H. and Alan M. Taylor. 1998. Introduction in *Latin America and the World Economy Since 1800,* ed. John H. Coatsworth and Alan M. Taylor, 1–17. Cambridge, MA: David Rockefeller Center for Latin American Studies, Harvard University.

Coatsworth, John H. and Jeffrey G. Williamson. 2002. "The Roots of Latin American Protectionism: Looking Before the Great Depression." NBER Working Paper No. 8999.

Coatsworth, John H. and Jeffrey G. Williamson. 2004. "Always Protectionist? Latin American Tariffs from Independence to Great Depression." *Journal of Latin American Studies* 36, no. 2: 205–32.

Coleman, D. C. 1973. "Gentlemen and Players." *Economic History Review* 26: 92–116.

Coleman, D. C. and C. Macleod. 1986. "Attitudes and New Techniques: British Businessmen, 1800–1950." *Economic History Review* 39: 588–611.

Collins, B. and K. Robbins, eds. 1990. *British Culture and Economic Decline*. London: Weidenfeld and Nicholson.

Collins, Michael. 1995. *Banks and Industrial Finance in Britain, 1800–1939*. 2nd ed. Cambridge: Cambridge University Press.

——. 1998. "English Bank Development Within a European Perspective, 1870–1939." *Economic History Review* 51: 1–24.

Conant, Charles A. 1900. *The United States and the Orient: The Nature of the Economic Problem*. Boston: Houghton Mifflin.

——. 1905. *The Principles of Money and Banking*. Vol. 1. New York and London: Harper and Brothers.

Conkin, Paul. 1980. *Prophets of Prosperity: America's First Political Economists*. Bloomington: Indiana University Press.

Cooper, Richard N. 1982. "The Gold Standard: Historical Facts and Future Prospects." *Brookings Papers on Economic Activity* vol. 1: 1–56.

Cortés Conde, Roberto. 1979. *El progreso Argentino, 1880–1914*. Buenos Aires: Sudamericana.

———. 1989. *Dinero, deuda y crisis: Evolución fiscal y monetaria en la Argentina*. Buenos Aires: Sudamericana.

———. 1996. *La economía Argentina en el largo plaza*. Buenos Aires: Sudamericana.

Cottrell, P. L. 1975. *British Overseas Investment in the Nineteenth Century*. London: Macmillan.

———. 1980. *Industrial Finance, 1830–1914: The Finance and Organization of British Manufacturing Industry*. London: Methuen.

Crafts, Nicholas F. R. 1997. *Britain's Relative Economic Decline, 1870–1995*. London: Social Market Foundation.

———. 1998. "Forging Ahead and Falling Behind: The Rise and Relative Decline of the First Industrial Nation." *Journal of Economic Perspectives* 12, no. 2: 193–210.

Crafts, Nicholas F. R., S. J. Leybourne, and Terence C. Mills. 1989. "The Climacteric in Late Victorian Britain and France: A Reappraisal." *Journal of Applied Econometrics* 4, no. 2: 103–17.

Crafts, Nicholas F. R. and Anthony J. Venables. 2003. "Globalization in History: A Geographical Perspective." In *Globalization in Historical Perspective*, ed. Michael D. Bordo, Alan M. Taylor, and Jeffrey G. Williamson, 323–70. Chicago: University of Chicago Press.

Crawcour, E. Sydney. 1988. "Industrialization and Technological Change, 1885–1920." In *The Twentieth Century*, ed. Peter Duss, 385–450. Vol. 6 of *The Cambridge History of Japan*. Cambridge: Cambridge University Press.

Crisp, Olga. 1953. "Russian Financial Policy and the Gold Standard at the End of the Nineteenth Century." *Economic History Review* new series, 6, no. 2: 156–72.

———. 1976. *Studies in the Russian Economy Before 1914*. London: Macmillan Press.

Davis, Lance E. and Robert A. Huttenback. 1987. *Mammon and the Pursuit of Empire: The Political Economy of British Imperialism, 1860–1912*. Cambridge: Cambridge University Press.

Dawson, Andrew. 2000. "Reassessing Henry Carey (1793–1879): The Problems of Writing Political Economy in Nineteenth-Century America." *Journal of American Studies* 34: 465–85.

de Cecco, Marcello. 1974. *Money and Empire: The International Gold Standard, 1890–1914*. Oxford: Basil Blackwell.

de Cecco, Marcello. 1996. "Short-Term Capital Movements Under the Gold Standard." In *Currency Convertibility: The Gold Standard and Beyond*, ed. J. Braga de Macedo, Barry Eichengreen, and Jaime Reis, 102–12. London: Routledge.

——. 1997. "The Gold Standard." In *Monetary Standards and Exchange Rates*, ed. M. Marcuzzo and A. Rosselli, 62–77. London: Routledge.

Della Paolera, Gerardo. 1988. "How the Argentine Economy Performed During the International Gold Standard: A Reexamination." Ph.D. dissertation, University of Chicago.

——. 1994. "Experimentos monetarios y bancarios en Argentina, 1861–1930." *Revista de Historia Económica* 12: 539–89.

Della Paolera, Gerardo and Alan M. Taylor. 2001. *Straining at the Anchor: The Argentine Currency Board and the Search for Macroeconomic Stability, 1880–1935*. Chicago: University of Chicago Press.

Della Paolera, Gerardo and Alan M. Taylor, eds. 2003. *A New Economic History of Argentina*. Cambridge: Cambridge University Press.

DeLong, J. Bradford. 1990. "'Liquidation' Cycles: Old-Fashioned Real Business Cycle Theory and the Great Depression." NBER Working Paper No. 3546.

——. 2009. "DeLong: The Modern Revival of the 'Treasury View.'" Draft. January 18. Brad DeLong's Scrapbook. http://braddelong.posterous.com/delong-the-modern-revival-of-t.

DSCD (*Diario de Sesiones de la Honorable Cámara de Diputados*), 1899.

DSCS (*Diario de Sesiones de la Honorable Cámara de Senadores*), 1899.

Díaz Alejandro, Carlos. 1970. *Essays on the Economic History of the Argentine Republic*. New Haven: Yale University Press.

Díaz Fuentes, Daniel. 1994. *Crisis y cambios estructurales en América Latina: México, Brasil y Argentina durante el período de entreguerras*. México: Fondo de Cultura Económico.

——. 1998. "Latin America During the Interwar Period: The Rise and Fall of the Gold Standard in Argentina, Brazil, and Mexico." In *Latin America and the World Economy Since 1800*, ed. John H. Coatsworth and Alan M. Taylor, 443–69. Cambridge, MA: David Rockefeller Center for Latin American Studies, Harvard University.

Diéguez, Héctor L. 1969. "Argentina y Australia: Algunos aspectos de su desarrollo económico comparado." *Desarrollo Económico* 8, no. 32: 543–63.

Dintenfass, Michael. 1988. "Entrepreneurial Failure Reconsidered: The Case of the Interwar British Coal Industry." *Business History Review* 62: 1–34.

Di Tella, Guido, and Manuel Zymelman. 1967. *Las etapas del desarrollo económico argentino*. Buenos Aires: Editorial de Universitaria de Buenos Aires.

Dorfman, Adolfo. 1942. *Historia de la Industria Argentina*. Buenos Aires: Solar-Hachette.

Droppers, Garrett. 1895. "Silver in Japan." *Transactions of the Asiatic Society of Japan* 23: vi-xxix.

——. 1898. "Monetary Changes in Japan." *Quarterly Journal of Economics* 12, no. 2: 153–85.

Drummond, Ian M. 1976. "The Russian Gold Standard, 1897–1914." *Journal of Economic History* 36, no. 3: 663–88.

Duncan, Tim. 1981. "Government by Audacity: Politics and the Argentine Economy, 1885–1892." Ph.D. dissertation, University of Melbourne.

——. 1983. "La política fiscal durante el gobierno de Juárez Celman, 1886–1890: Una audaz estrategia financiera internacional." *Desarrollo Económico* 23, no. 89: 11–34.

Duncan, Tim and John Fogarty. 1984. *Australia and Argentina: On Parallel Paths.* Melbourne: University of Melbourne Press.

Dyster, Barrie. 1979. "Argentine and Australian Development Compared." *Past and Present* 84, no. 1: 91–110.

Edelstein, Michael. 1982. *Overseas Investment in the Age of High Imperialism: The United Kingdom, 1850–1914.* New York: Methuen.

——. 1994a. "Foreign Investment and Accumulation, 1860–1914." In *1860–1939,* ed. Roderick Floud and Deirdre McCloskey, 173–96. Vol. 2 of *The Economic History of Britain Since 1700.* 2nd ed. Cambridge: Cambridge University Press.

——. 1994b. "Imperialism: Cost and Benefit. " In *1860–1939,* ed. Roderick Floud and Deirdre McCloskey, 197–216. Vol. 2 of *The Economic History of Britain Since 1700.* 2nd ed. Cambridge: Cambridge University Press.

Edgeworth, Francis Y. 1895. "Thoughts on Monetary Reform." *Economic Journal* 5 (September): 434–51.

Eichengreen, Barry. 1984. "Central Bank Cooperation Under the Interwar Gold Standard." *Explorations in Economic History* 21: 64–87.

——. 1987a. "Conducting the International Orchestra: Bank of England Leadership Under the Classical Gold Standard, 1880–1913." *Journal of International Money and Finance* 6: 5–29.

——. 1987b. "Hegemonic Stability Theories of the International Monetary System." NBER Working Paper No. 2193.

——. 1992. *Golden Fetters: The Gold Standard and the Great Depression, 1919–1939.* New York: Oxford University Press.

——. 1996. *Globalizing Capital: A History of the International Monetary System.* Princeton: Princeton University Press.

Eichengreen, Barry and Marc Flandreau. 1996. "The Geography of the Gold Standard." In *Currency Convertibility: The Gold Standard and Beyond,* ed. J. Braga de Macedo, B. Eichengreen, and J. Reis, 113–43. London: Routledge.

Eichengreen, Barry and Jeffrey Sachs. 1985. "Exchange Rates and Economic Recovery in the 1930s." *Journal of Economic History* 45: 925–46.

Eichengreen, Barry and Peter Temin. 1997. "The Gold Standard and the Great Depression." NBER Working Paper No. 6060.

Einaudi, Luca. 2000. "From the Franc to the 'Europe': The Attempted Transformation of the Latin Monetary Union Into a European Monetary Union, 1865–1873." *Economic History Review* 53, no. 2: 284–308.

——. 2001. *Money and Politics: European Monetary Unification and the International Gold Standard, 1865–1873.* Oxford: Oxford University Press.

Elbaum, Bernard and William Lazonick. 1984. "The Decline of the British Economy: An Institutional Perspective." *Journal of Economic History* 44: 567–83.

Elbaum, Bernard and William Lazonick, eds. 1985. *The Decline of the British Economy: An Institutional Perspective.* Oxford: Oxford University Press.

Etchepareborda, Roberto. 1980. "Las presidencias de Uriburu y Roca." In *La Argentina del Ochenta al Centenario*, ed. Gustavo Ferrari and Ezequiel Gallo, 255–90. Buenos Aires: Sudamericana.

Fallows, James. 1994. *Looking at the Sun: The Rise of the New East Asian Economic and Political System.* New York: Pantheon.

Fechter, Ursula. 1974. *Schutzzoll und Goldstandard im Deutschen Reich (1879–1914): Der Einfluss der Schutzzollpolitik auf den internationale Goldwährungsmechanismus.* Vienna: Köln.

Ferguson, Niall. 1998. *The House of Rothschild: The World's Banker, 1849–1999.* London: Penguin.

——. 2001. *The Cash Nexus: Money and Power in the Modern World, 1700–2000.* New York: Basic Books.

——. 2003. *Empire: The Rise and Demise of the British World Order and the Lessons for Global Power.* New York: Basic Books.

——. 2005. "Sinking Globalization." *Foreign Affairs* (March–April): 64–77.

——. 2006. *The War of the World: History's Age of Hatred.* New York: Penguin Press.

——. 2009. *The Ascent of Money: A Financial History of the World.* New York: Penguin.

Ferns, H. S. 1960. *Britain and Argentina in the Nineteenth Century.* Oxford: Clarendon Press.

Ferrer, Aldo. 1963. *La economía Argentina: Etapas de su desarrollo y problemas actuales.* Buenos Aires: Fondo de Cultura Económica.

Fieldhouse, D. K. 1973. *Economics and Empire, 1830–1914.* London: Weidenfeld and Nicolson.

Findlay, Ronald and Kevin H. O'Rourke. 2003. "Commodity Market Integration, 1500–2000." In *Globalization in Historical Perspective*, ed. Michael D. Bordo, Alan M. Taylor, and Jeffrey G. Williamson, 13–62. Chicago: University of Chicago Press.

——. 2008. *Power and Plenty: Trade, War, and the World Economy in the Second Millennium.* Princeton: Princeton University Press.

Fingleton, Eamonn. 1995. *Blindside: Why Japan Is Still on Track to Overtake the U.S. by the Year 2000.* New York: Houghton Mifflin.

——. 2008. *In the Jaws of the Dragon: America's Fate in the Coming Era of Chinese Hegemony.* New York: Thomas Dunne Books.

Fisher, Irving. 1911. *The Purchasing Power of Money.* New York: Macmillan.

——. 1933. "The Debt-Deflation Theory of Great Depressions." *Econometrica* 1: 337–57.

Flandreau, Marc. 1996a. "Adjusting to the Gold Rush: Endogenous Bullion Points and the French Balance of Payments, 1846–1870." *Explorations in Economic History* 33: 417–39.

——. 1996b. "The French Crime of 1873: An Essay on the Emergence of the International Gold Standard, 1870–1880." *Journal of Economic History* 56, no. 4: 862–97.

——. 1997a. "As Good as Gold? Bimetallism in Equilibrium, 1850–70." In *Monetary Standards and Exchange Rates*, ed. M. Marcuzzo and A. Rosselli, 150–76. London: Routledge.

——. 1997b. "Central Bank Cooperation in Historical Perspective: A Skeptical View." *Economic History Review* 50, no. 4: 735–63.

——. 2000a. "The Economics and Politics of Monetary Unions: A Reassessment of the Latin Monetary Union, 1865–71." *Financial History Review* 7, no. 1: 25–43.

——. 2000b. *L'or du monde: La France et la stabilité du système monétaire international, 1848–1873*. Paris: Editions L'Harmattan.

——. 2004. *The Glitter of Gold: France, Bimetallism, and the Emergence of the International Gold Standard, 1848–1873*. New York: Oxford University Press.

Flandreau, Marc, Carl-Ludwig Holtfrerich, and Harold James, eds. 2003. *International Financial History in the Twentieth Century: System and Anarchy*. Cambridge: Cambridge University Press.

Flandreau, Marc, Jacques Le Cacheux, and Frédéric Zumer. 1998. "Stability Without a Pact? Lessons from the European Gold Standard, 1880–1914." *Economic Policy: A European Forum* 26: 115–49.

Flandreau, Marc and Frédéric Zumer. 2004. *The Making of Global Finance*. Paris: OECD.

Fleming, J. M. 1962. "Domestic Financial Policies Under Fixed and Under Floating Exchange Rates." *IMF Staff Papers* 9, no. 3 (November): 369–79.

Floud, Roderick and Deirdre McCloskey, eds. 1994. *1860–1939*. Vol. 2 of *The Economic History of Britain Since 1700*. 2nd ed. Cambridge: Cambridge University Press.

Flynn, Dennis O. and Arturo Giráldez. 1995. "Born with a 'Silver Spoon': The Origin of World Trade in 1571." *Journal of World History* 6: 201–22.

Fogarty, John. 1979. "Argentina y Australia en el período de 1914–1933." In *Argentina y Australia*, ed. J. Fogarty, E. Gallo, and H. Diéguez. Buenos Aires: Serie Jornadas Instituto Torcuato Di Tella.

Ford, A. G. 1962. *The Gold Standard, 1880–1914: Britain and Argentina*. Oxford: Clarendon Press.

——. 1965. "Overseas Lending and Internal Fluctuations, 1870–1914." *Yorkshire Bulletin of Economic and Social Research* 17, no. 1: 19–31.

Foreman-Peck, J. S., ed. 1991. *New Perspectives on the Late Victorian Economy: Essays in Quantitative Economic History, 1860–1914*. Cambridge: Cambridge University Press.

Fox, Alan. 1985. *History and Heritage: The Social Origins of the British Industrial Relations System*. London: Unwin Hyman.

Fox, Justin. 2009. *The Myth of the Rational Market: A History of Risk, Reward, and Delusion on Wall Street*. New York: Harper Collins.

Francks, Penelope. 2001. *Japanese Economic Development*. London: Routledge.

Frieden, Jeffry A. 1996. "The Dynamics of International Monetary Systems: International and Domestic Factors in the Rise, Reign, and Demise of the Classical Gold Standard." In *Coping with Complexity in the International System*, ed. J. Snyder and R. Jervis, 137–62. San Francisco: Westview Press.

———. 2006. *Global Capitalism: Its Fall and Rise in the Twentieth Century*. New York: Norton.

Friedman, Milton. 1990a. "Bimetallism Revisited." *Journal of Economic Perspectives* 4, no. 4: 85–104.

———. 1990b. "The Crime of 1873." *Journal of Political Economy* 98, no. 6: 1159–94.

Friedman, Milton and Rose Friedman. 1980. *Free to Choose: A Personal Statement*. New York: Harcourt Brace Jovanovich.

Friedman, Milton and Ann J. Schwartz. 1963. *A Monetary History of the United States, 1867–1960*. Princeton: Princeton University Press.

Friedman, Thomas L. 1999. *The Lexus and the Olive Tree: Understanding Globalization*. New York: Farrar, Straus, and Giroux.

———. 2005. *The World Is Flat: A Brief History of the Twenty-first Century*. New York: Farrar, Straus, and Giroux.

Frost, Peter K. 1970. *The Bakumatsu Currency Crisis*. Cambridge, MA: East Asian Research Center, Harvard University.

Fujimura, Tōru, ed. 1982. *Matsukata Masayoshi kankei bunsho*. Tokyo: Tōkyō Bunka-daigaku Tōyō Kenkyūjo.

Fukai, Eigo. 1938. *Kin hon'isei ridatsugo no tsūka seisaku*. Tokyo: Chikura Shobō.

———. 1941. *Kaiko 70 nen*. Tokyo: Iwanami Shoten.

Fukuzawa, Yukichi. 1958–64. *Fukuzawa Yukichi zenshū*. Tokyo: Iwanami Shoten.

Fussell, Paul. 1975. *The Great War and Modern Memory*. Oxford: Oxford University Press.

Gallarotti, Giulio. 1993. "The Scramble for Gold: Monetary Regime Transformation in the 1870s." In *Monetary Regimes in Transition*, ed. Michael Bordo and Forrest Capie, 15–67. Cambridge: Cambridge University Press.

———. 1995. *The Anatomy of an International Monetary Regime: The Classical Gold Standard, 1880–1914*. New York: Oxford University Press.

Gallo, Ezequiel. 1979. "El método comparativo en historia: Argentina y Australia (1850–1914)." In *Argentina y Australia*, ed. J. Fogarty, E. Gallo, and H. Diéguez, 3–18. Buenos Aires: Serie Jornadas Instituto Torcuato Di Tella.

———. 1983. *La pampa gringa*. Buenos Aires: Sudamericana.

———. 1988. "La expansión agraria y el desarrollo industrial en la Argentina (1880–1930)." *Anuario del IEHS* 13.

———. 1993. "Society and Politics, 1880–1916." In *Argentina Since Independence*, ed. Leslie Bethell, 79–112. Cambridge: Cambridge University Press.

———. 1996. "El contexto histórico de la ley de convertibilidad de 1899." In *Aspectos analíticos e históricos de la convertibilidad monetaria*, ed. Ana M. Martirena-Mantel, 69–81. Buenos Aires: Academia Nacional de Ciencias.

———. 1997. *Carlos Pellegrini*. Buenos Aires: Fondo de Cultura Economica.

Garon, Sheldon. 1997. *Molding Japanese Minds: The State in Everyday Life*. Princeton: Princeton University Press.

———. 1998. "Fashioning a Culture of Diligence and Thrift: Savings and Frugality Campaigns in Japan, 1900–1931." In *Japan's Competing Modernities: Issues in Culture and Democracy, 1900–1930*, ed. Sharon Minichiello, 312–34. Honolulu: University of Hawaii Press.

Gerchunoff, Pablo and Pablo Fajgelbaum. 2006. *¿Por qué Argentina no fue Australia? Una hipótesis sobre un cambio de rumbo*. Buenos Aires: Siglo XXI Editores.

Gerchunoff, Pablo and Lucas Llach. 2003. *El ciclo de la ilusión y el desencanto*. Buenos Aires: Ariel.

———. 2004. *Entre la equidad y el crecimiento: Ascenso y caída de la economía argentina, 1880–2002*. Buenos Aires: Siglo XXI Editores.

Gerchunoff, Pablo, Fernando Rocchi, and Gastón Rossi. 2008. *Desorden y progreso: Las crisis económicas argentinas, 1870–1905*. Buenos Aires: Edhasa.

Gerschenkron, Alexander. 1943. *Bread and Democracy in Germany*. Berkeley: University of California Press.

———. 1962. *Economic Backwardness in Historical Perspective: A Book of Essays*. Cambridge, MA: Belknap Press of Harvard University Press.

Gesell, Silvio. 1898. *Anemia monetaria*. Buenos Aires.

Gide, Charles. 1883. *Principes d'économie politique*. Paris.

Gilpin, Robert. 1987. *The Political Economy of International Relations*. Princeton: Princeton University Press.

Girault, René. 1997. *Diplomatie européenne: Nations et imperialismes, 1871–1914*. Paris: Armand Colin.

Gluck, Carol. 1985. *Japan's Modern Myths: Ideology in the Late Meiji Period*. Princeton: Princeton University Press.

Goldin, Claudia. 1994. "The Political Economy of Immigration Restriction in the United Staes, 1890–1921." In *The Regulated Economy: A Historical Approach to Political Economy*, ed. Claudia Goldin and Gary D. Libecap, 223–57. Chicago: University of Chicago Press.

Golob, Eugene. 1944. *The Méline Tariff: French Agriculture and Nationalist Economic Policy*. New York: Columbia University Press.

Goodwyn, Lawrence. 1976. *Democratic Promise: The Populist Moment in America.* New York: Oxford University Press.

Gordon, Scott. 1991. *The History and Philosophy of Social Science.* London: Routledge.

Gourevitch, Peter. 1977. "International Trade, Domestic Coalitions, and Liberty: Comparative Responses to the Crisis of 1873–1896." *Journal of Interdisciplinary History* 8, no. 2: 281–313.

——. 1986. *Politics in Hard Times: Comparative Responses to International Economic Crises.* Ithaca: Cornell University Press.

Graham, Thomas. 1990. *Charles H. Jones: Journalist and Politician of the Gilded Age.* Tallahassee: Florida A&M University Press.

Green, E. H. H. 1988. "Rentiers v. Producers? The Political Economy of the Bimetallic Controversy, c. 1880–98." *English Historical Review* 103: 588–612.

——. 1990. "The Bimetallic Controversy: Empiricism Belimed or the Case for the Issues." *English Historical Review* 105: 673–83.

Greenspan, Alan. 1986. "Gold and Economic Freedom." In *Capitalism: The Unknown Ideal* by Ayn Rand. New York: Signet, 101–7. The article originally appeared in the magazine *The Objectivist* in 1966.

Gregory, Paul. 1979. "The Russian Balance of Payments, the Gold Standard, and Monetary Policy: A Historical Example of Foreign Capital Movements." *Journal of Economic History* 39: 379–400.

Gregory, Paul and Joel W. Sailors. 1976. "Russian Monetary Policy and Industrialization, 1861–1913." *Journal of Economic History* 36, no. 4: 836–51.

Grimes, William W. 2001. *Unmaking the Japanese Miracle: Macroecnoomic Politics, 1985–2000.* Ithaca: Cornell University Press.

Grimmer-Solem, Erik. 2003. *The Rise of Historical Economics and Social Reform in Germany, 1864–1894.* Oxford: Oxford University Press.

Guy, Donna. 1976. "Tucuman Sugar Politics and the Generation of Eighty." *Americas* 32, no. 4: 566–84.

——. 1979. "Carlos Pellegrini and the Politics of Early Industrialization in Argentina, 1876–1906." *Journal of Latin American Studies* 11, no. 1: 123–44.

——. 1980. *Argentine Sugar Politics: Tucuman and the Generation of Eighty.* Tempe: Arizona State University, Center for Latin American Studies.

——. 1982. "La indústria argentina, 1870–1940: Legislación comercial, mercado de acciones y capitalización extranjera." *Desarrollo Económico* 22, no. 87: 351–74.

——. 1984. "Dependency, the Credit Market, and Argentine Industrialization, 1860–1940." *Business History Review* 58, no. 4: 532–61.

Halperín Donghi, Tulio. 1987a. "1880: Un nuevo clima de ideas." In *El espejo de la historia: Problemas Argentinos y perspectivas Latinoamericanas*, 239–52. Buenos Aires: Sudamericana.

———. 1987b. "¿Para que la inmigración? Ideologia y política inmigratoria en la Argentina, 1810–1914." In *El espejo de la historia: Problemas Argentinos y perspectivas Latinoamericanas*, 189–238. Buenos Aires: Sudamericana.

———. 1995a. *Una nación para el desierto argentino*. Buenos Aires: CEAL.

———. 1995b. *Proyecto y construcción de una nación, 1846–1880*. Buenos Aires: Ariel.

Hamashita, Takeshi. 1983. "A History of the Japanese Silver Yen and the Hongkong and Shanghai Banking Corporation, 1871–1913." In *Eastern Banking: Essays in the History of the Hongkong and Shanghai Banking Corporation*, ed. Frank H. H. King, 321–49. London: Athlone Press.

Hamilton, Alexander. 1791. *Report on Manufactures*.

Hamilton, James D. 1987. "Monetary Factors in the Great Depression." *Journal of Monetary Economics* 13: 1–25.

———. 1988. "The Role of the International Gold Standard in Propagating the Great Depression." *Contemporary Policy Issues* 6: 67–89.

Harcave, Sidney. 2004. *Count Sergei Witte and the Twilight of Imperial Russia*. Armonk, NY: M. E. Sharpe.

Harlen, Christine. 1999. "A Reappraisal of Classical Economic Liberalism and Economic Nationalism." *International Studies Quarterly* 43, no. 4: 733–44.

Harley, C. K. 1974. "Skilled Labour and the Choice of Technique in Edwardian Industry." *Explorations in Economic History* 11, no. 4: 391–414.

Hashimoto, Jurō, and Ōsugi Yuka. 2000. *Kindai Nihon keizai shi*. Tokyo: Iwanami Shoten.

Hayek, Friedrich von. 1931. "The 'Paradox' of Saving." *Economica* 32 (May): 125–69.

Hayek, Friedrich von. 1935. *Prices and Production*. London: Routledge.

Helleiner, Eric. 2002. "Economic Nationalism as a Challenge to Economic Liberalism? Lessons from the Nineteenth Century." *International Studies Quarterly* 46: 307–29.

———. 2003. *The Making of National Money: Territorial Currencies in Historical Perspective*. Ithaca: Cornell University Press.

Heller, Anne C. 2009. *Ayn Rand and the World She Made*. New York: Doubleday.

Hobsbawm, Eric. 1987. *The Age of Empire*. New York: Vintage Books.

Hobsbawm, Eric and Terence Ranger, eds. 1983. *The Invention of Tradition*. Cambridge: Cambridge University Press.

Hora, Roy. 2000. "Terratenientes, empresarios industriales y crecimiento industrial en la Argentina: Los estancieros y el debate sobre el proteccionismo (1890–1914)." *Desarrollo Económico* 40, no. 159: 465–92.

———. 2001. *The Landowners of the Argentine Pampas: A Social and Political History, 1860–1945*. Oxford: Clarendon Press, Oxford Historical Monographs.

———. 2003a. "Autonomistas, radicales y mitristas: El Orden oligarquico en la provincia de Buenos Aires, 1880–1912." *Boletín del Instituto de Historia Argentina y Americana "Dr. Emilio Ravignani"* 23: 39–78.

——. 2003b. "Empresarios y política en la Argentina, 1880–1916." In *La vida política en la Argentina del siglo XIX: Armas, votos y voces*, ed. Hilda Sabato and Alberto Lettieri. Mexico City: Fondo de Cultura Economica.

Howe, Anthony C. 1990. "Bimetallism: A Controversy Reopened." *English Historical Review* 105: 377–91.

——. 1997. *Free Trade and Liberal England, 1846–1946*. Oxford: Oxford University Press.

Hunter, Janet. 1993. "The Limits of Financial Power: Japanese Foreign Borrowing and the Russo-Japanese War." In *Great Powers and Little Wars: The Limits of Power*, ed. A. H. Ion and E. J. Errington, 145–65. Westport, CT: Praeger.

——. 2004. "Bankers, Investors, and Risk: British Capital and Japan During the Years of the Anglo-Japanese Alliance." In *The Anglo-Japanese Alliance, 1902–1922*, ed. Phillips Payson O'Brien, 176–98. London: Routledge.

Hutchison, Michael M., and Frank Westermann, eds. 2006. *Japan's Great Stagnation: Financial and Monetary Policy Lessons for Advanced Economies*. Cambridge, MA: MIT Press.

Imlah, A. H. 1958. *Economic Elements in the Pax Britannica: Studies in British Foreign Trade in the Nineteenth Century*. Cambridge, MA: Harvard University Press.

Inoue [Inouye], Junnosuke. 1926. *Waga kokusai kinyū no genjō oyobi kaizensaku*. Tokyo: Iwanami Shoten.

——. 1929. *Kin kaikin—zen Nihon ni sakebu*. Tokyo: Senshinsha.

——. 1931. *Problems of the Japanese Exchange, 1914–1926*. London: Macmillan. (Translation of Inoue 1926).

Irigoin, Maria Alejandra. 2000. "Inconvertible Paper Money, Inflation, and Economic Performance in Early Nineteenth Century Argentina." *Journal of Latin American Studies* 32, no. 2: 333–59.

Irwin, Douglas A. 1996. *Against the Tide: An Intellectual History of Free Trade*. Princeton: Princeton University Press.

——. 1997. "Higher Tariffs, Lower Revenues? Analyzing the Fiscal Aspects of the Great Tariff Debate of 1888." NBER Working Paper No. 6239.

——. 1998. "Did Late Nineteenth Century U.S. Tariffs Promote Infant Industries? Evidence from the Tinplate Industry." NBER Working Paper No. 6835.

——. 2002. "Interpreting the Tariff-Growth Correlation of the Late 19th Century." *American Economic Review* 92, no. 2: 165–69.

Itō, Masanao. 1989. *Nihon no taigai kinyū to kinyū seisaki, 1914–1936*. Nagoya: Nagoya Daigaku Shuppankai.

Itō, Masanao. 2009. *Sengo Nihon no taigai kinyū: 360 en raito no seiritsu to shūen*. Nagoya: Nagoya Daigaku Shuppankai.

Iwata, Kikuo, ed. 2004. *Shōwa kyōkō no kenkyū*. Tokyo: Tōyō Keizai Shinpōsha.

James, Harold. 2001. *The End of Globalization: Lessons from the Great Depression*. Cambridge, MA: Harvard University Press.

Jevons, William Stanley. 1875. *Money and the Mechanism of Exchange*. London: Henry S. King.

Johnson, Harry G. 1967. *Economic Nationalism in Old and New States*. Chicago: University of Chicago Press.

Jones, Stanley. 1964. *The Presidential Election of 1896*. Madison: University of Wisconsin Press.

Kaminski, Arnold P. 1980. "'Lombard Street' and India: Currency Problems in the Late Nineteenth Century." *Indian Economic and Social History Review* 17, no. 3: 307–27.

Kazin, Michael. 2006. *A Godly Hero: The Life of William Jennings Bryan*. New York: Knopf.

Kemp, John and Ted Wilson. 1999. "Monetary Regime Transformation: The Scramble to Gold in the Late Nineteenth Century." *Review of Political Economy* 11, no. 2: 125–49.

Kennedy, Paul. 1987. *The Rise and Fall of the Great Powers: Economic Change and Military Conflict from 1500 to 2000*. New York: Random House.

Kennedy, William P. 1976. "Institutional Response to Economic Growth: Capital Markets in Britain to 1914." In *Management Strategy and Business Development*, ed. L. Hannah, 151–83. London: Macmillan.

——. 1987. *Industrial Structure, Capital Markets, and the Origins of British Economic Decline*. Cambridge: Cambridge University Press.

Keynes, John Maynard. 1913. *Indian Currency and Finance*. London: MacMillan.

——. 1920. *The Economic Consequences of the Peace*. London: Macmillan.

——. 1925. *The Economic Consequences of Mr. Churchill*. London: Hogarth Press.

Kindleberger, Charles P. 1973. *The World in Depression, 1929–1939*. Berkeley: University of California Press.

Kinghorn, Janice Rye and John Nye. 1996. "The Scale of Production in Western Economic Development: A Comparison of Official Industry Statistics in the United States, Britain, France, and Germany, 1905–1913." *Journal of Economic History* 56, no. 1: 90–112.

Kirby, M. W. 1992. "Institutional Rigidities and Economic Decline: Reflections on the British Experience." *Economic History Review* 45, no. 4: 637–60.

Ko Sakatani Shishaku Kinen Jigyōkai. 1951. *Sakatani Yoshio den*. Tokyo: Ko Sakatani Shishaku Kinen Jigyōkai.

Kojima, Hitoshi. 1981. *Nihon no kin hon'isei jidai (1897–1917)—en no taigai kankei o chūshin to suru kōsatsu*. Tokyo: Nihon Keizai Hyōronsha.

Korol, Juan Carlos. 1992. "El Desarrollo Argentino y la Historia Comparada." *Boletín del Instituto de Historia Argentina y Americana "Dr. Emilio Ravignani"* 5, no. 3: 113–25.

Kotegawa, Toyojirō. 1897. *Kinka hon'isei/Bankoku fukuhon'isei*. Tokyo: Hashio Shoten.

Kydland, Finn, and Edward Prescott. 1977. "Rules Rather than Discretion: The Inconsistency of Optimal Plans." *Journal of Political Economy* 85 (June): 473–90.

Laidler, David. 1991. *The Golden Age of the Quantity Theory*. Princeton: Princeton University Press.

——. 1999. *Fabricating the Keynesian Revolution: Studies of the Inter-war Literature on Money, the Cycle, and Unemployment*. Cambridge: Cambridge University Press.

Lake, David A. 1988. *Power, Protection, and Free Trade: International Sources of U.S. Commercial Strategy, 1887–1939*. Ithaca: Cornell University Press.

Lamont, Thomas W. Papers. Baker Library, Harvard Business School.

Lamoreaux, Naomi R. 1985. *The Great Merger Movement in American Business, 1895–1904*. Cambridge: Cambridge University Press.

Landes, David S. 1969. *The Unbound Prometheus: Technological Change and Industrial Development in Western Europe from 1750 to the Present*. Cambridge: Cambridge University Press.

——. 1998. *The Wealth and Poverty of Nations: Why Some Are So Rich and Some So Poor*. New York: Norton.

Laughlin, J. Laurence. 1886. *The History of Bimetallism in the United States*. New York: Appleton.

——. 1931. *A New Exposition of Money, Credit, and Prices*. 2 vols. Chicago: University of Chicago Press.

Lawrence, Robert Z., Albert Bressand, and Takatoshi Ito. 1996. *A Vision for the World Economy: Openness, Diversity, and Cohesion*. Washington, DC: Brookings Institution.

Lazonick, William. 1981. "Competition, Specialization, and Industrial Decline." *Journal of Economic History* 41, no. 1: 31–38.

——. 1994. "Employment Relations in Manufacturing and International Competition." In *1860–1939*, ed. Roderick Floud and Deirdre McCloskey, 90–116. Vol. 2 of *The Economic History of Britain Since 1700*. 2nd ed. Cambridge: Cambridge University Press.

Lebovics, Herman. 1988. *The Alliance of Iron and Wheat in the Third French Republic, 1860–1914: Origins of the New Conservatism*. Baton Rouge: Louisiana State University Press.

Lebra, Joyce. 1959. "Okuma Shigenobu and the 1881 Political Crisis." *Journal of Asian Studies* 18: 4.

——. 1973. *Okuma Shigenobu: Statesman of Meiji Japan*. Canberra: Australian National University Press.

Leroy-Beaulieu, Paul. 1874. *De la colonisation chez les peuples modernes*. Paris: Guillaumin.

Levi-Faur, David. 1997a. "Economic Nationalism: From Friedrich List to Robert Reich." *Review of International Studies* 23: 359–70.

——. 1997b. "Friedrich List and the Political Economy of the Nation-State." *Review of International Political Economy* 4: 154–78.

Levine, A. L. 1967. *Industrial Retardation in Britain, 1880–1914*. London: Weidenfeld and Nicolson.

Lewchuck, William. 1987. *American Technology and the British Vehicle Industry*. Cambridge: Cambridge University Press.

Lewis, Colin. 1983. *British Railways in Argentina, 1857–1914: A Case Study of Foreign Investment*. London: Athlone.

Lewis, W. A. 1978. *Growth and Fluctuations, 1870–1913*. London: Allen and Unwin.

Lind, Michael. 1998. "The Time Is Ripe for the Third Man." *Nation* 267 (October 5).

Lindert, Peter H. 1969. *Key Currencies and Gold, 1900–1913*. Princeton: Princeton University Press.

Lindsey, Brink. 2001. *Against the Dead Hand: The Uncertain Struggle for Global Capitalism*. New York: John Wiley and Sons.

List, Friedrich. 1841. *The National System of Political Economy*. (The current U.S. edition, published by Cosimo Classics [2006], divided into 3 vols.)

Llach, Lucas. 2007. "The Wealth of the Provinces: The Rise and Fall of the Interior in the Political Economy of Argentina, 1880–1910." Ph.D. dissertation, Harvard University.

Maddison, Angus. 2003. *The World Economy: Historical Statistics*. Paris: OECD.

Marichal, Carlos. 1989. *A Century of Debt Crises in Latin America: From Independence to the Great Depression, 1820–1930*. Princeton: Princeton University Press.

Marrison, Andrew, ed. 1998. *Free Trade and Its Reception, 1815–1960*. London: Routledge.

Marshall, Alfred. 1925. *Memorials of Alfred Marshall*. Ed. Alfred C. Pigou. London: Macmillan.

——. 1926. *Official Papers*. London: Macmillan.

Matsukata, Masayoshi. 1899. *Report on the Adoption of the Gold Standard in Japan*. Tokyo: Government Press.

——. 1900. *Report on the Post-Bellum Financial Administration in Japan*. Tokyo: Government Press.

Mauro, Paulo, Nathan Sussman, and Yishay Yafeh. 2006a. "Bloodshed or Reforms? The Determinants of Sovereign Bond Spreads in 1870–1913 and Today." CEPR Discussion Paper No. 5528.

——. 2006b. *Emerging Markets and Financial Globalization: Sovereign Bond Spreads in 1870–1913 and Today*. Oxford: Oxford University Press.

McCloskey, Donald and Lars Sandberg. 1971. "From Damnation to Redemption: Judgments on the Late Victorian Entrepreneur." *Explorations in Economic History* 9: 89–108.

McKenzie, Frederick. 1902. *American Invaders*. London: G. Richards.

McKeown, Adam. 2008. *Melancholy Order: Asian Migration and the Globalization of Borders*. New York: Columbia University Press.

McKinnon, Ronald. 2005. *Exchange Rates Under the East Asian Dollar Standard: Living with Conflicted Virtue*. Cambridge, MA: MIT Press.

McKinnon, Ronald and Kenichi Ohno. 1997. *Dollar and Yen: Resolving Economic Conflict Between the United States and Japan*. Cambridge, MA: MIT Press.

——. 2001. "The Foreign Exchange Origins of Japan's Economic Slump and Low Interest Liquidity Trap." *World Economy* 24, no. 3: 279–315.

McLean, Ian. 2006. "Recovery from Depression: Australia in an Argentina Mirror, 1895–1913." *Australian Economic History Review* 46, no. 3: 215–41.

Meiji nyūsu jiten. 1983–86. Tokyo: Mainichi Komyunikeshonzu.

Meissner, Christopher M. 2005. "A New World Order: Explaining the International Diffusion of the Gold Standard, 1870–1913." *Journal of International Economics* 66: 385–406.

Meltzer, Allan. 1989. *Keynes's Monetary Theory: A Different Interpretation*. Cambridge: Cambridge University Press.

Metzler, Mark. 2004. "Woman's Place in Japan's Great Depression: Reflections on the Moral Economy of Deflation." *Journal of Japanese Studies* 30, no. 2: 315–51.

——. 2006a. "The Cosmopolitanism of National Economics: Friedrich List in a Japanese Mirror." In *Global History: Interactions Between the Universal and the Local*, ed. A. G. Hopkins, 98–130. Basingstoke: Palgrave Macmillan.

——. 2006b. *Lever of Empire: The International Gold Standard and the Crisis of Liberalism in Prewar Japan*. Berkeley: University of California Press.

Michie, Ranald C. 1986. "The Myth of the Gold Standard: An Historian's Approach." *Revue Internationale d'Histoire de la Banque* no. 32–33: 167–97.

——. 1987. *The London and New York Stock Exchanges, 1850–1914*. London: Allen and Unwin.

——. 1988. "The Finance of Innovation in Late Victorian and Edwardian Britain: Possibilities and Constraints." *Journal of European Economic History* 17: 491–530.

Middleton, Roger. 2005. *Toward the Managed Economy*. London: Routledge.

Mill, John Stuart. 1848. *Principles of Political Economy*. London.

Milward, Alan. 1996. "The Origins of the Gold Standard." In *Currency Convertibility: The Gold Standard and Beyond*, ed. J. Braga de Macedo, B. Eichengreen, and J. Reis, 87–102. London: Routledge.

Minami, Ryoshin. 1986. *The Economic Development of Japan: A Quantitative Study*. New York: St. Martin's Press.

Mises, Ludwig von. 1953. *The Theory of Money and Credit*. New Haven: Yale University Press.

Mishkin, Frederic S. 1978. "The Household Balance Sheet and the Great Depression." *Journal of Economic History* 38 (December): 918–37.

——. 1991. "Asymmetric Information and Financial Crises: A Historical Perspective." In *Financial Markets and Financial Crises*, ed. Glenn Hubbard, 69–108. Chicago: University of Chicago Press.

——. 1997. "Understanding Financial Crises: A Developing Country Perspective." *Annual World Bank Conference on Development Economics*, 29–62.

Mitchener, Kris James and Marc D. Weidenmier. 2008. "Trade and Empire." NBER Working Paper No. 13765.

Miwa, Ryōichi. 2003. *Senkanki Nihon no keizai seisakushiteki kenkyū*. Tokyo: Tōkyō Daigaku Shuppankai.

Moggridge, Donald. 1969. *The Return to Gold, 1925: The Formulation of Economic Policy and Its Critics*. Cambridge: Cambridge University Press.

——. 1972. *British Monetary Policy, 1924–1931*. Cambridge: Cambridge University Press.

Moran, Theodore. 1970. "The 'Development' of Argentina and Australia: The Radical Party of Argentina and the Labor Party of Australia in the Process of Economic and Political Development." *Comparative Politics* 3, no. 1: 71–92.

More, Charles. 1980. *Skill and the English Working Class, 1870–1914*. London: Croom Helm.

Morris-Suzuki, Tessa. 1989. *A History of Japanese Economic Thought*. London: Routledge.

Mouré, Kenneth. 1991. *Managing the Franc Poincaré*. Cambridge: Cambridge University Press.

——. 2002. *The Gold Standard Illusion: France, the Bank of France, and the International Gold Standard, 1914–1939*. Oxford: Oxford University Press.

Mundell, Robert. 1960. "The Monetary Dynamics of International Adjustment Under Fixed and Flexible Exchange Rates." *Quarterly Journal of Economics* 74, no. 2 (May): 227–57.

——. 1961a. "The International Disequilibrium System." *Kyklos* 14: 153–71.

——. 1961b. "A Theory of Optimum Currency Areas." *American Economic Review* 51, no. 4 (September): 657–65.

——. 1961c. "Flexible Exchange Rates and Employment Policy." *Canadian Journal of Economics and Political Science* 27, no. 4 (November): 509–17.

——. 1962. "The Appropriate Use of Monetary and Fiscal Policy for Internal and External Stability." *IMF Staff Papers* 9, no. 1 (March): 70–79.

——. 1963. "Capital Mobility and Stabilization Policy Under Fixed and Flexible Exchange Rates." *Canadian Journal of Economics and Political Science* 29, no. 4 (November): 475–85.

——. 1968. *International Economics*. New York: MacMillan.

Muroyama, Yoshimasa. 1984. *Kindai Nihon no gunji to zaisei*. Tokyo: Tōkyō Daigaku Shuppankai.

——. 2004. *Matsukata zaisei kenkyū—futaiten no seisaku kōdō to keizai kiki kokufuku no jissō*. Kyoto: Minerva Shobō.

———. 2005. *Matsukata Masayoshi*. Kyoto: Minerva Shobō.

Murphy, Agnes. 1948. *The Ideology of French Imperialism, 1817–1881*. Washington, DC: Catholic University of America Press.

Nakamura, Takafusa. 1983. *Economic Growth in Prewar Japan*. New Haven: Yale University Press.

———. 1985. *Meiji Taishō-ki no keizai*. Tokyo: Tōkyō Daigaku Shuppankai.

———. 1987. "The Japanese Economy in the Interwar Period: A Brief Summary." In *Japan and World Depression*, ed. R. Dore and R. Sinha, 52–67. Basingstoke: Macmillan.

———. 1990. "Macro keizai to sengo keiei." In *Sangyōka no Jidai (ge)*, ed. S. Nishikawa and Y. Yamamoto, 1–36. Vol. 5 of *Nihon Keizaishi*. Tokyo: Iwanami Shoten.

———. 1994. *Shōwa kyōkō to keizai seisaku*. Tokyo: Kōdansha.

Nakamura, Takafusa and Umemura Mataji. 1983. *Matsukata zaisei to shokusan kōgyō seisaku*. Tokyo: Tōkyō Daigaku Shuppankai.

Nicholas, Tom. 1999. "Clogs to Clogs in Three Generations? Explaining Entrepreneurial Performance in Britain Since 1850." *Journal of Economic History* 59, no. 3: 688–713.

NKS-M (Nihon kin'yūshi shiryō, Meiji-Taishō hen). 1955–61. Ed. Nihon Ginkō Chōsakyoku. 26 vols. Tokyo: Ōkurashō Insatsukyoku..

Nipperdey, Thomas. 1992. *Machtstaat vor der Demokratie*. Vol. 2 of *Deutsche Geschichte, 1866–1918*. Munich: C. H. Beck.

Nish, Ian. 1966. *The Anglo-Japanese Alliance: The Diplomacy of Two Island Empires, 1894–1907*. London: Athlone Press.

———. 1972. *Alliance in Decline: A Study of Anglo-Japanese Relations, 1908–1923*. London: Athlone Press.

Nishikawa, Shunsaku and Abe Takeshi. 1990. "Gaisetsu, 1885–1914." In *Sangyōka no jidai (jō)*, ed. S. Nishikawa and A. Takeshi, 1–77. Vol. 4 of *Nihon Keizaishi*. Tokyo: Iwanami Shoten.

Nocken, Ulrich. 1998. "Die Große Deflation: Goldstandard, Geldmenge und Preise in den USA und Deutschland 1870 bis 1896." In *Geld und Währung vom 16. Jahrhundert bis zur Gegenwart*, ed. E. Schremmer, 157–89. Stuttgart: Steiner Franz Verlag.

Nugent, J. B. 1973. "Exchange Rate Movements and Economic Development in the Late Nineteenth Century." *Journal of Political Economy* 81, no. 5: 1110–35.

Nurkse, Ragnar. 1944. *International Currency Experience: Lessons of the Inter-War Period*. Princeton: Princeton University Press for the League of Nations.

Offer, Avner. 1993. "The British Empire, 1870–1914: A Waste of Money?" *Economic History Review* 46, no. 2: 215–38.

Official Proceedings of the Democratic National Convention held in Chicago, Ill., July 7th, 8th, 9th, 10th, and 11th, 1896. 1896. Logansport, IN: Wilson, Humphreys.

Ohkawa, Kazushi, and Miyohei Shinohara, eds. 1979. *Patterns of Japanese Economic Development: A Quantitative Appraisal*. New Haven: Yale University Press.

Ōishi, Kaichirō. 1989. *Jiyūminken to Ōkuma/Matsukata zaisei*. Tokyo: Tōkyō Daigaku Shuppankai.

O'Rourke, Kevin. 2000. "Tariffs and Growth in the Late Nineteenth Century." *Economic Journal* 110 (April): 456–83.

O'Rourke, Kevin and Jeffrey G. Williamson. 1999. *Globalization and History: The Evolution of a Nineteenth-Century Atlantic Economy*. Cambridge, MA: MIT Press.

Patrick, Hugh T. 1965. "External Equilibrium and Internal Convertibility: Financial Policy in Meiji Japan." *Journal of Economic History* 25, no. 2: 187–213.

———. 1971. "The Economic Muddle of the 1920s." In *Dilemmas of Growth in Prewar Japan*, ed. James Morley, 211–66. Princeton: Princeton University Press.

Payne, P. L. 1988. *British Entrepreneurship in the Nineteenth Century*. 2nd ed. London: Macmillan.

Peden, G.. C. 1988. *Keynes, the Treasury, and British Economic Policy*. London: Macmillan.

———. 2005. *Keynes and His Critics: Treasury Responses to the Keynesian Revolution, 1925–1946*. London: British Academy.

Phillips, Kevin. 2003. *William McKinley*. New York: Times Books.

Platt, D. C. M. 1972. *Latin America and British Trade, 1806–1914*. London: Adam and Charles Black.

———. 1977. *Business Imperialism, 1840–1930*. Oxford: Clarendon Press.

Platt, D. C. M. and Guido Di Tella, eds. 1985. *Argentina, Australia, and Canada: Studies in Comparative Development, 1870–1965*. London: MacMillan.

Poinsard, Léon. 1893. *La politique douanière de tous les pays expliquée par les circonstances de leur état social et économique*. Paris: Firmin Didot.

Polanyi, Karl. 1944. *The Great Transformation*. New York: Rinehart.

Pollard, Sidney. 1982. *The Wasting of the British Economy*. London: Palgrave Macmillan.

———. 1985. "Capital Exports, 1870–1914: Harmful or Beneficial?" *Economic History Review* 38: 489–514.

———. 1994. "Entrepreneurship." In *1860–1939*, ed. Roderick Floud and Deirdre McCloskey, 62–89. Vol. 2 of *The Economic History of Britain Since 1700*. 2nd ed. Cambridge: Cambridge University Press.

Pomeranz, Kenneth. 2000. *The Great Divergence: China, Europe, and the Making of the Modern World Economy*. Princeton: Princeton University Press.

Prados de la Escosura, Leandro, and Isabel Sanz-Villarroya. 2004. "Institutional Instability and Growth in Argentina: A Long-Run View." Universidad Carlos III, Departamento de Historia Económica e Instituciones, Working Papers in Economic History No. wh046705.

Prestowitz, Clyde V., Jr. 1993. *Trading Places: How We Are Giving Our Future to Japan and How to Reclaim It.* New York: Basic Books.

Price, Richard. 1986. *Labour in British Society: An Interpretive History.* London: Croom Helm.

Ramseyer, J. Mark, and Frances M. Rosenbluth. 1995. *The Politics of Oligarchy: Institutional Choice in Imperial Japan.* Cambridge: Cambridge University Press.

Rand, Ayn. 1943. *The Fountainhead.* New York: Bobbs-Merrill.

——. 1957. *Atlas Shrugged.* New York: Random House.

——. 1986. *Capitalism: The Unknown Ideal.* New York: Signet.

Redish, Angela. 1990. "The Evolution of the Gold Standard in England." *Journal of Economic History* 50, no. 4: 789–805.

——. 2000. *Bimetallism: An Economic and Historical Analysis.* Cambridge: Cambridge University Press.

Regalsky, Andrés. 1994. "La evolución de la banca privada nacional en Argentina, 1880–1914: una introducción a su estudio." In *Suramerica y el Caribe*, ed. Pedro Tedde and Carlos Marichal, 35–60. Vol. 2 of *La formación de los bancos centrales en España y América Latina: siglos XIX y XX.* Madrid: Banco de España.

——. 1997. "Banking, Trade, and the Rise of Capitalism in Argentina, 1850–1930." In *Banking, Trade, and Industry: Europe, America, and Asia from the Thirteenth to the Twentieth Century*, ed. Alice Teichova, Ginette Kurgan-van Henenryk, and Dieter Ziegler, 359–77. Cambridge: Cambridge University Press.

——. 2001. "¿Una experiencia de banca industrial en la Argentina exportadora? El Banco Francés del Río de la Plata, 1905–1914." *Anuario del Centro de Estudios Históricos de Córdoba* 1, no. 1: 219–45.

——. 2002. *Mercados, inversores y elites: Las inversiones francesas en la Argentina, 1880–1914.* Buenos Aires: Editorial de la Universidad Nacional de Tres de Febrero.

Reitano, Joanne. 1994. *The Tariff Question in the Gilded Age: The Great Debate of 1888.* University Park: Pennsylvania State University Press.

Ritter, Gretchen. 1997. *Goldbugs and Greenbacks: The Antimonopoly Tradition and the Politics of Finance in America, 1865–1896.* Cambridge: Cambridge University Press.

Rocchi, Fernando. 2006. *Chimneys in the Desert: Industrialization in Argentina During the Export Boom Years, 1870–1930.* Stanford: Stanford University Press.

Rock, David. 1975. *Politics in Argentina, 1890–1930: The Rise and Fall of Radicalism.* Cambridge: Cambridge University Press.

Rockoff, Hugh. 1990. "The Wizard of Oz as Monetary Allegory." *Journal of Political Economy* 98: 739–60.

Romer, Christina. 1992. "What Ended the Great Depression?" *Journal of Economic History* 52: 757–84.

Rosa, José María. 1909. *Conversión de la moneda, unidad monetaria, Caja de Conversión.* Buenos Aires: Imprenta de Coni Hermanos.

Rostow, W. W. 1960. *The Stages of Economic Growth: A Non-Communist Manifesto.* Cambridge: Cambridge University Press, 1960.

Rothermund, Diet. 1993. *An Economic History of India: From Pre-Colonial Times to 1991.* London: Routledge.

Rouseau, Peter L., and Richard Sylla. 2003. "Financial Systems, Economic Growth, and Globalization." In *Globalization in Historical Perspective*, ed. Michael D. Bordo, Alan M. Taylor, and Jeffrey G. Williamson, 373–413. Chicago: University of Chicago Press.

Rowthorn, Robert, and Solomos Solomou. 1991. "The Macroeconomic Effects of Overseas Investment on the UK Balance of Trade, 1870–1913." *Economic History Review* 44, no. 4: 654–64.

Rubinstein, W. D. 1993. *Capitalism, Culture, and Decline in Britain, 1750–1990.* London: Routledge.

Russell, Henry B. 1898. *International Monetary Conferences.* New York: Harper and Brothers.

Sachs, Jeffrey, and Andrew Warner. 1995. "Economic Reform and the Process of Global Integration." *Brookings Papers on Economic Activity* 1: 1–118.

Said, Edward. 1978. *Orientalism.* New York: Pantheon.

Sakairi, Chōtarō. 1988. *Meiji kōki zaiseishi.* Tokyo: Sakai Shoten.

Samuels, Richard J. 1994. *"Rich Nation, Strong Army": National Security and the Technological Transformation of Japan.* Ithaca: Cornell University Press.

Sanders, Elizabeth. 1999. *Roots of Reform: Farmers, Workers, and the American State, 1877–1917.* Chicago: University of Chicago Press.

Sanderson, Michael. 1972. *The Universities and British Industry, 1850–1970.* London: Routledge and Kegan Paul.

Sanz Villarroya, Isabel. 2003. "Los Procesos de Convergencia de Argentina con Australia y Canadá, 1875–2000." Universidad Carlos III, Departamento de Historia Económica e Instituciones, Working Papers in Economic History, No. dh030302.

Saul, S. B. 1985. *The Myth of the Great Depression, 1873–1896.* London: Macmillan.

Sayers, R. S. 1953. "The Bank in the Gold Market, 1890–1914." In *Papers in English Monetary History*, ed. R. S. Sayers and T. S. Ashton, 132–50. Oxford: Clarendon Press.

——. 1957. *Central Banking After Bagehot.* Oxford: Oxford University Press.

——. 1976. *The Bank of England, 1891–1944.* Cambridge: Cambridge University Press.

Schedvin, C. B. 1990. "Staples and Regions of Pax Britannica." *Economic History Review* 43, no. 4: 533–59.

Schlesinger, Arthur M., Jr. 2002. *History of American Presidential Elections, 1789–2001.* Philadelphia: Chelsea House.

Schumpeter, Joseph A. 1994. *A History of Economic Analysis*. London: Routledge. (Reprint of 1954 1st edition.)

Schwartz, Anna J. 1984. Introduction in *A Retrospective on the Classical Gold Standard*, ed. Michael Bordo and Anna J. Schwartz, 1–22. Chicago: University of Chicago Press.

Schwartz, Herman. 1989. "Foreign Creditors and the Politics of Development in Australia and Argentina, 1880–1913." *International Studies Quarterly* 33, no. 3: 281–301.

Scobie, James R. 1964. *Revolution in the Pampas: A Social History of Argentine Wheat, 1860–1910*. Austin, TX: Institute of Latin American Studies.

Senghaas, Dieter. 1991. "Friedrich List and the Basic Problems of Modern Development." *Review* (Fernand Braudel Center) 14, no.3: 451–67.

Semmel, Bernard. 1993. *The Liberal Ideal and the Demons of Empire: Theories of Imperialism from Adam Smith to Lenin*. Baltimore: Johns Hopkins University Press.

Simmons, Beth. 1994. *Who Adjusts? Domestic Sources of Foreign Economic Policy During the Interwar Years*. Princeton: Princeton University Press.

Sklar, Martin J. 1988. *The Corporate Reconstruction of American Capitalism, 1890–1916: The Market, the Law, and Politics*. Cambridge: Cambridge University Press.

Smethurst, Richard J. 2007. *From Foot Soldier to Finance Minister: Takahashi Korekiyo, Japan's Keynes*. Cambridge, MA: Harvard University Press.

Smith, Michael S. 1980. *Tariff Reform in France, 1860–1900*. Ithaca: Cornel University Press, 1980.

Smith, Thomas C. 1955. *Political Change and Industrial Development in Japan: Government Enterprise, 1868–1880*. Stanford: Stanford University Press.

Smithies, Arthur. 1965. "Argentina and Australia." *American Economic Review* 55, no. 1: 17–30.

Snowden, Kenneth. 1990. "Historical Returns and Security Market Development, 1872–1925." *Explorations in Economic History* 27: 381–420.

Soros, George. 1998. *The Crisis of Global Capitalism*. New York: Public Affairs Books.

Soyeda [Soeda], Juichi. 1896. "The History of Banking in Japan." In *A History of Banking in All the Leading Nations*. New York: Journal of Commerce and Commercial Bulletin. (Reprinted 2002 by RoutledgeCurzon, London.)

Sussman, Nathan and Yishay Yafeh. 2000. "Institutions, Reforms, and Country Risk: Lessons from Japanese Government Debt in the Meiji Period." *Journal of Economic History* 60, no. 2 (June): 442–67.

Suzuki, Toshio. 1994. *Japanese Government Loan Issues on the London Capital Market, 1870–1913*. London: Athlone Press.

Szporluk, Roman. 1988. *Communism and Nationalism: Karl Marx Versus Friedrich List*. Oxford: Oxford University Press.

Takahashi, Korekiyo. 1936. *Zuisōroku*. Tokyo: Chikura Shobō.

Takamura, Naosuke. 2006. *Meiji keizaishi saikō*. Kyoto: Minerva Shobō.

Takemori, Shunpei. 2006. *Sekai defure wa mitabi kitaru*. Tokyo: Kōdansha.

Tamaki, Norio. 1988. "Economists in Parliament: The Fall of Bimetallism." In *Enlightenment and Beyond: Political Economy Comes to Japan*, ed. C. Sugiyama and H. Mizuta, 223–36. Tokyo: University of Tokyo Press.

——. 1994. "Japan's Adoption of the Gold Standard and the London Money Market, 1881–1903: Matsukata, Nakai, and Takahashi." In *Britain and Japan: Biographical Portraits*, ed. Ian Nish, 121–32. Folkstone, Kent: Japan Library.

Tanaka, Ikuo. 1969. "Kin kaikin ronsō." In *Kindai Nihon keizai shisōshi*, ed. Yukio Chō and Sumiya Kazuhiko, 357–79. Tokyo: Yūhikaku.

Taussig, Frank W. 1905. "The Present Position of the Doctrine of Free Trade." *Publications of the American Economic Association* 3, no. 6 (February): 29–65.

Taylor, Alan M. 1992a. "Argentine Economic Growth in Comparative Perspective." Ph.D. dissertation, Harvard University.

——. 1992b. "External Dependence, Demographic Burdens, and the Argentine Economic Decline After the Belle Epoque." *Journal of Economic History* 52, no. 4: 907–36.

Temin, Peter. 1976. *Did Monetary Forces Cause the Great Depression?* New York: Norton.

Temin, Peter. 1989. *Lessons from the Great Depression*. Cambridge, MA: MIT Press.

Teranishi, Jūrō. 1990. "Kinyū no Kindaika to Sangyōka." In *Sangyōka no Jidai (ge)*, ed. S. Nishikawa and Y. Yamamoto, 37–84. Vol. 5 of *Nihon Keizaishi*. Tokyo: Iwanami Sho ten.

Teranishi, Jūrō and Uchino Yūko. 1986. "Kinhon'isei to geemu no ruuru." In *Nihon no kin'yū shisutemu*, ed. Kaizuka Keimi and Ono Eisuke, 55–68. Tokyo: Tōkyō Daigaku Shuppankai.

Thurow, Lester. 1992. *Head to Head: The Coming Economic Battle Among Japan, Europe, and America*. New York: William Morrow.

Todd, Emmanuel. 1998. Préface in *Système national d'économie politique*, by Friedrich List, 9–35. Paris: Gallimard.

Tokutomi, Ichirō, ed. 1935. *Kōshaku Matsukata Masayoshi den*. Vol. 2. Tokyo: Matsukata Masayoshi Biographical Association.

Tolchin, Martin and Susan Tolchin. 1988. *Buying Into America: How Foreign Money Is Changing the Face of Our Nation*. New York: Crown.

Tomlinson, B. R. 1993. *The Economy of Modern India, 1860–1970*. Cambridge: Cambridge University Press.

Triffin, Robert. 1997. "The Myth and Realities of the So-called Gold Standard." In *The Gold Standard in Theory and History*, ed. Barry Eichengreen and Marc Flandreau, 140–60. 2nd ed. London: Routledge.

U.S. House of Representatives. 1903. *Stability of International Exchange*. Washington, DC: Government Printing Office.

U.S. House of Representatives. 1912. *Report of the Tariff Board: Cotton Manufactures.* Washington, DC: Government Printing Office.

Van Helten, Jean-Jaques, and Youseff Cassis, eds. 1990. *Capitalism in a Mature Economy: Financial Institutions, Capital Exports, and British Industry, 1870–1939.* London: Edward Elgar.

Verdier, Daniel. 1994. *Democracy and International Trade: Britain, France, and the United States, 1860–1990.* Princeton: Princeton University Press.

Villanueva, Javier. 1972. "El origen de la industrialización argentina." *Desarrollo Económico* 12 (October–December): 451–76.

Von Laue, Theodore H. 1963. *Sergei Witte and the Industrialization of Russia.* New York: Columbia University Press.

Walras, Léon. 1874. *Éléments d'économie politique pure; ou, Théorie de la richesse sociale.* Lausanne: Corbaz.

Watson, Katherine. 1996. "Banks and Industrial Finance: The Experience of Brewers, 1880–1913." *Economic History Review* 49, no. 1: 58–81.

Wehler, Hans-Ulrich. 1995. *Von der "Deutsche Doppelrevolution" bis zum Beginn des Ersten Weltkrieges, 1849–1914.* Vol. 3 of *Deutsche Gesellschaftsgeschichte.* Munich: C. H. Beck.

Weiner, M. J. 2004. *English Culture and the Decline of the Industrial Spirit, 1850–1980.* 2nd ed. Cambridge: Cambridge University Press.

Williams, Ernest. 1896. *Made in Germany.* London: William Heinemann.

Williams, John H. 1920. *Argentine International Trade Under Inconvertible Paper Currency, 1880–1900.* Cambridge, MA: Harvard University Press.

Williams, Karel, John Williams, and Dennis Thomas. 1983. *Why Are the British Bad at Manufacturing?* London: Routledge and Kegan Paul.

Williamson, Jeffrey G. 2003. "Stolper-Samuelson, Strategic Tariffs, and Revenue Needs: World Tariffs, 1789–1938." www.economics.harvard.edu/faculty/williamson/files/Stolper-Samuelson.pdf.

Wilson, Ted. 2000. *Battles for the Standard: Bimetallism and the Spread of the Gold Standard in the Nineteenth Century.* Aldershot, Hampshire: Ashgate.

Winch, Christopher. 1998. "Listian Political Economy: Social Capitalism Conceptualised?" *New Political Economy* 3, no. 2: 301–16.

Winkler, Heinrich August. 1997. "Demokratie und Nation in der deutschen Geschichte." In *Streitfragen der deutschen Geschichte,* 31–51. Munich: C. H. Beck.

Witte, Sergei. 1889. *Po povodu natsionalizma: Natsionalnaia ekonomiia i Fridrikh List.* Moscow: Evropa.

———. 1960. *Vospominaniia.* Ed. A. L. Sidorov. Moscow: Economic Literature Publishing House.

———. 1990. *The Memoirs of Count Witte.* Trans. and ed. Sidney Harcave. Armonk, NY: M. E. Sharpe.

Wolters, Willem. 2005. "Southeast Asia in the Asian Setting: Shifting Geographies of Currencies and Networks." In *Locating Southeast Asia: Geographies of Knowledge and Politics of Space*, ed. Paul H. Kratoska, Remco Raben, and Henk Schulte Nordholt, 175–202. Singapore: Singapore University Press.

Wright, Maurice. 2002. *Japan's Fiscal Crisis: The Ministry of Finance and the Politics of Public Spending, 1975–2000*. New York: Oxford University Press.

Yamamoto, Yoshihiko. 1989. *Senkanki Nihon shihonshugi to keizai seisaku—kinkaikin mondai o meguru kokka to keizai*. Tokyo: Hakushobō.

Yamamoto, Yūzō. 1989. "Meiji isshinki no zaisei to tsūka." In *Kaiko to Ishin*, ed. M. Mataji and Y. Yamamoto, 111–72. Vol. 3 of *Nihon Keizaishi*. . Tokyo: Iwanami Shoten.

——. 1994. *Ryō kara en e: Bakumatsu Meiji zenki kahei mondai kenkyū*. Tokyo: Minerva Shobō.

Yamamura, Kozo. 1974. "The Japanese Economy, 1911–1930: Concentration, Conflicts, and Crises." In *Japan in Crisis: Essays in Taisho Democracy*, ed. B. Silberman and H. Harootunian, 299–328. Princeton: Princeton University Press.

Yeager, L. B. 1984. "The Image of the Gold Standard." In *A Retrospective on the Classical Gold Standard, 1821–1931*, ed. Michael Bordo and A. J. Schwartz, 651–70. Chicago: University of Chicago Press.

Yergin, Daniel and Joseph Stanislaw. 1998. *The Commanding Heights: The Battle Between Government and the Marketplace That Is Remaking the Modern World*. New York: Simon and Schuster.

Yoshino, Toshihiko. 1975–79. *Nihon ginkō shi*. Tokyo: Bank of Japan.

Young, Louise. 1998. *Japan's Total Empire: Manchuria and the Culture of Wartime Imperialism*. Berkeley: University of California Press.

Zevin, Robert. 1992. "Are World Financial Markets More Open? If So, Why and With What Effects?" In *Financial Openness and National Autonomy*, ed. Tariq Banuri and Juliet B. Schor, 43–83. Oxford: Clarendon Press.

Zoellick, Robert B. 2002. "So What Is There to Cover? Globalization, Politics, and the U.S. Trade Strategy." Address to the Society of American Business Editors and Writers, Phoenix, AZ, April 30. http://ustraderep.gov/assets/Document_Library/USTR_Speeches/2002/asset_upload_file718_4245.pdf.

Periodicals

Argentina (Buenos Aires)
Caras y Caretas
Don Quijote
El Correo Español

El Diario
El Economista Argentino
El Tiempo
La Argentina Económica
La Italia al Plata
La Nación
La Prensa
La Tribuna
Revista Económica (del Río de la Plata)

Britain (London)
Economic Journal
Economist
Financial Times
Times

France (Paris)
L'Economiste français

Japan (Tokyo except as noted)
Chūgai shōgyō shinpō
Jiji shinpō
Kokumin shinbun
Nihon shinbun
Ōsaka mainichi shinbun (Osaka)
Tōkyō asahi shinbun
Tōyō keizai shinpō
Yorozu chōhō

United States
Bloomberg
Commercial and Financial Chronicle
National Interest
New York Times
Wall Street Journal

Index

and silver standard, 34, 119, 124–27,
132, 133, 141, 142, 143, 145, 148, 157,
160, 219n20; treaty port system of,
155; and Western imperialism, 168
Australia: and free trade, 75; gold
production in, 19, 29, 35, 128; and
gold standard, 34, 44; and grain
production, 27; and late nineteenth-
century world economy, 27
Austria, 34, 178
Austria-Hungary: and bimetallic
system, 45; and exchange rate, 33;
and gold standard of 1890s, 36;
military expenditures of, 28; and
protectionism, 22, 24
Austro-Hungarian Bank, 33

Banco de La Nación (Argentina), 78,
89–90, 105
Bank of England, 45, 180, 191n10
Bank of France, 35–36, 45–46
Bank of Italy, 33
Bank of Japan, 33, 121, 123, 131, 160, 171,
213n15
Barro, Robert, 197n5
Baum, L. Frank, 40
Belgium: and bimetallic system, 34,
45; and foreign exchange reserves,
178; and free trade, 18, 22; and
gold conversion, 208n10; and gold
standard, 36; industrial output of, 18;
interest rates of, 37
Bensel, Richard, 200n6, 201nn8, 9, 10, 11
Berduc, Emilio, 64
Berlin Wall, 1
Bernanke, Ben, 5, 190–91n9
Bértola, Luis, 192n12, 202n12
Bimetallic system: and Britain, 40,
44; and Europe, 36, 128, 143; and
exchange rates, 119, 142–43; and

France, 34, 36, 45–46, 175; and India,
53; and international conferences,
20–21, 39, 135, 138, 139, 144; and
Japan, 122–23, 128, 138, 141, 142–44,
152, 160; and nationalism, 41, 144;
proposals for, 40, 199n27; and United
States, 34, 50, 51, 138, 142; and world
standard, 141, 142, 143–45, 198n8
Bismarck, Otto von, 11, 24, 31, 35, 46, 48,
107, 123
Bloomfield, Arthur, 6, 191n10
Boer War of 1899–1902, 28, 62, 170
Bordo, Michael D., 198n15, 201n15,
212n4, 220n55
Botana, Natalio, 6, 201n1, 202nn2, 3
Braga de Macedo, Jorge, 6
Brave new world theme, and change, 2,
190n2
Brazil: and currency depreciation, 41;
and gold standard, 34, 36, 40, 44; and
protectionism, 22
Bretton Woods system, 33, 39, 41, 144,
181, 187
Britain: capital exports of, 37; and
civilizational development, 157,
218n20; and exchange rates, 131; and
exports, 102, 136, 216n11; financial
power of, 17–18, 36, 37–38, 44–45, 50,
54, 150, 154, 167–70, 175, 179; and free
trade, 18, 21, 22–23, 24, 30, 65, 75, 88,
180; and gold appreciation, 40; gold
exports blocked by, 176; and gold
standard, 34, 43, 44–45, 46, 55, 88, 99,
100, 103, 119, 128, 175, 178–79, 186,
197n4, 200n1; and grain imports, 27,
28; and great power politics, 44–45,
153; industrial power of, 17, 18–19, 21,
23, 61, 75; and interest rates, 37–38,
149, 169–70, 172, 180; and Japan, 149,
153–54, 157, 166–67, 169–72; military